MW01520114

MERRY HELL

The Story of the 25th Battalion
(Nova Scotia Regiment)

Canadian Expeditionary Force 1914–1919

Merry Hell

*The Story of the 25th Battalion
(Nova Scotia Regiment)*

Canadian Expeditionary Force 1914–1919

CAPTAIN ROBERT N. CLEMENTS, MC

Edited by Brian Douglas Tennyson

UNIVERSITY OF TORONTO PRESS
Toronto Buffalo London

© University of Toronto Press 2013
Toronto Buffalo London
www.utppublishing.com
Printed in Canada

ISBN 978-1-4426-4496-0

Printed on acid-free, 100% post-consumer recycled paper with
vegetable-based inks.

Library and Archives Canada Cataloguing in Publication

Clements, Robert N.
Merry hell : the story of the 25th Battalion (Nova Scotia Regiment),
Canadian Expeditionary Force 1914–1919 / Robert N. Clements ;
edited by Brian Douglas Tennyson.

Includes bibliographical references and index.
ISBN 978-1-4426-4496-0

1. Canada. Canadian Army. Battalion, 25th – History. 2. World War,
1914–1918 – Regimental histories – Canada. 3. World War, 1914–1918
– Canada. I. Tennyson, B. D. II. Title.

D547.C2C537 2013   940.4'12716   c2012-907220-6

University of Toronto Press acknowledges the financial assistance
to its publishing program of the Canada Council for the Arts
and the Ontario Arts Council.

Canada Council   Conseil des Arts
for the Arts   du Canada

ONTARIO ARTS COUNCIL
CONSEIL DES ARTS DE L'ONTARIO
50 YEARS OF ONTARIO GOVERNMENT SUPPORT OF THE ARTS
50 ANS DE SOUTIEN DU GOUVERNEMENT DE L'ONTARIO AUX ARTS

University of Toronto Press acknowledges the financial support of the
Government of Canada through the Canada Book Fund
for its publishing activities.

Dedicated
to the brave men
of the 25th Battalion
and to
R.C. Tennyson
who has finally discovered
the importance of history

Contents

Contents

Introduction

The Great War was probably the most significant event in modern history. Its impact on Western civilization, and indeed the world, was profound, while it was taking place, in its immediate aftermath, and even today, nearly a century later. As Winston Churchill rather dramatically put it:

> The Great War ... differed from all ancient wars in the immense power of the combatants and their fearful agencies of destruction, and from all modern wars in the utter ruthlessness with which it was fought. All the horrors of all the ages were brought together, and not only armies but whole populations were thrust into the midst of them ... Every outrage against humanity or international law was repaid by reprisals often on a greater scale and of longer duration ... Europe and large parts of Asia and Africa became one vast battlefield on which after years of struggle not armies but nations broke and ran. When all was over, Torture and Cannibalism were the only two expedients that the civilized, scientific, Christian States had been able to deny themselves: and these were of doubtful utility.[1]

It was, moreover, as John Keegan and others have concluded, 'a tragic and unnecessary conflict,' which not only killed some ten million people but

> tortured the emotional lives of millions more, destroyed the benevolent and optimistic culture of the European continent and left ... a legacy of political rancour and racial hatred so intense that no explanation of the causes of the Second World War can stand without reference to those roots.[2]

The respected military historian C.P. Stacey thought it was the 'greatest event' in Canadian history.[3] Historians and others, perhaps especially Québécois with long memories, may debate that, but there is no denying it shook the country to its very foundations while at the same time expediting its transition from a largely rural Dominion in the British Empire to a largely urban industrial and independent nation.[4]

Its outbreak in August 1914 was greeted with wild enthusiasm, not only in London and Berlin but also in cities and towns throughout Canada. Here, it seemed, was an unexpected but brilliant opportunity to escape the humdrum existence of life on the family farm or in a deadening office, to see the world, to participate in a great adventure, and to actively contribute to the by now well established ideology of British – and Canadian – imperialism, serving king and empire in a noble cause.[5] Politicians of all parties set aside their factiousness to unite in supporting the mother country in its hour of need, and newspapers across the country, including francophone Quebec, provided a stirring chorus.

When the call for volunteers came, indeed before it came, thousands of Canadian men, young and not-so-young, rushed to enlist, fearful that they might miss this once-in-a-lifetime opportunity if the war ended before they got to Europe. They came from the farms and fishing villages of the Maritimes, from the farms and factories of Quebec, both anglophones and francophones, from the mines of northern Ontario, from the wheat farms of Saskatchewan and the cattle ranches of Alberta, from the fruit farms of the Okanagan Valley and the coastal fisheries of British Columbia, from the gold fields of the Yukon, and an astonishing number of 'clerks' came from everywhere. They even came from Newfoundland, despite that Dominion's own major contribution, and they came in significant numbers from the United States. There were women as well, who volunteered as nurses and nursing assistants or worked for the YMCA and other organizations supporting the troops. Before it all came to an end, an appalling four years later, more than 600,000 men had enlisted, almost all of them voluntarily. Some 424,000 of them went overseas, and nearly half of them were wounded or injured in some way. This, in a population of less than eight million.

Canada was a very small country in terms of population, but it was a very large country in terms of geography. This meant that the population was thinly spread across the country and there were large spaces consisting of forest, farmland, or wasteland between urban centres, most of which were small. Canada was, inevitably, a very regional country, to a much greater extent than it is today. The war changed that because the overseas army was organized in battalions that increasingly, because of

the insatiable demand for more and yet more men, had to draw reinforcements who did not come from the communities in which they
were originally recruited. This meant that those who served overseas
and shared the unique experience of combat, the horror of the trenches,
and the insanity of the first technologically modern war, not only met
but forged a sacred bond with men from other parts of the country. The
cliché that Canada became a nation at Vimy Ridge is well known, but
really, the men of the Maritimes, Quebec, Ontario, the Prairies, British
Columbia, and the northern territories became true Canadians through
their shared experience, which no one who wasn't there will ever fully
comprehend. In typically Canadian fashion, this happened at the same
time that their war experience reinforced regional identities, as veterans
and communities took pride in their contributions to the war, and especially in locally based battalions like the 25th, while grieving at the cost.
Meanwhile, social and cultural divisions generated by the demands of
the war, especially the conscription crisis, created deep wounds that
would take years of sensitive management to heal.

When these men were demobilized following the armistice, they
faced another major practical and psychological problem: trying to
adapt to civilian life, returning to previous occupations or seeking new
ones, returning to their home communities or going elsewhere. At the
same time, they had to grapple with the fact that what they had experienced was incomprehensible to those who had remained at home.
These were very young men, for the most part, whose lives had been
changed forever. While they needed to reintegrate into society and did
so, they carried with them for the rest of their lives a sense of separate-
ness if not alienation from those around them.

The Canadian Legion provided a profoundly important service to
these men because it not only represented their interests in dealing with
governments, it also constituted a kind of club in which the price of
membership was both high and unique. This was not enough, of course.
While many veterans wanted to put the war behind them, many others
wanted to keep alive the memory of what they had done, the price they
had paid, and especially the price that had been paid by those who had
not returned. Many who had not served agreed that the memory of sacrifice had to be kept alive, with the result that monuments were built in
communities throughout the land, a national war memorial was built,
the Peace Tower was included in the rebuilt Parliament Buildings to
house the national book of remembrance, and November 11th quickly
became a solemn day of respect and thanksgiving.[6]

This was not enough either. Many veterans wanted their stories to be told, and some wanted to tell their own stories. Between 1919 and 1939 more than sixty regimental histories were published, although less than half were full-length monographs. Since, with few exceptions, they were written by officers who had served in the war in the battalions about which they were writing, this was a case of soldiers writing for soldiers.[7] These books understandably tended to glorify the heroism and sacrifice of the soldiers, if not the war itself. But the late 1920s and early 1930s were a period of intense and painful controversy. The bitter anti-war poetry of men like Siegfried Sassoon and Wilfred Owen, and the more popular disillusionist wartime memoirs of men like Sassoon and Robert Graves, resonated with a public that increasingly suspected that the Great War had been either a ghastly mistake or just a continuation of traditional European national rivalries. These suspicions were powerfully reinforced by such popular sensationalist novels as Erich Maria Remarque's *All Quiet on the Western Front*, Peregrine Acland's *All Else Is Folly*, and, most controversial of all, Charles Yale Harrison's *Generals Die in Bed*.

With the coming of the Second World War, which clearly was a 'just' war necessary to stop the spread of the Nazi obscenity, the controversy over the Great War subsided, at least for a few years. While it revived in later years with historians analyzing and debating strategy and the quality of military leadership, the more than twenty Canadian regimental histories that have been published in Canada since 1945 have been more widely accepted because they tell their stories in the by now generally accepted context of the inhuman horrors and insanity of the western front.

The early regimental histories were (and remain) valuable because they were based not just on official records but on the recollections of veterans. At the same time, their authors sought and received much advice from the Army Historical Section, which possessed the official records and controlled access to them, and particularly from Colonel A.F. Duguid, the official historian. His primary assignment was to write the official history, but he also took upon himself the responsibility of exercising his influence to ensure that the regimental histories were not 'controversial.' While this effectively prevented any overt criticism of commanding officers, these regimental histories nonetheless did recall the horrendous conditions in which the war was fought, and they did, as Tim Cook says, 'challenge wilder accusations that the infantry consisted of rampaging lunatics or that the generals were butchering incompetents.'[8] The more recent histories are, inevitably, quite different because their authors are not veterans (at least not of the Great War) and they have access to all the official and unofficial records, the vast literature that has been built up over the years, and the perspective of ninety years' separation from the war. As well, they are writing for an audience that knows the war only as an historical event.[9]

Is there a need for yet another regimental history? If one wants to know what Canadian soldiers were doing and experiencing in the Great War, are there not enough battalion histories already to provide that information, not to mention the several broader histories of Canadian involvement, most notably Tim Cook's recent two volumes on the Canadian army in the war?[10] The reader will not be surprised to discover that I think there is a need for another one, indeed, many more, for the simple reason that, while there is a sameness to the experience of all soldiers in the war and all battalions, there is also a uniqueness. Battalions had their own 'culture,' reflecting the communities in which they were originally raised and with which they identified themselves. As well, while battalions fought alongside other battalions in battles, their roles in those battles varied. For example, one battalion might lead an assault, while another battalion was held in reserve to join the battle after the initial gains had been made. As Tim Cook says, regimental histories

> offer unparalleled insight into particular aspects of the Canadian battle experience ... There is, quite simply, no better way to grasp where a particular battalion was engaged and what its men did, than to study the regimental histories ... In short, the regimental histories provide a valuable window for those attempting to understand and reconstruct the social history of Canadian soldiers and the units that shaped their wartime experiences.[11]

Clements, the author of this history, makes the same point equally well, if less eloquently, when he observes that 'no two people ever had exactly the same experience. Even where at times these were closely shared with a number of others, reactions were never completely the same, nor later memories identical.'[12]

One battalion whose history has never been written is the 25th, which was recruited in Nova Scotia in the winter of 1914–15 as part of the Second Contingent. It went to England in April 1915, then in September 1915 to France and Belgium, where it served throughout the war, and finally to Germany to serve in the occupation after the armistice. Gerald McElhenny, who served in the battalion, published a brief history of the 25th as a chapter in M.S. Hunt's *Nova Scotia's Part in the Great War*, published in 1920. It is a good narrative summary, typical of the battalion histories being written in the early post-war period, but it is only twenty-one pages in length. Many years later, in 1983, F.B. MacDonald and John J. Gardiner published *The Twenty-Fifth Battalion, Canadian Expeditionary Force: Nova Scotia's Famous Regiment in World War One*. Unfortunately, it is poorly written, thin, and reflects no research, its chief contribution being to publish the battalion's nominal roll and war diary, and to include regrettably brief interviews with ten veterans. There is one good first-hand personal memoir; Ralph Lewis, a Newfoundlander who served in the battalion, published *Over the Top with the 25th* in 1918, but it is only fifty-four pages in length and ends in April 1917 when he was wounded near Vimy Ridge. Francis MacGregor, a Cape Bretoner, included a very general account of his experience in the 25th in his 1976 autobiography, *Days That I Remember*, but it is only five pages in length.[13] More useful are the letters of Percy Willmot, an Englishman who grew up in Cape Breton, which relate his experiences in England and France. Their value is also limited, however, because he was a staff sergeant during most of the war and did not take part in the actual fighting until August 1918, and because he was generally careful about what he included in his letters.[14]

There is, however, the present unique history of the battalion, which was written in the 1970s by Robert Nehemiah Clements, who served in the 25th throughout the war. His manuscript, which until now has never been published, is unusual in that it is obviously an eye-witness account based on his personal experiences and observations, but it is written as a unit history, although it makes no claim to being a traditional regimental history because Clements did no research other than to consult Nicholson's *Canadian Expeditionary Force, 1914–1919* to assist him with the general narrative. It is unique, however, in that it gives a complete history of the 25th Battalion, written by a man who served in it from its creation to demobilization. And whereas most regimental histories, at least the early ones, were written by officers at the request and under the supervision of other officers, Clements's account reflects the experiences of a man who started out as a private, although he rose to the rank of captain, and was writing independently, many years later. Being part history and part memoir, his book constitutes an exceptional contribution to our knowledge of the war and those who fought in it.

I discovered Clements's unpublished manuscript in the Public

Archives of Nova Scotia when I was working on Percy Willmot's letters. As readers of that book will know, I used material from Clements's manuscript to flesh out some of the history of the battalion as necessary background to the letters. *Merry Hell* deserves to be published in full, however, because it is an exceptionally lively personal history of the battalion, filled with anecdotes and accounts of events not included in official histories such as Nicholson's *Canadian Expeditionary Force, 1914–1919* and certainly not included in the briefer accounts mentioned earlier. As well, it includes several of Clements's entertaining poems, which are similar in style, content, and quality to those of Robert Service.

One wonders why he wrote *Merry Hell* so many years after the war, and for whom he was writing. In his own words, it was

> not intended to be just another war history, or to make any attempt to justify war as such ... *Merry Hell* has been written solely on behalf of the men in the ranks who with their officers served in the infantry battalions of the CEF 1914–1919. For the first time it tells their full story in their own words.

At the same time, he hoped that all veterans, including those who served in the Second World War, 'will find a mirror of their army service and that of the comrades with whom those years were shared.' He also hoped that his history 'will truly reflect my great love and respect for those grand young Canadians and help to preserve their memory in the hearts of their countrymen.'[15] Clements appears to have been stimulated to write the book because he was troubled by the 'dissension and unrest in our wonderful country' in the late 1960s and early 1970s, when, it will be remembered, the Quebec crisis was raging, with a sovereignist political party calling for independence, the radical FLQ engaging in violence, the War Measures Act proclaimed, and armed troops patrolling the streets of Montreal. It was in this environment that Clements wrote *Merry Hell*, pleading that 'we must never forget the honour and pride they [the soldiers of the Great War] felt in facing the world with the word "CANADA" on their shoulders.'[16]

These comments raise the question of whether Clements might have written his memoir differently if he had written it forty years earlier, just after the war. It seems likely that he would have, but one of the remarkable things about this manuscript is that Clements's recollections of events remained sharp despite the passage of time. At the same time, it is strengthened, I think, by the fact that he was looking back from a perspective of so many years during which he had obviously matured and perhaps mellowed and now felt, as he said, that it was time to tell not just his story but the story of the 5,000 young Canadians who had served in the largest and most brutal war in history.

Why was *Merry Hell* never published? We will never know, as Clements did not include any personal papers when he donated copies of the manuscript to the Public Archives of Canada (now Library and Archives Canada) and the Nova Scotia Archives. It seems likely that he would have submitted it to a few publishers, and we can only surmise that they turned it down. It must be remembered that there were very few small community-oriented publishers in the 1970s and getting published was much more difficult than it is today. Clements was a retired businessman, probably with little knowledge of the publishing world. We can only be grateful that he wrote the manuscript and did send copies to two archives, perhaps hoping that sooner or later someone would resurrect it.

Because this book was not written until the 1970s, Clements had had lots of time to reflect on and contextualize his wartime experiences. Did the passage of so many years have an influence on the way he tells his story? The amount of detail which he includes suggests that it did not, and his goal clearly was to tell the story, as he experienced it, but without any desire either to glorify war or to shock his readers. One senses that he was aware of the revisionist historiography of the war, but he did not allow it to make him wise *ex post facto*. There is no reflection of Remarque, Acland, or Harrison here. At the same time, he was clearly writing, not for his fellow veterans – although some of his humorous anecdotes about men he does not name would surely have been best appreciated by those who could remember them – but for readers of the 1970s and later, who lived in a world vastly different and far removed from the period he was writing about. He was careful, for example, to explain the pay system and terms like 'the awkward squad,' and to describe the food, things not usually included in regimental histories because they were deemed unnecessary, and which tend not to be found in modern academic studies either. In a nutshell, Clements's book is important because it was written without trying to be important: there is nothing self-conscious about it, and his sense of humour and folksy poetry add to its unique charm.

Who was Robert Clements? Born in Yarmouth, Nova Scotia, on 12 May 1894, Robert Nehemiah Clements was the son of Edgar Norwood and Charlotte Van Norden Clements. The Clements family could trace its history back to John and Mary Clements of Salem, Massachusetts. Although not one of the famous thirteen original settlers who founded Yarmouth in 1761, their son, also called John, was among the earliest settlers of the Chebogue-Yarmouth area, arriving in 1769.[17] These New Englanders moved to the area, at the invitation of the Nova Scotian government following the expulsion of the Acadians, to establish a fishery. John and his descendants prospered, becoming shipbuilders and -owners, culminating in Nehemiah Kelly Clements (1816-80), who achieved considerable prominence and wealth. One of his business partners was his uncle, Reubin Z. Clements (1783–1868), whose daughter, Caroline, married George Killam, a member of the most prominent shipping dynasty in Yarmouth. Nehemiah was a remarkably far-sighted businessman who, unlike many others, successfully made the transition to the emerging industrial economy. He built and owned steamships, founding the Clements Steamship Company, supported Confederation in the 1860s, and was one of the founders of the Western Counties Railway Company in 1871. At the time of his death, he was busily promoting the establishment of a woollen mill in Yarmouth. One of his sons was Edgar Norwood Clements, who became a prominent lawyer in Yarmouth and was the father of Robert Nehemiah Clements.

After graduating from Yarmouth Academy in 1911, Clements began working at the Bank of Montreal in Yarmouth, but in November 1914 he enlisted in the 25th Battalion. He served in it throughout the war, was promoted to quartermaster sergeant of 'A' Company in February 1915, and was commissioned in the field in September 1916. Mentioned in dispatches in August 1917, he was wounded in August 1918, awarded the Military Cross, and promoted to the rank of captain.

Following the battalion's demobilization, Clements returned to Yarmouth and began his business career as a student apprentice at Cosmos Imperial Mills Limited, a cotton mill which was then the major employer in Yarmouth. In 1921 he attended the Municipal School of Technology in Manchester, England, taking two accelerated courses in cotton manufacturing, after which he returned to the Cosmos mill as assistant manufacturing superintendent from 1921 to 1925. At some point, he married Ann Winnifred Mitchell, then went to work for Ayers Limited, which operated a textile mill at Lachute, Quebec. In 1931 he established the Textile Machinery and Sales Agency in Montreal, which supplied production machinery to the textile industry. He retired in 1965 but remained involved in the company until 1969, when he severed his last remaining connections with it.

After his first retirement, Clements and his wife moved to Rexdale, Ontario, where he wrote this history of the 25th Battalion. He subsequently revised the manuscript in 1975–6 and donated copies to the Public Archives of Nova Scotia and Library and Archives Canada. At some point, following Ann's death on 16 July 1975, he returned to Nova Scotia and died at the Camp Hill Veterans' Hospital in Halifax on 31 January 1983. They appear to have had no children.[18]

The 25th Battalion was authorized shortly after the dispatch of the First Contingent to England in October 1914. It was one of the fifteen battalions that comprised the Second Contingent, two of which were raised in the Maritime provinces. One, the 26th, was raised in New Brunswick, and the 25th was the other, which therefore became the first battalion organized and raised entirely in Nova Scotia.[19] Lieutenant Colonel George Augustus Le Cain of the 69th Militia Regiment was given command, headquarters were established in Halifax, and recruiting took place throughout the province. By Christmas 1914 the battalion had reached full strength.

Unlike the First Contingent, which had been called to Valcartier Camp in Quebec for training, the Second Contingent battalions remained in their respective military districts for training. Because of a shortage of training facilities in England and the demands on shipping for the transportation of reinforcements for the First Contingent, the British government did not want the new force to cross the Atlantic until the troops already there had gone to France.[20] Accordingly, three battalions sailed in February, and the twelve battalions that remained in Canada were organized into three brigades on a territorial basis. The 25th Battalion was included in the Fifth Brigade, along with the 22nd, 24th, and 26th Battalions, which had been raised in Quebec and New Brunswick.[21]

As the Halifax armoury could not accommodate that many men, some were housed in tents on the North Common. Even so, 350 men had to be moved to the federal immigration building at Deepwater Terminals in February because of overcrowding at the armoury. The battalion trained daily on the Common and on the slopes of nearby Citadel Hill.[22] Daily musketry training took place at McNab's Island, and route marches and manoeuvres took place around the North West Arm, at Chain Lake, and across the harbour in Dartmouth. By spring, the men were anxious to go overseas, the big day finally arriving on 20 May, when the 25th Battalion marched from the armoury to Pier Two. Huge crowds lined the streets to watch the dramatic and emotional spectacle. After the battalion had boarded the Cunard Steamship Company's *Saxonia*, the 22nd Battalion arrived by train and boarded as well.

Unlike the First Contingent, which had been sent to Salisbury Plain for training and had endured a brutal wet and muddy winter, the Second Contingent troops were posted to East Sandling military camp, which was situated just outside of Folkestone on England's south coast. Once there, the 25th was engaged from May to September 1915 in further training. In the middle of September, it crossed to France and almost immediately went into action. It saw continuous service, participating in all of the major battles for which the Canadian Expeditionary Force became justly famous, until it found itself on the morning of 11 November 1918 entering the city of Mons, site of the first clash between British and German troops in August 1914. Following the armistice, it went on to participate in the occupation of Germany until, in April 1919, it finally returned to England, and a month later sailed home to Halifax, almost precisely four years after its departure.

Merry Hell is presented here exactly as Clements wrote it except that I have corrected his appalling spelling and eccentric grammar, combined paragraphs to make the text flow more smoothly, and omitted several pages of operational orders that he included at the beginning of chapter 20. I have also added explanatory notes where they seemed necessary and a short bibliography for those who may wish to read further on the subject.

I'm sure that all who read and enjoy this book will join me in thanking Robert Clements for writing it. I also wish to express my deep appreciation to the Public Archives of Nova Scotia, which gave me permission to copy the manuscript with a view to publishing it. I am grateful also to the anonymous readers who evaluated this manuscript for their insightful and constructive suggestions, which have greatly improved the final result. I am especially grateful to Len Husband at University of Toronto Press, whose belief in the importance of this project made this publication possible, to Ken Lewis, whose skilful copy-editing significantly improved the text, and to Frances Mundy for guiding the book (and me) through the production process. Sandra Atwell-Tennyson helped with background research, proofread the manuscript, and as always was supportive of yet another project.

Portions of the first two chapters were previously published as 'Pre-paring for War: The 25th Battalion in Halifax, 1914–15,' in *Canadian Military History* 20.1 (Winter 2011): 61–73.

Brian Douglas Tennyson
Bridgewater, Nova Scotia
6 June 2012

NOTES

1 Winston S. Churchill, *The World Crisis, 1911–1918* (London, 1939), vol. 1, p. 2.
2 John Keegan, *The First World War* (Toronto, 1998), p. 3.
3 Cited in Tim Cook, *Clio's Warriors: Canadian Historians and the Writing of the World Wars* (Vancouver, 2006), p. 10. Desmond Morton and J.L. Granatstein describe the war years as ' a great divide' in Canada. 'In the aftermath, Canadians tried to return to their old ways but found they could not do so. The war cost them their innocence' (Desmond Morton and J.L. Granat-stein, *Marching to Armageddon: Canadians and the Great War, 1914–1919* [Toronto, 1989], p. 1).
4 On the transition from a rural agricultural society to an increasingly urban industrial society, see Kenneth Norrie and Douglas Owram, *A History of the Canadian Economy* (Toronto, 1991), pp. 411–40; Paul-Andre Linteau, Rene Durocher, and Jean-Claude Robert, *Quebec: A History, 1867–1929* (Toronto, 1983), pp. 116–38; Paul Voisey, 'The Urbanization of the Canadian Prairies, 1871–1916,' *Histoire sociale / Social History* 8.15 (May 1975): 77–101; N.H. Lithwick, 'The Process of Urbanization in Canada,' in *Readings in Cana-dian Geography*, ed. R.M. Irving (Toronto, 1972), pp. 130–45; and Richard Preston, 'The Evolution of Urban Canada: The post-1867 Period,' in Irving, ed., *Readings in Canadian Geography*, pp. 19–46. On Canada's evolution to autonomy, see Robert Craig Brown and Ramsay Cook, *Canada, 1896–1921: A Nation Transformed* (Toronto, 1974); and C.P. Stacey, *Canada and the Age of Conflict*, 2 vols (Toronto, 1977–81).
5 The popular enthusiasm for the war displayed by the crowds in London and Berlin was not reflected in Paris, where it was understood that France must bear the brunt of the first attacks in the west by the world's domi-nant military power, and there were very real doubts about the attitudes of revolutionary syndicalists, socialists, and the workers generally. The public displays of militant jingoism in London were somewhat misleading as well, as there were very real divisions within the political class, includ-

ing the government, about the wisdom of going to war, as well as outright opposition by some labour leaders and pacifists. See Arthur Marwick, *The Deluge: British Society and the First World War* (London, 1965), pp. 15–35. In Germany, according to Roger Chickering, 'as the crisis intensified, the crowds grew; and in many places the mood grew euphoric to the accompaniment of military and civilian bands, the singing of patriotic songs, the waving of flags, and spontaneous processions through the centers of cities, particularly in university towns, where students provided the lead ... The spectacle had already taken on the air of a public festival' when Russia mobilized and 'the exhilaration of early August was captured in innumerable scenes ... of flag-bedecked public squares ... where crowds gathered in increasing numbers as the crisis reached its climax' (*Imperial Germany and the Great War, 1914–1918* [Cambridge, 1998], p. 13). Jeffrey Verhey agrees that the outbreak of war was 'a moment of powerful intensity and sharpness' and that 'some Germans, especially German intellectuals, experienced the August days as a liminal experience, as a moment when individual and collective identities were transformed, as a miracle, a renewal of oneself, a liberation, a rebirth.' He argues, however, that enthusiasm should not be confused with excitement and that 'the only shared emotion of the August experiences was not enthusiasm but excitement, a depth of emotion, an intensity of feeling.' In reality, the outbreak of war 'did not produce any noticeable changes in attitudes and beliefs. The working class accepted the war, hoped that Germany would win, but remained unenthusiastic and sceptical' (*The Spirit of 1914: Militarism, Myth, and Mobilization in Germany* [Cambridge, 2000], pp. 231, 232). As for Canada, the public displays of enthusiasm were also somewhat misleading. While there undoubtedly was an excited outpouring of patriotism and excitement at the prospect of great adventure, these attitudes largely represented the urban communities more than rural Canada. As Tim Cook rightly points out, 'English and French were united behind the war at first, the true gulf being between rural and urban centres. Most farmers continued to stoically work the land, assuming – and rightly at first – that this was a big-city war' (*At the Sharp End: Canadians Fighting the Great War, 1914–1916* [Toronto, 2007], p. 23). While political leaders and newspapers in Quebec did initially support the war, their statements were somewhat qualified, recognizing that Québécois, mindful of the South African war, were understandably less enthusiastic about participating in another, and much larger, imperial war. Cf. Ian Hugh MacLean Miller, *Our Glory and Our Grief: Torontonians and the Great War* (Toronto, 2002); Robert Rutherdale, *Hometown Horizons: Local Responses to Canada's Great War* (Vancouver,

2004), which examines attitudes in Guelph, Lethbridge, and Trois Rivières; and James M. Pitsula, *For All We Have and Are: Regina and the Experience of the Great War* (Winnipeg, 2008). On Québécois attitudes, see Gérard Filteau, *Le Québec, le Canada, et la guerre, 1914–1918* (Montreal, 1977), pp. 15–25.

6 On the history of the memory of the war, see Paul Fussell, *The Great War and Modern Memory* (London, 1975); Jonathan Vance, *Death So Noble: Memory, Meaning and the First World War* (Vancouver, 1997); Suzanne Evans, *Mothers of Heroes, Mothers of Martyrs: World War I and the Politics of Grief* (Montreal/Kingston, 2007); and David Macfarlane, *The Danger Tree: Memory, War, and the Search for a Family's Past* (Toronto, 1991).

7 Notable exceptions were R.C. Fetherstonhaugh's histories of the 13th, 14th, and 24th Battalions, the Royal Canadian Dragoons, and the Royal Canadian Regiment. Fetherstonhaugh had a physical disability and did not serve. Another exception was S.G. Bennett's *The 4th Canadian Mounted Regiment, 1914–1919* (Toronto, 1926). Bennett was a veteran, but he had served as a captain in the Royal Engineers.

8 Cook, *Clio's Warriors*, p. 66.

9 See, for example, G.W.L. Nicholson, *The Fighting Newfoundlanders: A History of the Royal Newfoundland Regiment* (St John's, 1964); James L. McWilliams and James Steel, *The [46th] Suicide Battalion* (Edmonton, 1978); Daniel G. Dancocks, *Gallant Canadians: The Story of the Tenth Canadian Infantry Battalion, 1914–1919* (Calgary, 1990); S. Douglas MacGowan, Henry Heckbert, and Byron O'Leary, *New Brunswick's 'Fighting 26th': A History of the 26th New Brunswick Battalion, C.E.F., 1914–1919* (Saint John, 1994); Bruce Tascona, *From the Forks to Flanders Fields: The Story of the 27th City of Winnipeg Battalion, 1914–1919* (Winnipeg, 1995); David Bercuson, *The Patricias: The Proud History of a Fighting Regiment* (New York, 2001); and Mark Zuehlke, *Brave Battalion: The Remarkable Saga of the 16th Battalion (Canadian Scottish) in the First World War* (Toronto, 2008).

10 Tim Cook, *At the Sharp End: Canadians Fighting the Great War, 1914–1916* (Toronto, 2007) and *Shock Troops: Canadians Fighting the Great War, 1917–1918* (Toronto, 2008). Cf. Kenneth Radley, *We Lead, Others Follow: First Canadian Division, 1914–1918* (St Catharines, 2008); and Andrew Iarocci, *Shoestring Soldiers: The 1st Canadian Division at War, 1914–1915* (Toronto, 2008).

11 Cook, *Clio's Warriors*, pp. 67–8.

12 Preface, p. 3. On the various factors – from command structure and personalities down to group identities – influencing the wartime experience of individuals and battalions, see David Campbell, 'The Divisional Experience in the C.E.F.: A Social and Operational History of the 2nd Canadian Division, 1915–1918' (PhD diss., University of Calgary, 2004).

13 Francis MacGregor (1883–1968) was born in Stellarton, Nova Scotia, but
    grew up on a farm at Baddeck River. He was working in northern Ontario
    as a miner but happened to be in Boston on vacation when the war broke
    out. He immediately went to Halifax and joined the 25th Battalion, enlist-
    ing under the name 'Frank McGregor.'
14 Brian Tennyson, *Percy Willmot: A Cape Bretoner at War* (Sydney, 2007). Will-
    mot enlisted in the 25th in November 1914 and served until October 1918,
    when, having been promoted to lieutenant, he was wounded at Cambrai.
    His account through his letters is limited, however, because he went to
    England in September 1917 for officer training and did not return to the
    front until August 1918.
15 Preface, pp. 3–4.
16 Ch. 1, p. 7.
17 Interestingly, he brought the family home with him. It was dismantled and
    brought to Chebogue, where it was reassembled. It survives to this day
    and is thought to be the oldest house in Chebogue and possibly the oldest
    in Yarmouth County.
18 Ann's obituary appeared in the *Globe & Mail* on 19 July 1975, Robert's in
    the Halifax *Chronicle-Herald* on 1 February 1983 and the Yarmouth *Van-
    guard* on 9 February 1983. None of the obituaries mentions any children,
    living or dead.
19 G.C. McElhenny, 'The 25th Battalion,' in *Nova Scotia's Part in the Great War*,
    ed. M.S. Hunt (Halifax, 1920), p. 71.
20 G.W.L. Nicholson, *Canadian Expeditionary Force, 1914–1919* (Ottawa, 1962),
    p. 109.
21 Ibid., p. 110.
22 Francis MacGregor, *Days That I Remember* (Windsor, 1976), p. 38.

MERRY HELL

The Story of the 25th Battalion
(Nova Scotia Regiment)

Canadian Expeditionary Force 1914–1919

Preface

In the great wars of 1914–1919 and 1939–1945 millions of men and women were engaged. No two people ever had exactly the same experience. Even where at times these were closely shared with a number of others, reactions were never completely the same, nor later memories identical.

Merry Hell is a record of 1,100 young Canadians and a further 4,500 who followed them into the 25th Battalion, Nova Scotia Regiment, Fifth Brigade, Second Division, CEF, through four and one half years of World War I, from November 1914 to May 1919.

The locale and record of one particular battalion, while important, has to be taken as incidental. The primary purpose is to supply the framework in which the narrative is developed. With relative variations the writing relates intimately to every unit in the CEF.

The book is not intended to be just another war history, or to make any attempt to justify war as such. Many excellent historical accounts already exist. *Merry Hell* has been written solely on behalf of the men in the ranks who with their officers served in the infantry battalions of the CEF 1914–1919. For the first time it tells their full story in their own words.

It is astonishing how many of those men still survive. In this volume all will find a mirror of their army service and that of the comrades with whom those years were shared. This is equally true of the men and women who served from 1939 to 1945 in World War II. The book and its contents will have a strong appeal to them, no matter what part of Canada they now call home.

I am very grateful for the encouragement received from many old comrades and friends. I was also most fortunate through the kindness of Mrs W.J. Evans of Montreal for her permission to examine and take notes from the personal papers of her father, the late Sir David Watson, KCB, CMG, covering the time from his enlistment in 1914 through to his position at the end of the war commanding the Fourth Division.[1]

Reference to a book put out by the 24th Battalion, Victoria Rifles of Montreal, some time after its return to Canada, enabled me to check and sort out many dates and places.[2] Examination of other books and records in the military museum at the Citadel in Halifax, Nova Scotia, was also helpful. Copies of old letters and discussions with many former Fifth Brigade men added details and refreshed my memory. Finally, continued reference to Colonel G.W.L. Nicholson's magnificent book, *Canadian Expeditionary Force 1914–1919*,[3] enabled me to keep the narrative in correct sequence and add many references beyond my own personal knowledge.

I can only hope what I have tried to create will truly reflect my great love and respect for those grand young Canadians and help to preserve their memory in the hearts of their countrymen.

The freedoms we still possess were kept secure by their courage and the sacrifices they and men and women like them made through those dreadful years of World Wars I and II.

For record purposes an appendix provides the nominal roll of the officers and men of the 25th Battalion at the muster parade of June 6th, 1915, immediately following the arrival in England.[4]

Manpower

From November 1914 to May 1919 more than 5,500 men passed

---

1 David Watson (1871–1922) was a journalist who became managing director of the Quebec *Chronicle*. He was also active in the militia and by 1910 was lieutenant colonel of the 8th Royal Rifles of Quebec. He has been described as an old 'crony' of Sam Hughes, the minister of militia in the Borden government (Desmond Morton and J.L. Granatstein, *Marching to Armageddon* [Toronto, 1989], 107). On the outbreak of war, he was appointed lieutenant colonel in command of the 2nd Battalion. In 1915 he was promoted to brigadier general commanding the Fifth Brigade in the Second Division. In May 1916 he was promoted to major general and replaced Lord Brooke in command of the Fourth Division, which position he retained until the end of the war. He was knighted in 1918.

2 R.C. Fetherstonaugh, *The 24th Battalion, CEF, Victoria Rifles of Canada, 1914–1919* (Montreal, 1930).

3 Ottawa: Queen's Printer, 1962.

4 Editor's note: the original manuscript separated the officers and men into two appendices. I have combined them into one.

through the ranks of the 25th Battalion. Of these, thirty-two officers and 686 other ranks were killed. A further two officers and sixty-four other ranks were reported missing and presumed killed.

There were 156 officers and 2,557 other ranks reported wounded.

The strength of the battalion on its return to Halifax on 16 May 1919 was forty-five officers and 975 other ranks.

Decorations[5]

The following decorations were awarded to members of the battalion during its three years and seven months of service in France and Belgium from September 1915 to April 1919:

Distinguished Service Order	5
Bar to DSO	2
Military Cross	40
Bar to Military Cross	7
Distinguished Conduct Medal	13
Bar to DCM	2
Military Medal	156
1st Bar to MM	22
2nd Bar to MM	1
Mentioned in Dispatches	25
Military Service Medal	7

---

5 Clements does not mention that one soldier in the 25th Battalion was executed for desertion. Elsworth Young, who was born in Halifax in 1895, enlisted in the 25th Battalion in November 1914. He went to France with the battalion in September 1915 and served as an officer's batman until, during the battle for Courcelette, he was ordered into action. He failed to report for duty until later that evening, when the fighting was over. A year later, in September 1916, he went absent again and was arrested by military police some miles behind the front lines. He was dressed in the uniform of a corporal in an artillery unit and initially gave false details to the MPs when they questioned him. He was charged with desertion, found guilty, and was executed on the morning of 29 October 1916, near Bully-Grenay.

Chapter One

In the Beginning

There is not any such thing as a nice, clean, polite war. War is always a mean dirty business. It is particularly tough on the men in the ranks and their junior officers who are exposed in the forward areas to all the worst hazards of the fighting fronts.

Courage takes many forms and is drawn from many sources. Not the least is the part which humour plays in maintaining sanity and self-control under extreme pressure. The ability to laugh and make a joke of their circumstances sustained these men at times when everything else failed. This helps to explain the title of this story, *Merry Hell*.

They desperately needed all the humour and relaxation they could find to control the tensions and endure the hells they had to face and overcome. Without these they would have failed. Their enemies did, partly at least through the lack of these very qualities.

Today, with so much dissension and unrest in our wonderful country, we must never forget the honour and pride they felt in facing the world with the word 'Canada' on their shoulders. The 25th Battalion started recruiting at Halifax, Nova Scotia, following the call from Ottawa in November 1914 for men to form part of the Second Division, supplementary to the first Canadian troops already en route to England. The response was rapid and effective. Large numbers of men quickly came forward from every part of the province.[6]

Some recruits came from the docks and shipping in port, others from local militia regiments with a small amount of peacetime training. There were salt bank fishermen from Lunenburg and Newfoundland, farmers

---

6 Actually, the call from Ottawa was made in October. The 25th Battalion was recruited solely in Nova Scotia.

from the Annapolis Valley, coal miners and men from the steel works at
Sydney and Glace Bay in Cape Breton, some as much at home in Gaelic
as in English. From the southwestern counties came deep sea sailors
and lumbermen, many with Acadian names marking their French origins. Others came from Cumberland and Colchester with early family
origins in the dales of Yorkshire. More men arrived from Antigonish
and Pictou, where the landing of the original settlers from the famous
ship *Hector* was still a sacred memory.

At that time British consuls in the New England states, being resident
in a neutral country, could not do any active recruiting. They did, however, direct several small groups of British-born young men to Halifax.
Some went right on through to England but quite a few enlisted in the
25th Battalion where they found a ready welcome.

Recruits on arrival were checked by medical examination and if
found acceptable were recorded by name and given numbers. They
were then issued with two blankets, a mattress cover known in army
language as a 'palliasse,' together with a pillow case of similar material.
Both the latter were stuffed by the prospective soldier with straw from
a large pile in a corner of the armory. Each was assigned to a company
and given a bunk located in one or other of the hastily prepared barrack
rooms.

At first there were not any uniforms. The men paraded and were
given preliminary drill instruction as they stood on arrival. Gradually,
uniforms began to appear from that mysterious source, the quartermaster's stores. The NCOs got first pick as usual. It was several weeks
before the entire unit of some 1,200 men was completely and uniformly
covered.

Each temporarily possessed two suits of Stanfield's 'Unshrinkable'
woollen combinations (quickly christened Stanfield's Unstinkables),
two pair of woollen socks, one top shirt, one sweater coat, officially
known as a cardigan jacket, one pair of pants, one regulation jacket,
one overcoat (called a greatcoat), one cap, one pair of woollen gloves,
and one pair of strong non-elastic braces to hold up the pants. A metal
maple leaf cap badge plus two smaller collar badges and two shoulder
badges marked 'Canada' appeared about the same time.

Oh yes, one other item: the famous puttees, consisting of two long
rolls of cloth some three inches wide, to be wound around the legs
from boot tops to below the knees. It took long and painful training
to acquaint the entire assembly with the proper system of applying
these attachments. Some never did learn and one such became gener-

ally known as 'Feather Legs.' He was a smallish man with an 'Old Bill' mustache and among other virtues he had a weak bladder, so care was always necessary to see that he was kept in the lower tier of bunks. One night he found relief in one of the company sergeant major's boots, which had been carefully polished and set out near a hot water pipe to be kept warm for the morning. The resulting explosion provided a news item for the whole unit for several days thereafter but no one squealed in spite of considerable pressure and Feather Legs escaped the threatened dire punishment. He made the grade as far as England but it is not clear that he ever got to France. In any case he disappeared somewhere along the way and was never heard from again. The foregoing deed remains his one claim to fame.

The old army game of 'one man one shirt' prevailed from the start. A small 5' 7" 135 pounder received with the quartermaster's blessing a garment large enough for someone 6' 2", weighing upwards of 200 pounds and vice versa. After much trading and help from Sergeant Jack Henry,[7] the regimental tailor, and his staff, the unit gradually reached a point where it was reasonably fit to be seen in public. All civilian clothing was flogged for beer money to the second-hand dealers on Water Street or sent back to the old home for use by younger members of the family not yet old enough to enlist.

One of the main problems was boots. The current style for the well-dressed young blade of those days was a brilliant yellow creation with sharply pointed toes, a sad choice for pounding the armory parade square and even sadder for training on the Common and the slopes of Citadel Hill during the snow and slush of a Halifax winter. Naturally, that is exactly what was issued to the troops. They came in large wooden cases and assorted sizes. Again, the usual scramble trying to match a size eight boot to a size eleven foot was followed by more horse trading and not a few unusual combinations, complicated further by the fact that several cases contained sample boots, all for one foot.

Winter was well under way. One hour outside completely wrecked the footwear of all so unfortunately exposed to the elements. The soles of that first issue were made of pressed paper, not even the cheapest leather. One soaking was enough to make them fall apart completely. Fortunately, most of the men had kept their own original boots. With these they managed to avoid becoming entirely barefooted. Others in

7 John Francis Henry (b. 1890) was a Halifax tailor before enlisting in the 25th Battalion in November 1914.

desperation bought good stout boots from local stores with their own money. New supplies of better service quality and design effectively shod the battalion prior to leaving for overseas on May 20th, 1915.

Further items of presumed utility were issued early on. These included one heavy clasp knife (good quality), one each metal knife, fork and spoon, one cloth folder containing needles, thread and spare buttons (officially described as a housewife, shortened by tradition to 'Hussif'). Mess tins were not needed at that time. The troops were fed off enamel plates, with heavy mugs for tea, served in large mess halls in the basement of the armory building. Issue of rubber ground sheets was delayed until movement to England some months later.

Other extra items were razors and shaving brushes. These were real dillies. The blades were soft steel or tin, disgracing even the Woolworth stores of that era. It was impossible to cut even a soft piece of cheese with them. The brushes were made out of some sort of rope fibre. They fell to bits at the first wetting, another case of buy your own and like it. Many had safety razors but good straight razors were not uncommon. Unlike today's generation, most men knew how to use a straight razor without cutting their own throats or generally making an unholy mess of their chin.

A cloth roll arrangement was given out to carry the eating utensils, razor and brush and other small items. All this list plus such personal effects as the individual desired to retain were kept in a canvas kit bag supplied along with the bedding at time of enlistment.

Lacking any real war experience the authorities had to look for guidance to records of the South African war. After a few weeks of foot drill instruction and preliminary organization, the process of turning men into pack mules got under way. This involved issue of an outfit officially known as the Oliver equipment. It comprised a leather belt and an assortment of straps in various shapes, all held together by buckles and rings. The ball pouch for ammunition fitted on the belt in front. A bayonet in scabbard also hung on the belt on the left side. The water bottle in its sling hung on the right side supported by a long strap over the left shoulder crossing the wearer's chest. A fabric haversack for small items including emergency rations (one can of corned beef and a few rock-hard biscuits) hung on the left side over the bayonet position. Its strap crossed the chest in the opposite direction to the water bottle strap. These two straps effectively restricted the soldier's breathing, particularly when the bottle was full and the haversack loaded.

When complete, the man's kit bag carrying all his other possessions was supported in straps on his back. In full marching order it was expected that his blanket or blankets would be rolled and strapped on his load above the kit bag. Added to all this was the long Ross rifle (rated to weigh nine and a half pounds but actually more nearly twelve to fourteen pounds). How any man could be in shape for effective fighting after several hours on the road under such a load has never been clearly established.

Training with this equipment went some distance in separating the boys from the men. It brought out physical defects not evident through the medical examinations at the time of enlistment. Those who could not make the grade were honourably discharged and sent home. Their places were quickly taken by other new recruits, at that time readily available.

This equipment was used throughout the training period in Halifax from November 1914 to May 1915. Taken overseas, it continued in use until replaced by the web model just a few days before movement to France on September 15th, 1915. It is certain that no man temporarily decorated and loaded with that Oliver equipment will ever completely forget it.

Chapter Two

Growing Pains

Oh they dressed us up in khaki in the very latest styles,
Then marched us round the Common for miles and miles and miles.
Till our feet were flat and weary and beyond all ways and means,
So they took us back to barracks, to feed us tea and beans.

At the start the battalion was organized on the South African war model, with a headquarters staff and eight companies of about 120 men each. After some weeks this was modernized, changing to four companies of roughly 250 men per company, each then divided into four platoons.

Before the change, several interesting situations developed. According to tradition, each company commander was held responsible for preparing his own company payroll. Drawing the funds through battalion HQ cheque, he paid his own men. Whatever their other talents, most of these officers had little previous experience of such duties. Previous banking experience could quickly lift a private to three stripes and a sergeant's rank.[8] This meant welcome relief from parade duties two days each week, to draw up the company payroll, go to the bank with the officer to count the money, and later pay it out to the worthy rank and file. Shortly after the change to four-company formation, a regular paymaster and staff were supplied from district headquarters and the company officers were relieved of that responsibility.

Rates of pay started with privates at $1.10 per day, followed by lance

---

8 Clements was one of those so promoted because of his previous employment at the Bank of Montreal in Yarmouth in February 1915. He was promoted to quartermaster sergeant of 'A' Company.

corporals at $1.20, corporals at $1.35, sergeants at $1.50, company quar-
termaster sergeants at $1.65, company sergeant majors at $1.75, and 1st
class warrant officers at $2.00. Rum was $1.00 a quart. At a private's pay
of $7.70 a week he had about seventy cents for luxuries after providing
for the necessities of his temporary situation. The claim was that there
were fifty-seven barrooms in the city at that time, the same number as
the well known pickles. Whether true or false, it made a good story.
Certainly, there was not any lack of refuge for the weary in need of liquid refreshment and support.

Trial and Error

The South African war had ended about fourteen years before the start
of World War I. A number of the first recruits carried South African war
medal ribbons and laid claim to some degree of combat experience
and military knowledge. This led to some early decisions which rather
quickly required revision.

It was first thought that these veterans would be ideal candidates for
non-commissioned rank. Quite a few of the early sergeants and corporals were selected from that group. A second group originally from
parts of Great Britain also appeared to qualify for consideration, based
on various terms of peacetime service in the regular British army. A fair
proportion of both types really did make good. Their work helping in
training the totally inexperienced majority should be recognized and
acknowledged.

Alas, in spite of these advantages, quite a few were somewhat less
than successful. For various reasons some had to be returned to the
ranks. The history of one such South African worthy may be worth
a brief review. Promoted to sergeant's rank, he was given charge of a
squad of men from Cape Breton who were still in civilian clothes. Out on
the Common in front of the armory building, under his officer's supervision he started to teach them squad drill. When the officer was called
to the orderly room in the main building to answer a telephone, the sergeant moved his men at the double well south along the drill area.

Here he halted them, removed his cap, and passed through the ranks
taking up a collection. The recruits, yielding to his pressure, contributed reluctantly. This quickly changed to delight when the sergeant
marched them smartly down a side street into the nearby barroom.
After lining them up at the counter, he dumped the collection from his
cap and ordered drinks all around. Additional donations were quickly

forthcoming. A search party hastily organized following the officer's return finally located the missing group and persuaded them to return to barracks. Any possibility of further drill instruction that day had vanished. Result: one sergeant reduced to corporal and forty men confined to barracks for two days.

The second time the corporal, still acting as a drill instructor, tried the same thing he was caught before he could deploy his troops to advantage. That evening he took the proceeds to finance a two-day personal holiday. Finally apprehended by the military police, he was returned to the armory under escort. Result: one corporal reduced to private, fined, and confined to barracks for two weeks.

A few weeks later a third outbreak brought about his discharge and return to civilian life. That only lasted long enough for him to re-enlist in the 40th Battalion then organizing at Aldershot, Nova Scotia. When the 25th required a reinforcement draft prior to sailing for England in May 1915, our hero returned with other 40th Battalion men.

To hasten the early organization program, two senior colour sergeant instructors from the RCRs [Royal Canadian Regiment] were attached to the 25th.[9] Under their supervision all NCOs and junior officers were given intensive training. A series of lectures outlined their duties and responsibilities. NCOs were trained in special classes to act as drill instructors to the new recruits. All phases of military organization, starting with squad drill through company and battalion formations and movements were introduced and gradually perfected.

With the issue of the then Canadian army standard Ross rifles and bayonets, arms drill was started, together with training in the care and operation of this equipment. During the winter season it was not possible to practice with live ammunition at outside ranges. There were several shooting galleries in the basement of the armory where service rifles loaded with light power gallery ammunition could be safely used. In addition to drill movements carrying rifles on parade and in training marches, good progress in actual shooting and firing exercises with related instruction was possible. When the weather cleared in

9 Born in the Channel Islands in 1889, Frederick Gerald Lauzanne was a career soldier who immigrated to Canada and enlisted in the Royal Canadian Regiment. At the outbreak of war, he was seconded to the 25th Battalion as an instructor. In July 1915 he transferred into the unit and subsequently rose to the rank of captain. Similarly, Frank Goddard (b. 1882) was a native of Birmingham, England, who came to Canada and enlisted in the Royal Canadian Regiment. He, too, was seconded to the 25th Battalion and also in July 1915 transferred into the unit.

the spring the men were taken in suitable groups to outside ranges for more advanced training with full load live ammunition.

Manpower

In view of what developed later on, bringing about the conscription issue, creating tensions in Canada which still remain after over fifty years, it should be interesting to briefly review the manpower situation existing in 1914 and early 1915. The call for the first contingent assembled at Valcartier, Quebec, following August 4th, 1914, met with such rapid response that the authorities could readily pick and choose. This established very high standards of physical fitness and good conduct to qualify men for enlistment and continued service.

The age limits were set at from eighteen to forty-five years. Men under twenty-one were required to secure written permission from their fathers or surviving parent or guardian before being accepted. At both ends of this scale some stretching of the truth undoubtedly prevailed. In later years it was more readily overlooked. In the main, however, an honest attempt was made to enforce the age regulations.

When it became clear, shortly after the movement of the first contingent to England early in October, that additional troops would be needed, a second division was authorized. This included the 25th Battalion as one of the infantry units to be formed. Recruiting, which started early in November, proceeded rapidly with plenty of volunteers readily available.

The medical examinations prior to enlistment were fairly effective as far as they went, but quite often failed to reveal at once a variety of physical defects. These came to light rather quickly under the strains of the hard training which followed. Some wastage developed from the start. In all such cases these men were given honourable discharge and returned to their homes without delay.

There were other reasons which caused some loss of personnel and need for replacements. Continued bad conduct in a small number of instances resulted in dishonourable discharge and return to civilian life. The very few cases of desertion resulted in severe punishment when the offenders were caught and returned. A few got away completely and were never seen again, at least as far as any 25th Battalion record can be traced. Most of the losses were due to physical breakdown. Where bad conduct or desertion did develop it was usually due to inability to adjust to military discipline and the restrictions of army life.

There were many other reasons for desertion, some of which may seem hard to believe. For some time after the battalion was organized there were strong barrack-room rumours suggesting an early end to the war and forecasting that the 25th would never go overseas. Weeks passed without any definite indication of early movement. Two men of Scottish origin decided they would not wait any longer and disappeared without a trace.

At this point it is necessary to temporarily and briefly turn ahead to the early months of 1916. By that time the 25th had moved from Halifax to England, completed training there, and moved to France in September of 1915. Since then they had been steadily engaged in trench duty in the Kemmel sector at the south flank of the Ypres salient. At least a year had passed since the departure of the two Scotch lads. On a trip out of the front line to a tent camp in reserve near Locre, the men over the wire fence in the next section of tents were a battalion of the Gordon Highlanders.

They were newly arrived in Belgium following evacuation from the Dardanelles disaster a few weeks earlier. There was much visiting back and forth between the two camps. Shortly after dark the first night, two kilted Gordons quietly enquired their way to the tents of 'A' Company of the 25th. There, sharing whatever refreshment could be hastily procured, they told their story. Weary of delays and the uncertainties of the situation in Halifax and incidentally not too popular with their company commander, they had decided to hasten their personal quarrel with the Germans. They bought some second-hand clothes from a dealer on Water Street and then signed on as seamen on a freight ship for Britain. With seamen rather in short supply, no questions were asked.

Immediately on arrival they made their way to Scotland and enlisted with the Gordons. The action they got was quite a bit faster and more than they anticipated. In exchange for the Dardanelles tour, they had given up the Canadian rate of pay of $1.10 per day, equal to about five shillings and sixpence, for the British rate of little more than one shilling, possibly worth some thirty cents Canadian. To a good Scotsman the financial sacrifice was more of a blow than the other unfortunate results. There were one or two further visits before the 25th moved back for another tour in the front line.

There is not any record of later contact with these two heroes, or what their ultimate fate may have been. At least it showed that all deserters were not cowards. Later on there will be another mention of contacts with the Gordons but for the present a return to Halifax in 1914–15 is necessary.

Spit and Polish

Early and sustained attention was given to personal cleanliness and correct military appearance at all times. After reveille, usually no later than 7:00 a.m., there was a brief PT parade followed by breakfast. From then until 9:00 a.m. the time was spent in shaving, washing and cleaning clothing and equipment, preparing for the daily parade of the whole battalion in platoon and company formation.

All men were required to shave daily. No excuses were accepted for lack of attention to this detail. Clothing was expected to be brushed clean with nothing torn or out of place. Boots had to be thoroughly clean and polished. The same applied to belts and all other leather equipment worn on parade. All buttons and badges must be in place, with none missing. These, together with belt buckles and metal fittings must be cleaned and polished to an extra high shine. Rifles and bayonets when carried were to be completely cleaned, oiled and in first-class working order at all times.

At the 9:00 a.m. parade a careful check was carried out by the company commanders and platoon officers. Any unfortunate offenders failing to pass inspection had their names taken and were booked to appear at the 11:00 a.m. company office for disciplinary action. A first offence of a minor nature usually was settled by a strong lecture. If carelessness and lack of attention continued the culprits were handed various periods of being confined to barracks. Exceptional cases were given one or more parades of pack drill. Both these types of punishment will be described in more detail further on.

Normal working days were from 7:00 a.m. to 5:00 p.m., followed by supper. All those not detailed for some duty, or being confined to barracks for their presumed or proven sins, were then free to go out and follow their own devices until 10:00 p.m. Late leave until 12:00 midnight could be secured by a limited number each day. It had to be applied for and covered by a special pass issued from the orderly room. There were also a few men of Halifax residence who for a time were granted permanent sleeping-out passes. These had to report back no later than 7:00 a.m. each day.

There was only one official entrance and exit from the armory, through the front door on North Park Street. The guard room was located at this point. All men leaving or entering had to report to the sergeant of the guard. Part of his duty was to see that each man was properly dressed before passing through to the street. In this duty he was aided by the regimental provost sergeant stationed at the same post during most of the evening hours.

Clothing had to be properly worn, all buttons shining and fastened, no badges missing, belts in place, knitted woollen gloves on hands and not missing or in the pockets of their greatcoats. For a time, men were required to carry what were known as swagger sticks. These were short tapered sticks about two feet long, usually with a small metal cap at the top and a ferrule at the bottom. These were not a free issue and had to be purchased by the men themselves. The purpose was not really as the name seemed to suggest, to add a bit of swank to the soldier's appearance. It was simply that when he carried a stick in his hand he could not go along with that hand in his pocket, a practice which was considered to be most unmilitary. With stick in left hand and right hand busy saluting officers along the route of his wanderings, the problem of sloppy appearance with hands in pockets was largely eliminated. Senior NCOs and officers carried full-length canes.

Under some conditions, sergeants when walking out also carried side arms (bayonet in scabbard on the belt). This regulation concerning side arms was cancelled by army order early in 1916 following a severe riot at Bailleul in France, near the Belgian border. NCOs' bayonets were snatched and used by some of the rioters. A number of serious wounds resulted before the fighting was controlled. No one from the 25th had any part in that particular trouble. The battalion was in the trenches some miles away at the time. Through the usual channels of the cookhouse chronicle and the latrine gazette they did learn most of the important details soon after.

Guard Duty

In the first few weeks the number of qualified sergeants and corporals was limited. That meant that guard duty came around quite often. In spite of numerous rehearsals and instruction periods, the daily ceremony of changing the guard was for a time somewhat less than a finished military exercise. There was also the problem of teaching the men on sentry duty to make sure they knew their instructions and passed them on properly to their replacements when relieved. Usually the guard consisted of a sergeant, one or two corporals or lance corporals, and sixteen men. Four sentries were posted, one on each side of the armory. The other twelve were held in the guard room to control any prisoners under detention and supply relief every two hours to the sentries outside.

At irregular intervals, once each twenty-four hours, the whole guard was turned out for inspection by the orderly officer of the day. During his tour of duty he checked the condition of the guard room and prisoners' section. It was also customary for him to visit the sentries to see that they were carrying out their duties properly and understood their instructions. For the first few days the only arms available for the sentries were two old muskets of South African vintage. One of these was carried by the sentry on the beat on North Park Street in front of the building. The second was used by the man on the Cunard Street side. On the other two sides the sentries temporarily carried swagger sticks only.

One night the front-door sentry got curious and removed the bolt from his musket. He did not know how to put it back again. While seeking help from his friend on Cunard Street, they heard the orderly officer approaching, so quickly parted and resumed marching their beats. After the proper challenge the officer inspected the sentry and then demanded his musket, which the lad promptly passed over to him. This, of course, was completely contrary to correct military practice. The officer, in checking out this lapse, pointed out that he could have shot the sentry with his own weapon. The sentry replied politely while hiding a slight smile that the musket was not any good because 'I've got the bolt in my own pocket.'

The officer, being a good sport, called it a draw. He continued on his rounds but the story got around. In its way it made certain no other sentry was ever caught out by the same trick. Incidentally, that sentry returned with the battalion four years later as a commissioned officer with a fine combat record.

Guard Room Capers

When the building was hastily converted into a barracks it lacked a proper guard room. One was built inside along the wall near the front door. The structure was made of matchboard about one inch thick and in two parts. The inside room held the prisoners and the outside section was the guards' quarters. The prisoners' section had a low sloping platform of wood on the floor for sleeping purposes. Blankets were provided but any idea of comfort was not part of the arrangements.

One pay night this section was well filled. The heat from the stove evidently took effect on several of the new arrivals, already somewhat unsteady from their earlier travels. Shortly after midnight a group on the inside worked the stove loose from its moorings. With a mighty heave they threw it right through the light wooden wall and out onto the floor. At that time the floor in the building was made of wooden blocks saturated with creosote.

When the stove burst open it scattered live coals in all directions and started many fires. Fortunately, there was good fire protection with water valves and sections of good hose nearby. The guard was at once fully engaged in controlling the fires. All the prisoners promptly departed through the hole in the wall, seeking the greater comfort of their regular bunks in the sleeping rooms.

After order had been restored and the fires extinguished the sergeant of the guard checked his record list of prisoners. It took all the rest of the night to locate them, one by one. When found, they were winkled out of their warm bunks to return to the now heatless confines of the prisoners' quarters. Next day the hole was fully repaired, the wall reinforced and a new stove installed. This time it was out in the guards' quarters. Only the pipe extended through the inside room, high up along the ceiling. It gave out just enough heat to take off the chill.

Canteen

A canteen of sorts was opened along the wall at the back end of the main floor. It was operated under civilian management and control. Almost from the start this led to dissatisfaction. The men had good reason to feel they were being given poor quality at inflated prices. This developed into a threat to take matters into their own hands and tear the place to bits. Fortunately, the battalion command took some notice of these complaints. There were also adverse reports from the daily rounds of the orderly officers. Sufficient improvement was made to keep tempers under control.

At first the canteen operated dry but soon draft beer was made available. Here again, poor quality and weak strength caused a raging protest which threatened for a time to get out of hand. A better grade of beer with a bit more authority was soon provided. This canteen operated and served its purpose until the departure of the battalion for overseas in May of 1915. It could never be rated any great success. Barely adequate would about fit its utility and operation. No doubt the financial returns were extremely satisfactory to the promoters.

Regimental Dress

With such a large proportion of the total enlistment coming from the Cape Breton, Pictou and Antigonish areas, it was only natural that a strong feeling soon developed in favour of the kilt as the regimental dress. After all, the name Nova Scotia is literally New Scotland. Why indeed should not the first full infantry battalion ever organized for overseas service be equipped in accepted Scottish style?

Several factors combined to prevent this development. There were quite a few people, both officers and men, with some record of service in existing Halifax militia regiments. These had always been what were known in army language as 'flat cap' units. Their men still held some attachment to their previous traditional dress and a desire to in some way preserve a connection between the new battalion and their former associations. The authorities at Ottawa, comfortably aware that the desire for kilts was not altogether unanimous, while suitable recruits were still readily available in more than adequate numbers, were not under any immediate pressure to hold out additional inducements to meet such desires.

They were quick to point out the awful additional expense which would be involved in dressing a whole new battalion in kilted uniforms as against the much more moderate cost of straight 'flat cap' attire. Strangely enough, these same authorities, when recruiting began to get critical after the early part of 1916, did not have the slightest problem in finding the far more expensive kilted dress to cover not just one battalion but a whole brigade of four battalions, in complete and extravagant Scottish attire.

Those in charge of the 25th Battalion never seemed to quite understand the value of any form of organized publicity. Throughout its entire life no real sustained and effective program was maintained to create a favourable public image. Such publicity as did develop was intermittent and poorly presented. Part of this, no doubt, was due to the failure to realize and develop the advantages of strong political connections. After all, Halifax is a long way both in distance and politically from the seats of the mighty at Ottawa. Any lack of well-placed and powerful spokesmen at the centre of all wisdom must result in very slender pickings when the goodies are being handed out. Later units were more alert in these matters and consequently fared much better than the 25th ever did.

Music Hath Charms

Martial music is always an essential part of military life. Here again the division between those of strong Scottish tradition and others with different views led to the formation of three different bands. It was natural that the need for a group of qualified buglers to sound the various calls associated with the daily routine would in turn develop into a bugle band including a drum section. This band in its day was an essential part of the early training program. It provided about the only approach then available for marching purposes. Music of that sort was at least helpful, even if not tremendously inspiring.

A few weeks later a group favouring the regular type of military brass band succeeded in enlisting support of enough patriotic Halifax citizens to secure funds to purchase a collection of instruments for that purpose. The ranks were checked to discover any men with some brass band experience. In one way or another, including a few transfers from existing military bands in the area, the elements of such a band were assembled. Quoting entirely from memory subject to correction, the bandmaster was a Sergeant Slater.[10] In the ranks, the group was generally known as Tommy Slater's band. After quite a struggle and frequent practice sessions, they mastered a few well-known items of marching music to a point where they could lead the battalion on outside parades with an accepted measure of dignity. They even managed a few evening band concerts inside the armory.

It lasted through the rest of the stay in Halifax and the training period in England. When the battalion moved to France in September 1915, the band instruments were left behind. There does not seem to be any further record of what happened to them. Possibly they were turned over to the 17th Reserve Battalion, which became the base unit for the 25th and the RCRs, joined later by the 85th when that battalion moved to England in 1916 and to France early in 1917.

If this band deserves any claim to glory, it would relate first to its use at the Sandling camp in marching the men down to the rifle ranges near Hythe for musketry practice.[11] During that series of training sessions the troops were turned out at daylight. After a hasty breakfast, they started along the route down over the hills at the back of the camp headed by Tommy Slater's assorted players. Their daily contribution to the joy of nations consisted in banging out, over and over again, the old tune 'It's nice to get up in the morning, but it's nicer to lie in your bed.'

---

10 Thomas A. Slater (b. 1878) was born in Edinburgh but was living in Halifax when he enlisted in the 25th Battalion in November 1914. In civilian life, he was a boilermaker, married to Matilda Slater, and lived at 161 Creighton Street. He had previously served twelve years in the Royal Navy and two years in the band of the 63rd Militia Regiment. Although wounded during the war, he re-enlisted in 1918.
11 The 25th Battalion was stationed at East Sandling military base in England, which was situated in the hills above the seaside town of Hythe, near Folkestone.

This was accompanied by sundry hoots and rude remarks from the still sleepy and disgruntled assembly following along behind.

The Regimental March-Past

Time passed as it always does. Just for a moment let us turn ahead to Bramshott camp[12] in early 1919, several weeks after the fighting had ended. The camp at that time consisted of a headquarters staff and details, together with three reserve companies, one company each for the RCRs, the 25th and the 85th.

There was quite a bit of unrest among the men, who by then were anxious to get back to Canada and out of the army. In order to keep them occupied and out of trouble, arrangements were made for a formal inspection by some higher authority, to include a march-past. A brass band would be properly stationed to play the troops past the reviewing stand.

A problem then faced the organizers. The RCRs had a long-established 'march-past' to their own traditional music. The 85th also had previously selected a suitable tune for the same purpose. On the other hand, no one at HQ had any idea what the regimental march-past of the 25th might be. Early inquiries failed to produce any answer. Finally, a veteran officer of the 25th, recently arrived at the camp, was summoned for consultation. When the problem was put to him he was temporarily halted. He could not recall any such provision ever having been made by the 25th. From the time they had gone to France their only regimental music had been from their pipe band. Nothing in the nature of a traditional 'march-past' had been developed during the confusions of the training period.

In desperation, the 25th officer finally cast his thoughts back to Tommy Slater's band and the marches to the Hythe musketry ranges in 1915. He kept a straight face and advised headquarters that the proper music for the regimental march-past of the 25th was to the tune of 'It's nice to get up in the morning, but it's nicer to lie in your bed.' When the parade later took place and the 25th company reached the point of approach to the saluting base, the band broke out that tattered old tune and the lines went sailing by in true military fashion. What better tribute can be recorded to Tommy Slater and the members of his musi-

---

12 One of the largest Canadian army training camps in England was at Bramshott, which is approximately twenty-five kilometres southwest of Guildford in Kent.

cal assembly? To quote a French Canadian expression, 'they did their possible.' What more can anyone do?

Coming of the Pipes

Returning to Halifax in 1914, while the brass band was being organized the strong Scottish group was not idle. Although at this late date the details are not very clear, they did succeed in enlisting a highly qualified pipe major and enough pipers and drummers to form a pipe band of respectable size and quality.

This band also appeared on parade at times and accompanied the battalion on route marches during the training period. Some of their practice sessions in confined quarters within the armory building did not meet with unanimous approval but had to be endured in the interests of progress.

The men quickly came to realize that for marching purposes when on the road over long distances, the slower rhythm of the pipe music was much easier to move by than the quicker tempo of a regular brass band. For ceremonial duty on the parade ground, the short quick step at the rate of 180 to the minute with a brass band was very effective. Even when slowed to 100 to the minute on the line of march it could just about kill you over a long distance under full load. Against this, the cadence of the pipes at about eighty to ninety to the minute enabled men to use a longer and easier rolling stride with much less muscular strain. Over the years, under active combat conditions, it became clearly recognized that behind the pipes entire battalions could cover ground faster, for longer distances, and arrive at their destinations in better physical shape than by any other means.

The pipe band continued to grow and improve all through the training periods (six months in Halifax and four months in England). It was taken along intact in the movement to France and from then on became the accepted battalion musical formation. As finally established, it consisted of Pipe Major J. Carson,[13] sixteen pipers and eight drummers. For the greater part of the battalion service in France, with very few exceptions, all movement was by road on foot. The idea of moving infantry

---

13 John Carson (b. 1884) was born in Greenock, Scotland, but immigrated to Canada and was living in Halifax when he enlisted in the 25th Battalion in January 1915. He was a carpenter but had previously served eight years in the Argyll and Sutherland Highland Regiment of the British army.

by motor transport did not begin to penetrate the thinking at staff level until quite late in the proceedings.

Meanwhile, the PBI [poor bloody infantry] had to slug it out on their poor old dogs as best they could. Through experience it was found that movement by companies with working distance between was much easier and more effective. In such cases, the pipe band was often divided, with three or four pipers and one or two drummers heading each company. At other times the entire band marched in formation at the head of the battalion. During relief movements from the trenches, pipers were often sent up to the rallying points. As soon as a safe distance had been passed, they played the tired companies back to the rest camps in the rear areas behind the lines. Further reference to this pipe band and its activities will be found later in this story.

Chapter Three

Oh What a Lovely War

The Awkward Squads

As recruiting proceeded, the battalion was rapidly brought up to strength. The armory at one time held almost 1,400 men of all ranks. That was a bit over strength, providing some surplus for wastage, which developed as training got well under way.

A small number from this total found the drill instruction hard to understand. To use a going expression of the times, 'they had two left feet.' To avoid the more alert majority being delayed in their progress, the backward types were separated from the rest. These were temporarily formed into groups known as awkward squads. Each company had to cope with the problem and detail their best instructors to bring these squads along. One instructor in particular was truly remarkable. He took on assorted lots of the most unlikely candidates. In one week of intense drill training they would be moving in excellent style and formation. As these men improved they were sorted back into the companies. After the first few weeks awkward squads were no longer needed.

Pack Drill

The most common form of punishment for minor offences was CB (confined to barracks). This did not involve being excused from any parades or instruction periods. It meant that unfortunates were kept in barracks after the day's work was over. To make sure they did not slip out during the 5:00 p.m. to 10:00 p.m. liberty period, their names and numbers were lodged with the sergeant of the guard at the outlet door.

Whenever the bugler blew the defaulters' call, they had to report near the guard room at the double, to answer their names at a roll call.

For those whose transgressions were of a more serious nature, other methods of control were put into effect. For being absent without leave (AWOL), the sinners, whether following voluntary return or when caught by the military police, lost their pay for the time absent. They could be fined additional sums, depending on the length of time away and the seriousness of related breaches of military regulations.

Among other methods of bringing the more stubborn types down to earth, there was a system known as 'pack' drill. These poor souls, in addition to being confined to barracks, were paraded after the full day of general instruction. They were loaded down with all their equipment, including full packs and carrying rifles. Assembled in squad formation during evenings and weekends, they were marched up and down the length of the armory floor for periods of an hour or more with few rest breaks. A week or so of that treatment was enough to convince most of them of the error of their ways. As the battalion was sorted out and settled down to business, this form of discipline was discontinued. There were other more sensible methods developed for dealing with sinners where necessary.

It did not take long for the troops to adopt the old army code that 'the only crime in the army was in getting caught.' It was held clear that if caught, the punishment was to be taken like a man without whimpering or resentment. Where resentment did arise it was usually due to being wrongly accused and punished, or in feeling the sentence too severe or vicious when given for some minor offence.

Kit Inspection

Earlier in this record details are given of the various items of kit and equipment graciously bestowed by a kindly government on each eager candidate for military service. Having done so, the next problem was to convince the recipients of the importance of retaining possession of these gifts intact and carefully preserving them as custodians for the rightful owners, 'the Department of National Defence.'[14]

Thus, another burden was added to the already overloaded and disillusioned military infant class: kit inspection. At irregular intervals and calculated short notice, the men were made to produce and display for review all of their official possessions. Depending on the time and location, a pattern for laying out the items was prescribed. The inspecting

---

14 Actually, the department did not adopt this name until 1926. During the First World War it was called the Department of Militia and Defence.

party took careful note of all missing pieces. Shortages were replaced from quartermaster's stores and the cost charged to the unfortunate losers.

Numerous methods developed for avoiding the sacrifice of hard-earned cash under this type of official pressure. A convenient absence on duty elsewhere at the time of inspection was helpful, as was the temporary loan of missing items from some companion in another company already past this barrier a few hours or even a few minutes earlier. This involved quick sleight of hand, with the same or similar pieces being passed from one to another. This was doubtful, but worth trying as a last resort. A temporary loan from some sympathetic company quartermaster sergeant or his storeman, frequently at the subsequent cost of a couple of beers or a packet of cigarettes, also worked. Outright theft from some less alert or green recruit was not unknown.

This touched a borderline about what could or could not be stolen from a comrade. Officially, it was a severe army sin but was viewed with considerable lenience by the rank and file. It was alright to pinch his knife, fork or spoon, his 'hussif' or holdall, but God help you if you ever touched his food or water. Those two things were always sacred and any man who broke that code never did it a second time.

1914 Hippies

Many pictures taken at the time reveal a temporary leaning toward cultivation of mustaches as a distinctive touch. While beards were permitted if not encouraged in the navy, they were completely taboo under army regulations. On the contrary, mustaches were allowed and very much in style. No special permission was required, so the competition both as to size and variety provided a certain amount of interest throughout the ranks. It may now be hard to realize that in 1914 mustache wax was in fact a commercial commodity, quite widely used to achieve desired effects. Some were grown with the longest possible ends, then heavily waxed and turned up in real Kaiser Bill style. Others had the waxed ends extended straight out as far as they could be persuaded to grow. Many were what later became known through Bairnsfather's drawings[15] as the 'Old Bill' type: rather ragged and lack-

---

15 Bruce Bairnsfather (1888-1959) served in the British army during the war but became famous as the creator of 'Old Bill,' a cartoon character who represented the practical philosophy of the British private soldier during the war. His drawings, which appeared weekly in *The Bystander*, were subsequently published in six volumes enti-

ing any clearly defined contours. Another name for that lot was 'soup strainers.' Some were just plain busy, close cut and trimmed to suit the owner's ideas of comfort and manly appearance.

Advocates of these facial adornments sometimes justified their growth by claiming that shaving the upper lip was bad for the eyesight. Gradually interest slackened and most of the mustached group returned to the normal clean-shaven habit. A few old-timers stuck it out and treasured their facial masterpieces to the end of their army service.

As the Days Passed

When the session of the Nova Scotia legislature convened in the spring of 1915, the battalion had progressed far enough to be given the privilege of supplying the guard of honour for the opening ceremonies. In preparation for this event three officers and 100 other ranks were carefully selected and given special training for several weeks. They put on an excellent display, reflecting great credit on themselves and their instructors.

In the opening months of 1915 a movement developed and extended throughout the province to show appreciation of the people to the men of the 25th. This took the form of a subscription and donation from the proceeds of two completely equipped field kitchens. The presentation was officially made to the complete battalion on parade a short time prior to its movement to England on May 20th, 1915.

In the military museum at the Citadel in Halifax a brass plate is on display, which is dated May 10th, 1915. It was originally attached to the first of these two field kitchens. It records the names of the various Nova Scotia towns and villages which contributed to their cost. Fortunately, the plate was saved at the time the kitchens were finally worn out and demolished after a long period of useful service overseas.

Army Diet

Authorities of that period seemed to regard food simply as a supply of adequate and acceptable fuel to stoke the human boiler. Evidently it was expected to generate the necessary amount of energy to keep soldiers alive and strong enough to absorb the shocks of army existence.

---

tled *Fragments from France*. Later books included *Carry On Sergeant!* (1927), *Old Bill Looks at Europe* (1935), and *Old Bill Stands By* (1939). He also published two volumes of memoirs, *Bullets & Billets* (1916) and *From Mud to Mufty* (1919).

Such things as vitamins, proteins and balanced diets were unheard of and never mentioned.

The 25th did not suffer from any lack of sufficient nourishment. Compared to the standards of home-cooked choice and variety, there was a distinct difference. The catering, if so it could be called, leaned heavily on bread, bacon, cheese, jam, tea and baked beans. One meal per day usually was based on meat and vegetables, largely potatoes, turnips and cabbage. There was an occasional roast, but generally in the form of stew. Now and then a pie was offered. Those in the kitchens, while listed as cooks, would scarcely qualify for the title of chefs. Some of their efforts in the line of pastry were almost historical. Concerning cheese and jam particularly, most Canadians did not mind modest portions with other foods now and then. To be asked to consume these two items daily, in pound lots in order to survive, was more than most of them could endure.

In the men's search for variety, the local restaurants did a fine business whenever the cash position of the troops would permit. For some weeks at the start, the doctor and his staff entertained each morning a sick parade of upwards of 100 men, complaining of stomach disorders. The manufacturers of the standard army remedy, Number 9s,[16] must have been able to declare several extra dividends from the profits on the increased volume of business thus developed. Those with family connections or friends in the Halifax area were treated to home-cooked meals from time to time. For the majority it was army cooking all the way.

Many soldiers are never happy until they have something to growl or grouse about. Food is always a prime subject for complaint. Frequently the loudest protests come from those who in fact are getting more and better food than they ever previously enjoyed. In all fairness, it should be here recorded that the quality and quantity of the food was very good. It was monotonous at times and its preparation left much to be desired for flavour and service. Even so, the real proof was evident in the condition of the men as the weeks passed. At no time before or after were they in as fine physical shape as during the months of their training period. They stood erect and strong, without an ounce of excess fat, clear-eyed, clean-skinned and fit as men could be made. The test came when they were called upon to withstand the conditions they had to face and endure a few months later as they entered active service at the front in France and Belgium.

---

16 laxative pills.

Rum Doings

Other problems quickly developed as recruiting proceeded and the armory was filled with some 1,200 men. Contrary to all rules and regulations, those so inclined succeeded in bringing in bottles of assorted alcoholic beverages. In those days all liquors were more mature, smoother, and with greater authority than their current namesakes. It was long before Mackenzie King put water in the whisky and then taxed us on the water.[17]

In a hot and crowded barrack room, a couple of quarts of forty overproof Demerara rum uncorked and consumed to wash down tasty bits of dry salt cod or dried capelin could perfume the air beyond description. The effect on the proprietors was equally drastic and the resulting turmoil easy to imagine.

Every possible effort was made to control and prevent this practice. Every man was checked and searched at the guard room when returning from travels outside. A very few trying to get by at that point had their bottles taken from them and were made to answer to the authorities the next day. Extra men were posted at the sides of the building to prevent any attempt to hoist bottles by rope from the streets to the windows. In spite of all these precautions a considerable flow continued.

In pursuing our study of this situation, attention must turn to the design of the armory building. At the southwest corner near the intersection of North Park Street and Armory Place there is a round tower. Inside this tower is a circular staircase with steps going down to the basement and the main stairs leading up to the gallery and the rooms connecting to it. At the main floor level there were openings in the stonework about 12" wide by 24" high, evidently intended as ventilation inlets for a certain amount of fresh air. There is no record of who was the first bright soul to realize the possibilities of these openings.

Someone certainly did, because it was quite simple to place a bottle on the ground close to the least visible opening and then report to the guard room for return to barracks. After being well checked, searched and certified as beyond suspicion, the owner of the liquid merchandise only had to enter the tower out of sight of the guard room, reach through the opening and pull in his precious deposit. He could then proceed up the stairs to his quarters in perfect safety and receive a warm welcome

---

17 In December 1942 the government of William Lyon Mackenzie King adopted regulations requiring the dilution to 40 per cent of all spirits sold in Canada.

from his thirsty associates. This very effective procedure continued successfully for several weeks. Alas, like many other such arrangements
the good news gradually spread. Somewhere along the line the provost
sergeant discovered the details of the whole operation.

This suggested several interesting possibilities. After some thought
he consulted with a sergeant due for guard duty a day or two later.
Also, he enlisted the assistance of the sergeant tailor whose personal
quarters and tailoring shop were located in the basement not far from
the bottom of the tower stairs. It was arranged that when the sergeant
took over the guard the provost sergeant would watch the openings
from a safe position. When he saw a deposit being made, he would
rap twice with his cane on the entrance door. Then the sergeant of the
guard would take plenty of time to check the incoming man or men.
While this was going on, the provost sergeant would proceed to collect
the bottle or bottles, bring them in under his coat and deposit them for
safekeeping with the sergeant tailor in the basement.

It was not hard to foresee the result of these manoeuvres. First of all
the original owners nearly wrecked their arms reaching through the
openings, trying to find their bottles, which by then were long gone.
Then, they came back to the guard room with requests to be allowed
out for only a brief interval because of some forgotten errand which
demanded immediate attention. To all such pleadings the sergeant of
the guard refused any permission, which of course could only result
in loud protests and harsh words from the injured parties. In the end
the sergeant's weight prevailed and the disappointed and angry lower
ranks were forced to go to bed minus their anticipated night cap.

The harvest of that night's work kept the three sergeants supplied
with a private stock of assorted select brands of winter comfort for several weeks. The losers took their disaster without much personal ill-
will toward the group which had outguessed them. There could not
be any repeat, as with the former secret now common knowledge, the
openings were fixed with heavy iron bars leaded into the stone. The
openings between bars were much too small to permit any bottles to be
pulled through. It had been a fine idea while it worked, but like many
others it was too good to last. Once in a while an odd bottle did get
through the gate to the inside, but the main flow had been blocked. An
improved degree of nocturnal peace prevailed from then on.

The Officers

A quick look at the record shows that the original officers were drawn from the different then existing militia regiments in Halifax and throughout the province. The list included the 63rd and 66th from Halifax itself, together with the 68th, 69th, 75th, 78th, 81st, 93rd and 94th, all from outside centres. While all of them had some rough understanding of military organization and formation movement, it must be admitted that they were in most respects just as green as the men they were trying to train and command. It would hardly be correct to describe many of them as dedicated to the army as a profession.

Otherwise, in all fairness it must be said that within the limits of their knowledge and experience they worked faithfully and with serious concern to qualify themselves for the responsibilities they had undertaken. In these endeavours some were more successful than others, which was only to be expected. After all, they were human and thus no two quite alike in reacting to their surroundings.

Later experience proved that a few of the senior officers were overage and not physically able to withstand any prolonged exposure to active service conditions. This was not in any way a reflection on their personal courage or determination. In fact, quite the contrary: they deserved great praise for trying and for doing as well as they did, before being forced by circumstances to give way to younger men strong enough to stand the strain.

This condition was not confined just to the 25th Battalion. It was the same in every unit of the Canadian forces at that time. In 1914, with the possible exception of the Princess Pats and a small number of South African war veterans, none of the hastily recruited Canadian troops had seen any real combat action. The First Division was enduring the miseries of that English winter under canvas on Salisbury Plain. This did reveal to some degree the effective age limits for both officers and men. The same was not immediately evident among units of the Second Division. These had to be held and given preliminary training in Canada, through lack of even canvas shelter and supporting supply in England.

As there was not any suitable space in the armory building for officers' quarters, they all slept out and reported for duty early each morning. At the end of the day's training and instruction periods, they usually signed out. After about 6:00 p.m. only the orderly officer of the day was still on duty. His main duties were to supervise the changing of the guard, check at defaulters' parades, see that the canteen closed on time, visit the guard room and make a tour of inspection of the sentries. He remained readily available at the orderly room in case of any unusual development but not directly in touch with parts of the building where the men were housed.

These conditions prevented or at least delayed the full development of the close bond between officers and men so essential in building morale and true regimental character. To command respect and the confidence of his men, a good officer cannot rely on physical strength and personal courage alone. His first and greatest lesson is to realize clearly how impossible it is to ever fool his men. Moral or ethical considerations do not enter into it at all.

As a platoon commander he has some sixty men under his care. A company commander has about 250 men and a battalion commander 1,000 or more. Under any circumstances, these officers cannot possibly know where all their men are or what each one is doing twenty-four hours every day. In reverse, there is scarcely a minute at any time when an officer is not being watched by one or more of his men or their friends. Everything he does or does not do is known sooner or later. Generally sooner, and relayed through the grapevine of the ranks. He may be smarter than any one of them individually but he will never be smarter than the whole group.

The mass intelligence is always greater than that of any single individual. Men are usually very clever at concealing their thoughts when a true expression might get them into trouble. It beats all understanding how quickly they can size up an officer and measure him for exactly what he really is. Within two or three days they will know him better than he will ever know himself. They will assess his strengths and weaknesses and spot a phoney unbelievably fast. From then on every day adds a little something to their knowledge of him. It is only when he realizes this and adjusts himself to living with it that he has a chance to fully measure up to his job. If he succeeds he will have his reward in the confidence and respect of his men, which is something he can treasure as long as he lives. This same principle applies in civilian life. If you want to know a man's true character, do not bother too much with the opinions from his superiors. Try to get an honest expression from those who work under him. They are the people who know the man as he really is.

It is fair to say that the officers of the 25th Battalion as a group compared very favourably with those in other units of the Canadian army at the time. Naturally some were better than others. When the curtain finally went up and they faced active combat service, they fully justified the confidence which had been placed in them. Many of them were far better than just good and proved it at the cost of their own lives.

One or two incidents during the training period in Halifax are worth a brief review. In those days officers were required to own and periodically carry swords. In addition to their other duties they had to take instruction in sword drill and go through the prescribed motions on certain mock ceremonial parades. It gave the irreverent other ranks great entertainment to watch several of the shorter officers trying to draw and later sheath swords two or three inches too long for them. They were always a bit late in getting them and putting them back, which gave the whole performance a rather ragged appearance, scarcely up to the desired regimental standard. When movement was involved, their efforts to avoid getting the swords between their legs were an unending delight to their less exalted followers.

How anyone could imagine carrying a sword into the trenches is hard to understand. As time went on the swords were less often seen but they were taken along to England. In the end, just before movement to France they were carefully packed and marked with the owners' names for transfer to some central storage depot. It was never very clear if any of them were reclaimed by survivors or sent back to the next of kin of those who did not return.

After a rough weekend the Monday morning parade was more than usually tough to face without undesirable complications. In one platoon there was a man who stuttered so badly he could not say 'four' no matter how hard he tried. It was just impossible so, in some unexplained way he would end up in that position in the front rank. When the officer, leaning on his cane for necessary support and viewing the assembly through a slight morning-after haze, would try to get proceedings under way, the troubles would promptly start. On the command, 'platoon number,' numbers one, two and three would sound off in true military style. A slight pause and then 'fuff, fuff, fuff-fuff, fuff-fuff, fuff, fuff, fuff' until a halt was called.

While a second and third attempt ended in similar failure, the rest of the battalion would be all numbered, proved and standing at ease. The intervention of a furious company sergeant major would remove the offender from front rank to the rear and replace him with another who could comfortably say 'four.' The platoon would finally get organized properly and be ready to take part in further essential manoeuvres. By that time at least ten minutes had been deducted from the day's military hard labour and by several equally dubious schemes a full half-hour per day could be disposed of. Any success in this direction was an achievement well worth the effort.

Chapter Four

Under Way at Last

Foreign Travel

As the winter wore away and spring came along, activity quickened. Route marches were longer. Athletic competitions were encouraged. Trips to rifle ranges for firing practice with live ammunition developed. Rumours multiplied and kept everyone on edge. Some felt the Second Division would never leave Canada. Then the First Division moved from England to France early in February. By the end of that month it had joined the British forces in the trenches.

In the press, place names began to be mentioned: Neuve Chapelle in March, then on April 22nd, 1915, the second battle of Ypres began. In a few days details of the use of poison gas for the first time became known. At once, another rumour spread, this time that the Second Division would be broken up and the men used to replace casualties suffered by the First Division. Each day brought a new idea. Finally, uncertainty ended. The sailing date was set. Relatives from all over the province came to spend a last day or two and say farewell to their husbands and sons.

At last the day arrived. On May 20th, 1915, the first complete Nova Scotia infantry battalion said goodbye to the armory building which had been its home for nearly seven months. Loaded down in full marching order, it formed up for the last time on the great floor. Then, led by its bands, it marched out and down through the city to board the Cunard liner *Saxonia* at Pier Two. No one on that day could foresee the passage of four full years less only five days before this great battalion would return on the *Olympic* on May 15th, 1919, to once again march through the city on its way back to the same old building to be demobilized and take its place in history.

Along the route from the armory to Pier Two the whole city turned out to line the streets and cheer its men on their way. Many broke through and marched hand in hand with their loved one, only falling back when forced to do so at the barrier gate of the pier. It is doubtful if any person in Halifax able to stand failed to turn out and take part in that tremendous outburst of feeling. Many stayed nearby for hours until at last the great ship pulled away from its berth and slowly moved out through the harbour toward the open sea.

At this point one other event of great importance must be put on record. Engrossed with their own affairs, the men of the 25th had very scanty knowledge of the other battalions which had been selected to form the Fifth Brigade. They only knew the others to be the 22nd from St Jean, Quebec, the 24th Victoria Rifles from Montreal, and the 26th from Saint John, New Brunswick. They had not been told very much about any of them. The 22nd had first been assembled at St Jean, Quebec. It lacked suitable accommodation there to cope with the severe Quebec winter conditions. Essential outdoor training there would be difficult and unsatisfactory. After some weeks the government arranged to send the 22nd down to Amherst, Nova Scotia, where conditions were more favourable. For some time prior to May 20th, the 22nd had been in Nova Scotia, going through much the same routine as the 25th.

Almost before the last of the 25th were on board the *Saxonia*, special trains came alongside. It was then learned that the 22nd would be going along on the same ship. For the voyage, the first class staterooms were reserved for the officers of both units. The first class dining saloon became the joint officers' mess. The second class cabins were set aside for the senior NCOs, and the second class dining saloon became the joint sergeants' mess. The main body of the 25th occupied one half of the lower decks and the 22nd the other half. Thus began an intimate and significant association. It was to last through the remainder of the training period and all of the three and a half following years in the fighting areas in Belgium and France.

Late in the day the lines were cast off and the *Saxonia* steamed slowly out of Halifax harbour to face the hazards of a wartime crossing of the North Atlantic. The men of the 25th watched the shoreline slowly fade away. They began to partly understand and perhaps for the first time to realize that a great many of their number would never again see this land they loved so well.

The management and operation of a large ship during any transatlantic crossing is much the same from one ship to another. Wartime hazards simply complicated further an already complicated job. The crossing of the *Saxonia* carrying the 25th and the 22nd actually produced little of permanent interest. The crew was efficient and the food and service satisfactory. Immediately after sailing the usual boat drills were carried out. Troops were properly instructed concerning their boat stations and procedure in case of emergencies. Sentries were posted at various points to assist the regular crew in anti-submarine watch duties. The ship was completely blacked out. Extreme precautions were taken to prevent lights from showing during the hours of darkness.

There was the usual amount of seasickness, but with few exceptions the troops found their sea legs very quickly. They were able to find ways to occupy their time with some degree of comfort during the nine days of the voyage. Stabilizers, common today, were then unknown. When the wind and the sea kicked up a bit the ship began to roll and pitch. The old sea tale quickly circulated: in all his years at sea, this was the worst storm the captain had ever seen. The lower decks did not find it difficult to believe but somehow they all survived. For most of the voyage the ship travelled without any visible naval escort. No doubt, units of the Royal Navy were never far away in case of need.

The food must have been at least acceptable to all those who were interested in eating. Complaints were only minor and were quickly dealt with. On May 28th, after eight days out, first one and then a second destroyer came into sight and after circling the *Saxonia* took up positions, one on each side of the ship to escort it into Devonport for docking on May 29th.

Following the usual formalities the battalion was rapidly disembarked and loaded on trains at the dockside. The trains moved non-stop around London to a way station a few miles from the permanent camp in Kent. This Sandling camp was located back of the downs behind the English channel coast towns of Folkestone and Hythe. During the journey from Devonport the small size and design of the cars and the high speed of the English trains came as a great surprise to all the men not previously acquainted with British railway service.

The one outstanding result of the trip from Halifax to Sandling was the bond of friendship and understanding which developed between the 25th and 22nd battalion officers and men. In spite of differences in language and customs, they quickly came to know and respect each other. It was on the old *Saxonia* that the music and words of 'Alouette' made their first impact on the English-speaking troops. In the months and years which followed, the song spread throughout the whole Canadian Corps and became an established part of the World War I musical record. The whole of the Fifth Brigade was located in the Sandling area.

There was only a light wire fence between the lines of the 22nd and the 25th battalions. Friendships developed on the *Saxonia* continued and became a permanent part of the life of both units for the remainder of their overseas service.

On June 6th, 1915, a muster parade was held at the camp. The official list records the names of forty-four officers and the regimental numbers and names of 1,130 other ranks, for a total of 1,174 in all. The numbering allotted by the Defence Department to the 25th covered 67001 to 68999. Any man with a regimental number starting with 67 or 68 is automatically identified as a member of the original unit as it left Halifax.

The period of training in England last three and a half months, from arrival on May 29th, 1915, to departure for France on September 15th, 1915. During that time the weather was generally favourable: mostly warm bright sunny days and clear cool nights. Kent is well known for the fine quality of fruit and vegetables grown there. While the quantities available were limited, the fine strawberries and cherries then in season were greatly enjoyed when the men were able to buy them. Note: *they were not included in the army rations.*

Equipment Problems

Reference has already been made to the marches to the Hythe ranges for musketry instruction, led by Tommy Slater's remarkable collection of musicians. The usual procedure was to march that band outfit back and forth through the camp immediately after the bugler at the guard house sounded the reveille. This served to arouse all late sleepers and start preparations for the day's activities. No effort will be made at this time to record the joyful comments of the waking citizen soldiers.

After a quick PT workout followed by breakfast, the troops finished cleaning up and turned out on parade. From there, headed by Slater's Band manfully pounding out that old tune, 'It's nice to get up in the morning but it's nicer to lie in your bed,' they wound their way down over the dunes to the rifle ranges for their musketry training.

Based on experience from the second battle of Ypres in April 1915, the First Canadian Division in France on or about June 15th discarded the twelve to fourteen-pound Canadian-made long Ross rifle and rearmed with the British nine-and-a-half-pound short Lee-Enfield service model. Colonel Nicholson's official history of the First World War covers in some detail the conflict which raged throughout the Canadian army over the relative merits and demerits of the two models for active serv-

ice combat use. In this, as in many other cases, Sir Sam Hughes[18] stub-
bornly resisted all experienced and informed opinion. Both the Second
and Third Divisions continued officially to be armed with the Ross rifle
until just prior to their movement to the Somme battle in August 1916.
This was more than a year after they had been thrown out by the First
Division. During the musketry training on the Hythe ranges under ideal
weather conditions, the Ross rifle served well as a target weapon. The
25th reluctantly carried them along to France. They already knew from
contacts with returning First Division men about what to expect when
they got to the trenches but temporarily could not do anything about it.

In the general training program there were route marches under full
equipment, with the Oliver arrangement issued in Halifax still in use
for most of this period in England. On September 6th, just a few days
before leaving for France, the Oliver type was replaced by the far better
design of web equipment which was standard throughout all British
forces in the combat areas. At about the same time the standard British
army boots were issued to replace those brought from Halifax, which
had been worn through most of the training period.

Another official headache inflicted on the enthusiastic gathering during the stopover in England was their introduction to the MacAdam
shovel or so-called entrenching tool. This weird brainchild of some fractured imagination had the strong and active endorsement of Sir Sam
Hughes, possibly influenced by the fact that the patent rights were reg-
istered in the name of his own female secretary.[19] The shovel part was

---

18 Sir Sam Hughes (1853–1921) was minister of militia and defence in the government
of Sir Robert Borden from 1911 until 1916. Born at Darlington, Ontario, Hughes
joined the militia at University of Toronto and became a teacher, later switching to
journalism. He was editor of the Lindsay *Warder* from 1885 to 1897. He was active in
the Conservative Party and the Orange Order and was elected to parliament in 1892.
He served in the South African war and in 1911 was appointed minister of militia
and defence. He was knighted in 1915 and promoted to major general. An energetic
and forceful personality, he clashed frequently with Prime Minister Borden and was
dismissed in November 1916.
19 The MacAdam shovel, an implement modelled upon a pre-war Swiss invention and
patented in the name of Ena MacAdam, Hughes's secretary, was designed to serve
as a combined shield and entrenching tool. Twenty-five thousand MacAdam shovels
purchased in Philadelphia at $1.35 each were taken to England, where they proved
unsatisfactory. The commander of the First Division concluded that they were not
effective as shields, were too heavy for the men to carry, and were awkward to dig
with. He refused to take them to France. When trials in the field by the Second Division brought more adverse reports, all were withdrawn from use and were eventually sold for $1,400 as scrap metal.

roughly nine inches square by 3/16" thick, with a short hinged handle to enable it to be stuck into the ground, handle down. In this position it was supposed to form a shield for the soldier to crouch behind and protect his head from a direct hit by a rifle bullet. The rest of his carcass was apparently not considered of any importance.

The blade had two holes in it, one small one to peak through and the other a slot through which to shoot at the enemy. The First Division had turned this gift down flat before going to France but Sir Sam refused to give in to experienced advice and did his best to force the Second Division to accept it. No doubt the fact that a lot of 25,000 of these playthings had been purchased at $1.35 each had something to do with it. In spite of scornful dislike by the troops, some of these actually did get to France under the pretense of field trials. The men promptly threw them away and in the end any left on hand were sold off as scrap metal for a few hundred dollars. To be truthful, the British entrenching tool was itself of little practical value and was eventually discarded, but at least it was lighter in weight compared to the MacAdam masterpiece and conveniently fitted to the web equipment so it was not too hard to carry. When it came to digging trenches, the only tools of any real value were the old reliable picks and shovels.

Mr Dickinson's Downfall

It developed over the first few weeks at Sandling that the Canadian troops gave their official British hosts more than a little cause for concern. Individually, the men quickly made friends with the English people. Also, quite a few of the men were English-born and had families and relatives throughout the country. In this respect the 25th Battalion was much the same as other units in the Second Division.

Around the camps and nearby towns conditions at times led to different developments. As an example, the civilian-operated canteen in the armory at Halifax would never have taken a prize but it was at least adequate and the stocks and prices were comparable with those of outside city stores. On the contrary, the British War Office in its wisdom had leased the canteen concessions in the Sandling camp area to a civilian company called Dickinson's. When the 25th arrived late in May 1915 this firm was already established in a special size and design of hut. Similar canteens were located in the lines of all the other battalions.

Their stocks were in place and staffs on hand, ready and eager to extract the largest amount of money in the shortest time from the wealthy Canadian warriors. The Canadian private's pay of $1.10 per day worked out to about four shillings and sixpence, a rate unheard of in the English scale. The English lads were only paid about one shilling and threepence per day. Unfortunately, the Dickinson stocks were unbelievably bad and the beer poor and weak. The canteen manager in the 25th camp was an equally bad choice: loud-mouthed, insolent and just plain ignorant. Altogether, the place was a positive disgrace.

Before the end of the first week, angry protests began to develop. To make matters worse, the nearest pub was at least two miles away and was only a small village establishment. Except for weekends or by special pass, it was not possible to get to the nearest towns of Hythe and Folkestone. Most of the time the men did not have any choice. It was either put up with Dickinson's or do without. Under such circumstances real trouble was bound to occur and it did not take long to develop. The men quickly found that complaints to company and battalion headquarters did not bring any results. As far as they could judge, their officers were either indifferent or lacked any understanding of how to deal with the problem.

One night when the beer was particularly bad and the sweet biscuits and overpriced chocolate bars more than usually stale and mouldy, tempers broke. There is not any record of who started the outbreak. Some men simply took over and marched the manager and his staff to the main gate. They departed in haste down the road. That particular lot were never again seen in the 25th Battalion camp. Meanwhile, others set fire to the hut and stood by while it burned flat with all its contents. They made sure the fire did not spread to any of the other buildings and then retired to await the consequences.

These were not long in coming. As the following day developed the 25th men saw more red tabs and brass hats gathered together in one place than at any time before or after. They ranked all the way from junior staff officers up to brigadiers and major generals, both Canadian and London War Office types. Inspections were carried out, courts of inquiry held, and other ranks questioned singly and in groups.

Throughout it all the men stood their ground. They took full advantage of the chance to tell all and sundry their opinions of the Dickinson company and all its works. Eventually it was decided unwise to provoke the men further. No attempt was ever made to force them to pay for the damage and there were not any pay deductions. Probably the Canadian government paid the bill and buried it in the archives along with the cost of the MacAdam shovels and hundreds of other similar items.

The principal result was the immediate inspection of every other Dickinson canteen in the Canadian area. Men and officers were interviewed and closely questioned. When it was all over the improvement both as to quality and price of the stocks and civility of service had to be seen to be believed. A new hut was built in the 25th section with new men in charge. Peace returned to the canteen. For the remainder of the time at Sandling there was not any further serious trouble from that situation.

Watch Your Change

Probably for good reasons there does not seem to be any mention in the official records of a real hefty donnybrook which happened in the town of Folkestone shortly after the Second Division arrived in the Shorn-cliffe area. At the weekend following the first full payday in England the troops poured into town from all directions. The place was almost completely submerged by Canadians. All the limited places of entertainment were crowded. It is not a very large place. The cinemas and pubs, together with a few seaside facilities could not possibly contain all those trying to get in. Under such circumstances it only needed a spark to trigger an outbreak. Once started it would spread like fire and get out of control in a very few minutes.

It was the currency problem which started that particular Folkestone come-all-ye. Men of English origin did not have any difficulty converting Canadian dollar values to British pounds. Other Canadians quickly understood a sixpence as ten cents, a shilling as a quarter, and two shillings as fifty cents. The half crown was not too clear to some of them. It was thus not very hard for a quick-change artist to substitute change for two shillings. The real difficulty came in comparing the value of one British pound and one Canadian dollar. It took some time for many men to get away from the idea that one pound equalled one dollar. Actually it had cost him five Canadian dollars. The ten shilling note further compounded the mystery. There was just too much temptation for store clerks, pub waiters and others handling money to take in a pound and return change for ten shillings. By paying off the change in shilling and six-penny pieces, they could increase the appearance of a lot of silver in return for the paper.

Incidentally, the Canadian government was not above making a small bit of change on its currency transactions with the troops. The going rate of exchange between Canada and Britain was $4.86 2/3 per pound. There is not any doubt that the government could buy all the pounds it required at that price or better. When it came to turning those same pounds over to the troops it charged them a straight $5.00, a tidy bit of profit of thirteen cents or better per pound. It would be interesting to know how much that amounted to over about four years, with more than 400,000 men taken overseas.

Returning to the Folkestone episode, the cookhouse chronicle version indicated the start in a fish-and-chip shop on Tontine Street. This street was in the lower town and not far away from the waterfront. Some Canadians (no names, no pack drill) paid up with a one-pound note and were handed back change for ten shillings. They happened to know the difference and gently pointed it out to the proprietor. In the argument which followed, the Canadian and his friends took the shop apart and distributed its contents, including the shopkeeper, in the street. This citizen called on his nearby friends for support. While they reinforced him, someone called the police. Canadian help was readily on hand to increase the scope of the entertainment. This in turn brought out the fire department, which temporarily created a local advantage under the resulting water pressure.

The noise and excitement quickly drew more Canadians to the scene. Some turned off the water and took possession of the hose. This they chopped up into convenient lengths and, armed with these, took charge of the whole street. A large number of shop fronts were badly damaged and some looting took place. The looting was not extensive and certainly was not the original intention of the celebrating assembly. Finally, the army authorities called in two regiments of British cavalry, which arrived on horseback armed with their swords. They surrounded the area, preventing any further additions to the multitude. Mounted cutting-out parties were then sent in. Using their horses and the flats of their swords, they cut out groups of twenty or thirty men at a time. These were shoved into hastily gathered buses for return to their camps. It was long after midnight before the last of the gathering had been collected and order once more restored.

No doubt the Canadian government had another nice account to pay off. They must have felt it impossible to punish several thousand men because no pay deductions were ever attempted. The main result was a heavy increase in military police patrols in all the Folkestone area. The number of passes per day was drastically reduced. As training proceeded, six-day leave and weekend passes to London came into effect so the attractions of Folkestone diminished. Over the same period the Canadians learned to protect their money better and the public became more aware of the hazards of trying to shortchange them.[20]

---

20 This hitherto unreported incident may be the reason why Lieutenant Karl Wetherbe of the 6th Battalion Engineers noted on 5 June 1915 that 'A. Cozzie's fried fish shop ... has been placed out of bounds for all troops.' Wetherbe gave the address, however, as Beach Street, Folkestone (K. Wetherbe, *From the Rideau to the Rhine and Back* [Toronto, 1928], p. 25).

Chapter Five

Summer Days

Leaves

Soon after arrival at Sandling Camp, arrangements permitted six-day leaves for all officers and men. These provided free transportation to any part of the British Isles. Men of British birth took their time to visit their own families. Other Canadians with relatives or family friends in the country did likewise. As a result, people in every part of England, Scotland, Ireland and Wales saw men from Canada. Many lasting friendships were formed. Aside from London as the centre of attraction, Scotland had a strong pull for many of the men of the 25th Battalion, proud of their Scottish ancestry and tradition.

Many others spent time in the Midland and northern English districts, while some were able to enjoy a brief visit to Ireland in the time available. Additional to the single six-day leaves, it was possible to give fairly frequent weekend passes which allowed visits to London and other nearby centres several times during the period from June to September.

Most men found that the English system of bed and breakfast at a fixed rate suited them well and reasonably within their means. In London, the Union Jack Club on Waterloo Road was popular with some. For Canadians, the haven most appreciated was the Maple Leaf Club in Berkeley Square. Through the efforts of a group of Canadian ladies headed by Lady Drummond, a large house had been secured.[21] It was

---

21 Grace Julia Parker (1861–1942) was the second wife of Sir George Drummond (1829–1910), a Montreal businessman, banker, and senator. Over the years, she was active in such organizations as the National Council of Women, the Victorian Order of Nurses, and the Canadian Red Cross Society, as well as in the promotion of women's

equipped with as many good beds as possible, together with bath and washroom facilities and a kitchen and dining room. There were also writing and reading rooms. The charges were not in any way related to the actual cost of operation. Any Canadian soldier prepared to conduct himself properly could have a clean bed and a good breakfast for a very small charge. As the club became known it was necessary to book in early. Its capacity had a limit and could not possibly house all the Canadians on leave in London from day to day. Later on, preference was given as far as possible to men on leave from France. Special arrangements gave the men on arrival direct from the trenches a hot bath, complete change to clean new underwear, socks, etc, free of all cost. Also there were clean pajamas for the night.

There was a check-room locker service where all but necessary walking-out dress and belt could be left for safety. Any extra money could also be left at the office for safekeeping. The wise and experienced protected their good boots by placing them under two legs at the head of the bed before turning in. When a man was asleep his boots could not be moved without waking him. It was quite a sight to see all the beds in a dormitory, each wearing a pair of army boots under the head end. Another necessity was to protect all money and other personal articles of value by keeping them secured in the tunic with that carefully folded in place under the pillow. Lacking a pillow, a folded tunic was often the only available substitute serving two purposes at the same time.

That Maple Leaf Club was without doubt one of the most effective and useful patriotic projects of the war. No amount of thanks can ever fully express to Lady Drummond and the ladies associated with her the full appreciation of the hundreds of young Canadians far from home who were able to enjoy a few brief hours of comfort after long periods of active combat service.

Parades and Inspections

In any army there is a great gap between the top and the bottom. The

---

suffrage. During the war, she founded the Canadian Red Cross's Information Bureau in London, which, initially funded from her own substantial fortune, kept families in Canada informed of the location and condition of men who were hospitalized, missing, or killed. She was also one of the founders of the Maple Leaf Club in London. Her son, Guy Melfort Drummond, who had given up his rank of captain in the militia in order to get overseas more quickly, was killed in the second battle of Ypres in April 1915. In reporting his death on 26 April 1915, the Toronto *Star* described him as 'one of the wealthiest young men in Canada.'

private soldier is very much like the young bank clerk in the old story. After a few weeks of employment, his rich uncle during a family visit suggested that by now the boy must be at least a teller. The lad replied that as things stood he was still only the doer. Pressed to explain further, he stated as follows: the manager tells the assistant manager, the assistant manager tells the accountant, the accountant tells the teller, the teller tells the ledger keeper, the ledger keeper tells the discount clerk, the discount clerk tells me and I have no one to tell so I have to go do it. Start with the army supreme command and follow down through the chain of authority. You end up with the private soldier in much the same position as the young bank clerk.

The rank and file are close to their junior officers and know them inside out, far better than those officers ever know themselves. They are also near enough to their company commanders to size them up equally well. Knowledge of the battalion commander, while not quite so direct, is fairly accurate and extensive. His batman, along with sundry runners, HQ cooks and others like orderly room clerks are all sources with connections at the lower levels. The brigade commander is seen less often and usually at a distance, the divisional commander mostly on very formal occasions. When it comes to corp commanders and up through army commanders, to most men the break is complete. Beyond knowing that such people exist, and possibly their names and titles, they are regarded as living in a separate heaven, far removed from ordinary mortals.

The Canadian army was fortunate in the way it developed. The First Division with its auxiliary troops was still small enough to permit close contact everywhere. Many of the rankers knew the senior officers personally in pre-war life and on occasion could still approach them informally to mutual advantage. When the Second Division developed it was able to draw quite a number of experienced officers from the First Division. Later on, as the Third and Fourth Divisions came along, similar movement from the First and Second Divisions provided senior staff.

As these officers were promoted and moved from one division to another, they brought with them knowledge and experience gained in more junior positions. They were already well known with reputations firmly established by close contact with front-line service. To some extent this affected the feelings in the ranks toward more formal parades and inspections. Possibly, some of the men enjoyed taking part in these spectacles but in general they were rather less than popular. In certain cases that is putting it mildly.

The preparations usually started some time in advance, involving extra hours of marching and drills in various formations. These extended, where thought useful by higher authority, up to brigade and sometimes divisional movements. In addition, there was much shining of buttons, badges and equipment brass. Special attention was given to clothing and general equipment, together with frequent parades for inspection at the platoon and company levels. Much preaching over the necessity of upholding the honour and prestige of the battalion in particular and the brigade and the division in general did little to improve matters.

When the great day finally arrived, it meant being roused at some unearthly hour, fed and watered, washed and shined, and then rushed onto the local parade ground, loaded down with all the military gear which could be draped on their sagging backs and shoulders. At the appointed hour the battalion in route march formation took to the road, proceeding to a selected junction point for brigade formation, en route to the final inspection site.

After preliminary blasting away by the brass band or the pipe band in turn, these performers rather quickly ran out of wind. From then on such marching time as could be maintained depended on the drums only. To hold some reasonable degree of military step, the company sergeant majors and the platoon sergeants spent considerable energy shouting out the cadence of 'Right, Left, Right' at frequent intervals. General progress depended on the luck of the weather. From the ranker's point of view, the best thing which could happen was a combination hurricane and downpour bad enough to cancel the whole program. Lacking such good fortune, a clear sunny day in southern England during August or September can be really hot. The final assembly area was always several miles from the nearest camp. Covering the distance on foot over dusty dirt roads on a good hot morning, burdened with all their military attachments did not provide much joy to the loyal gathering. They could readily think of dozens of other activities they would like better.

During the first few weeks, formal parades and inspections at the battalion and brigade levels became part of general routine. These, being held on nearby camp grounds, did not require long route marches. They were organized more easily and quickly than later senior events. Late in July things began to stir in a different way. It became known that on August 4th the whole Second Division plus all nearby Canadian artillery and auxiliary troops would be assembled in a single grand parade for review by Sir Sam Hughes and Mr A. Bonar Law.[22]

22 Born in Canada, Andrew Bonar Law (1858–1923) was a Glasgow businessman who

The site chosen was a private estate with an area of level short grass-land large enough to assemble some 30,000 men in full marching order when paraded in close inspection formation. For once, the 25th Battalion was lucky. Its camp lines touched the main road at a point closer to the inspection area than that of any of the other units. Many of the battalions had to march several miles further each way to reach their review positions and return to camp. Even so, the place was still several miles away from the 25th Battalion starting point.

The general idea of marching all the way under full load, being held for several hours while arrangements were completed, standing through the full inspection ceremony and finally marching the same distance in return did not fill the souls of the unfortunate with any high degree of joy. There were other considerations related to this affair. While Mr Bonar Law was well known in political circles in Britain and Canada as a distinguished Canadian, his name and achievements did not matter very much to many of the men in the army. They neither liked nor disliked him. They just did not know him and could not see why they were being put to all this trouble on his account

So much has been written concerning Sir Sam Hughes that only limited further comment seems useful at this time. Possibly Sir Sam had to shoulder more than his share of blame for the many unfortunate results of haste and inexperience. The men mostly referred to him as 'Old Sam' and formed their opinions on the direct effects of his actions on their personal fortunes. The Ross rifle and the MacAdam shovel episodes did not tend to increase their respect for his wisdom and leadership. Knowledge of his quarrels with higher authorities on both sides of the Atlantic was widespread among the troops. In some cases these were viewed with more approval than otherwise. At the time there was little if any intense dislike for the old boy. It was largely the wish that he would stick to other matters and avoid bothering them any more than necessary.

And so the grand day approached. Fortunately, the weather was reasonably decent but very hot. With no more than the normal amount of confusion and unnecessary duplication of effort, the proceedings got under way as planned. The movement from the camp in the summer heat developed into a series of starts and stops at unscheduled

---

led the Conservative Party in the British House of Commons 1911–21. He served as colonial secretary (1915–16), chancellor of the exchequer (1916–18), lord privy seal (1919–21), and prime minister (1922–3). He lost two sons in the war.

intervals, not helpful to the tempers of the marchers. On reaching the inspection site they managed to find and assume their assigned position and settled down to get what rest they could while awaiting the arrival of the official party. Any food they had managed to bring with them went the way of all such luxuries.

Finally, more action developed. Various officials, including the usual surplus of junior staff officers, began to appear and hurry about. The parade was called to order. In the distance a procession of several large staff cars came into view. These drew up near the manor house to deliver their passengers, somewhat like a fleet of navy cutters coming alongside a dock. The newcomers sorted themselves out, exchanged greetings with the welcoming committee, and then mounted the reviewing stand. Those in the multitude with good eyesight could distinguish a tall figure in civilian attire, complete with high silk hat, presumably the Hon Mr A. Bonar Law. The heavy personage in the military uniform well adorned with assorted red staff tabs, gold badges, highly polished Sam Browne belt and Strathcona boots, complete with spurs, could not possibly be other than the great Sir Sam himself.

When the bugler at the stand sounded the prearranged signal, the parade was brought to attention and sloped arms. This movement must have appeared rather ragged to the inspecting party. The sound of the bugle took time to travel. Those furthest away heard it last. When all had finally performed as required and a brief pause completed, the bugle sounded again to call for the 'General Salute Present Arms.' The official band struck up 'God Save the King.' The military on the stand stood at the salute. The civilians took off their hats and everyone remained still, waiting for the band to finish. At another signal from the bugler the assembly returned to the slope, then ordered arms, stood at ease and finally stood easy.

The official inspection party, arranged in correct order, then proceeded to carry out the prescribed routine. That took considerable time as there were twelve complete infantry battalions, plus reserve units, along with artillery batteries and other auxiliary troop parties. Each unit was in turn called to attention as Sir Sam, accompanied by Mr Bonar Law and their escorting retinue of red-tabbed officers, approached. As they moved through the ranks, it became partly a question of who inspected whom. The sods in the ranks took a long hard look at all the brass. It was a good thing that many of the comments did not carry as far as the ears of the inspectors. It is reliably on record that one hero succeeded in pinning a medal of tobacco juice on the heel of Old Sam's Strathcona boot without being detected, thereby establishing his personal claim to immortality among his comrades.

When that part of the ordeal was finally completed, the inspection group returned to the manor house to partake of needed refresh- ment and enjoy a brief rest. After that interval, they again mounted the reviewing stand. The final exercise of the day was the march-past by battalions and other units in line formation. Each battalion in turn moved off to the right to the top end of the area, then wheeled into com- pany lines and came pounding down past the stand to give the 'Eyes Right' salute as they sailed by on their way to the exit gate. In spite of musical assistance, marching in line was not one of their better efforts at the best of times. The performance on that occasion had best be left to history, without further comment. When the long dry march back to the camp ended, the weary warriors were quite content to clean up any available solid and liquid rations and go to bed without any further waste of time.

So Endeth the First Lesson

News of the second time around received a more favourable response.[23] It was confirmed that on September 2nd a great gathering of all Cana- dian troops in the area would be assembled for review by King George V, accompanied by Lord Kitchener. This was indeed a far different cup of tea, as compared with a parade for Sam Hughes and Bonar Law. To be inspected by the king himself, together with Lord Kitchener was an honour to be taken seriously and anticipated with real pleasure. For all but a very few of the thousands of men it would be the once-in-a-life- time chance to be momentarily close enough to the king to really see

---

23 Clements's memory is at fault here. This was the third high-level inspection. The sec- ond had taken place on 16 August when the Canadian troops at Shorncliffe marched past Princess Alexander of Teck and her two daughters. Also present were Sir Sam Hughes, Sir Edward Carson, General J.C. MacDougall, and other officers. Princess Alexander of Teck (1883–1981) was a grand-daughter of Queen Victoria. She married Prince Alexander of Teck, Queen Mary's brother, who became the Earl of Athlone in 1917. He served as governor general of Canada from 1940 to 1946. Sir Edward Car- son (1854–1935) was a prominent Irish lawyer and politician who served as attorney general in the British government for five months in 1915, first lord of the admiralty from December 1916 to July 1917, then minister without portfolio until January 1918. He was appointed a judge and life peer in 1921. Brigadier General J.C. MacDougall commanded the Canadian training camp at Shorncliffe between September 1915 and early November 1916.

him as a living person. Their interest in Lord Kitchener was almost as great, so they were equally eager to see him at close range.

There was a keen desire by all ranks to make the best possible showing. The intensive preparations did not seem to be nearly as much trouble as on the previous occasion. Former mistakes were reviewed with efforts made to correct them and prevent their recurrence. Particular attention given to formation marching in line resulted in marked improvement over the August 4th exhibition. No doubt the Guards could still do it better but as non-professionals the Canadian units did not need to be at all ashamed of their performance.

The movement to the parade area was largely a duplicate of the August 4th march. There was one useful difference which greatly improved the temper and comfort of the men. An effort was made to profit by experience. Instead of full marching order, a much reduced and lighter load was draped on their weary shoulders. They still had to carry and perform with the clumsy long Ross rifles but that was a minor discomfort not too difficult to endure.

With good weather and a minimum of controlled confusion, the day was a pleasant success. The official party arrived on time and carried out its share of the affair in acceptable fashion. The king looked and acted as the troops expected a king should. Lord Kitchener was equally impressive in his own way. The troops put on a far better show than on the previous occasion. The event completed its moment of glory and then passed quietly into history. The official history of the Canadian army in the First World War covers it in one sentence. 'On 2 September HM the King, accompanied by Lord Kitchener, inspected the Division, a sure sign that embarkation would not long be delayed.'[24]

After the early settling-down period, training was intensified. There were route marches, two- and sometimes three-day and night exercises, including brigade and divisional schemes. Practices in attack and defence were frequent, including instruction in the digging of trenches and preparing defensive positions.

During one night exercise the noise of gunfire was heard coming from the direction of Dover. Several searchlight beams could be seen in the distance. Suddenly, as these converged a German Zeppelin returning from a raid on London came into view. Bursts of anti-aircraft shells appeared close to it. The troops on the ground let out a big cheer when it was hit. For a short while it seemed likely to crash but somehow the

24 G.W.L. Nicholson, *Canadian Expeditionary Force, 1914–1919* (Ottawa, 1962), p. 113.

crew managed to recover control. By climbing to a higher level it pulled out of range of the ground fire to continue on its way back across the channel. In the end, the damage from the anti-aircraft shells slowed its speed so that it failed to reach the Belgian coast until after daylight. This enabled British attack planes from the Dunkirk area to intercept and destroy it in the air. The success was confirmed in the London papers a day or two later.

A Classic Desertion

Mention has already been made of one such case from Halifax and its sequel months later in Belgium. Considering the hundreds of thousands of men enlisted in the Canadian forces, the total number of desertions was so small that it could scarcely be counted. Of those which did occur, very few were due to any extreme degree of cowardice. On the contrary, it often took a very brave man to risk such a chance. If caught, as most of them were, the punishment at the least would be very severe and under extreme conditions could result in a death sentence.

One case involved two men and had its beginnings in Halifax through a personal feud which developed between them and their company commander. There were, no doubt, faults on both sides. The men were definitely rebellious types, hard to manage and unwilling to adjust themselves to the discipline of military life. The officer was just as stubborn and undertook to use his position and authority to break them to his will. Whenever caught out, they were unmercifully tongue-lashed and given maximum punishment. This quarrel continued and became even more intense after arrival in England.

The climax came one rainy night following a payday. Toward midnight a long-distance call came through to the only civilian telephone in the 25th camp open at that hour. It was located in the guardroom at the main gate near the highway. The call was received by the sergeant of the guard as an urgent personal call for the commander of X Company. The sergeant explained that this officer was at the top end of the camp, at least a quarter of a mile away, and probably in bed. The calling party insisted the business was most urgent and demanded that he be brought to the guardroom phone to take the call personally.

Under further pressure the sergeant dispatched a messenger for the officer, meanwhile taking an operator's number in Folkestone for the call back later. Finally, after hastily dressing and plowing down through the muddy camp in the pouring rain, the officer arrived at the guardroom. After an interval, the sergeant succeeded in re-establishing the connection and the call proceeded somewhat as follows:

Voice from Folkestone: Is this the commander of X Company 25th Battalion at Sandling camp?
Company Commander: Yes, yes. Who is this calling? What do you want?
Voice from Folkestone: Did I get you out of bed and down through the camp in the rain? Are you very wet?
Company Commander: Yes, damn it. Who are you? What in hell is this all about?
Voice from Folkestone: This is Private Y, speaking for myself and Private Y2. I just called up to tell you to go to hell and I hope you drown before you get back to your billet.

Let us pass lightly over the next painful half-hour. This is not any place to record the language which fell upon the innocent ears of the sergeant of the guard and his assembled assistants. Even so, it was impossible to start any action from the camp at midnight to locate the callers and bring them back from Folkestone. The calls went out in all directions as early as possible the following morning. All efforts were futile and the two stalwarts simply vanished and were never caught.

Sequel

Several years after the war was over and deserters had been either pardoned or forgotten, a strange meeting took place. At the start of a baseball game a veteran of the 25th on one team got a good look at the second baseman of the rival club. The name was different but the face was Private Y and no one else. In a quiet meeting which followed, the truth came out. Before making the phone call from Folkestone, Private Y and his travelling companion had plans well established. Within minutes after hanging up with a nasty bang, they were on their way in civilian clothes. During a regular six-day leave they had set up a haven of refuge in Wales.

Once there, they watched their chance and succeeded in shipping out of Cardiff on a freighter bound for Philadelphia. Facing the hazards of the North Atlantic at that time, the shipping companies were not too fussy about the identity of able-bodied men willing to risk a seaman's job. The pair, using assumed names, were not questioned too closely before being signed on. On arrival in Philadelphia they jumped ship and put some distance between themselves and the seacoast without delay. As the USA was still neutral at that time, they were not in any danger of arrest. Both found work without much trouble and stayed safely in the US until the war ended. Later, when it was safe to do so, Private Y returned to Canada. As far as is known, Private Y2 did not come back and has not been heard from since.

Absence without Leave

Known historically as AWOL, the practice of extending a regular leave beyond its limits, or taking off without permission for a few days' personal holiday in no way indicated intention to desert. These cases were dealt with on different terms. If the absence was short and return voluntary, the penalties were less severe. It was more serious when the culprits unfortunately fell into the hands of the military police and were brought back under escort with the joys of their brief freedom rudely terminated.

It would take a substantial book by itself to record a good collection of the interesting reasons put forward by the defendants when answering to the charges they had to face. No one knows who first used the excuse that just as the last return train of the day was due to depart a band struck up 'God Save the King' so that the accused was forced by military tradition to stand stiffly at attention and (regretfully) watch the train pull slowly away without him. Uncounted numbers of clocks and watches went wrong, resulting in missed trains or connections delaying prompt return to the drudgeries of military life. In some cases, reference to out-of-date calendars was blamed for confusion of dates. Whatever the excuses put forward in hopeful self-defence, parting from the varied joys of London, animal, vegetable and mineral, or a combination of all three, was a mad blow at best. Frequently it became temporarily impossible to make the sorrowful decision, particularly if there was any money still available.

When lack of funds became a problem, a system of bumming prevailed. There were certain unwritten rules. Among others, it was understood that Canadians would avoid as far as possible putting a touch on their own officers. They would go for Australian or New Zealand types, less likely to ask awkward questions. In reverse, Canadian officers were considered fair game for the Anzac contingent. To avoid suspicion it was wise to keep up an excellent military appearance: clothes brushed, buttons bright, face shaved, belt in place and nothing out of order likely to attract the unwanted attention of the military police. It was sometimes useful to divide the territory and keep to one side of the street while a competitor or companion in crime was working the other side. Whatever the interval, the end was always the same: either voluntary return or being caught by the MPs and then payment of the penalties in proportion to the seriousness of the offence.

Holiday's End

The long warm summer days of July and August slipped quickly away. The end of the holiday seemed to come suddenly. At last, after ten months of intensive training, preparations for the final move into active combat service advanced rapidly. On September 6th, a few days following the inspection by King George V and Lord Kitchener, the old leather-type Oliver equipment was turned in and replaced by an issue of standard British web design. About the same time the Canadian-pattern boots were exchanged for the heavier black leather British model, complete with iron plate reinforced toes and heels. It is hard enough to fit boots to feet but it takes some doing to fit feet to boots. For the remainder of the time in England and the early weeks in France and Belgium there were more sore feet per thousand men than at any time in history. In the end, after the primary torture had subsided, it was gradually admitted that for real hard service and foot comfort these heavy-soled solidly built boots had no equal.

Some days before the date of movement from England a final pay was passed out. All records were transferred to the central Canadian pay office in London or sent forward to France. The exact date of departure was not made clear. Actually, it was a little further ahead than the troops expected. At the best of times any pay did not last very long. In this case it vanished promptly in one last celebration, with nearly everyone happy but flat broke. A small number of the thrifty who regularly operated unofficial small loan accounts did a land-office business at exceptionally profitable rates. With all records elsewhere, no amount of pressure could produce an extra few shillings. It also became clear that no relief from the severe lack of funds could be expected until some extended time after arrival in France. Meanwhile, all and sundry became broker and broker until even a single cigarette was a luxury to be carefully concealed for personal use. Odd surplus stocks of cheese and canned bully beef were quickly snatched and passed over to local outlets in return for small quantities of beer and tobacco. This state of financial misery prevailed until the day of departure arrived.

After one or two false starts, the move was set to be made on September 14th. Issue was completed of all equipment to be carried. The men prepared to leave their huts at Sandling for the last time. When assembled and ready to move off, they were loaded down like pack mules. Clothing included heavy woollen underwear and socks, flannel top shirt, regulation tunic, pants and putties. Heavy new boots completed that part of their outfits. The web equipment carried a water bottle with a full quart of water, a haversack with emergency rations (one can bully beef and some iron-hard biscuits) and such small items as knife, fork and spoon, hand towel, soap and shaving gear. The backpack contained a long overcoat, cardigan jacket, mess tin, spare underwear, spare socks, and other small items, woollen blanket rolled and strapped on top of the pack, and a rubber ground sheet folded in place under the blanket. In ball pouches in front they carried 150 rounds of .303 rifle ammunition. A spare pair of boots was also issued and if possible was jammed into the pack, otherwise was tied securely to it. The load was completed by the heavy long Ross rifle with bayonet in a scabbard on the belt at the side, and an entrenching tool with wooden handle slung in its carrier on the belt at back under the pack.

It may seem strange but the smaller and medium-sized men made a better job of supporting the load than many of the larger types. Men around 5'8" weighing about 150 pounds proved to be the best, probably because they had less weight of their own to carry on their poor sore feet. It was really tough on some of the big men. After a couple of hours under those small mountains of kit and equipment, their knees began to bend and they were in real distress. The whole Second Division was on the move. As the 25th Battalion took to the road toward Folkestone, the men stood up to the march from the camp to the dock very well, considering the loads they were carrying.

The ferry boat was packed with just enough room to stand or lie down on the decks. The men were able to unload their gear to relax as much as the cramped quarters and the filthy ship would permit. Crossing the Strait of Dover can be pretty grim in rough weather. There was a fresh breeze that night. Many men were sick, as much from the foul air and ship smells as from the motion of the sea. At one point halfway across, the fastenings on one of the side hatches gave way and the doors swung open. The sea washed in every time the ship rolled. For a brief time a number of the men near the doors were in danger of being washed overboard. They clung to each other while those further inside managed to pull them to safety. After a struggle, the ship's crew got the doors closed, leaving some fifty soldiers soaked to the skin and all their belongings also. Most of them were able to dry out at the gratings over the engine room before going ashore.

Fortunately, the distance was not great. Within two hours the ship docked in Boulogne early on the morning of September 15th, 1915. The battalion went ashore quickly and marched off on its way to the staging camp area on the heights above the city. No one who made that trip will ever forget the climb up the endless long hill from the water level to the top. In the dark night it seemed to be miles high. Carrying over eighty pounds of load some men collapsed and had to be partly carried by their stronger companions. When a man stumbled on the rough cobbled road in the dark, it took two others to lift him and his load and get him going again. Somehow, they all managed to make the hill and bed down in tents for the rest of the night.

Chapter Six

Away to the Races

Boulogne to Kemmel Hill

Early on September 15th, following the rough trip across the channel the previous night, preparations began to break camp and move on. Any thoughts of even a brief rest were quickly and rudely shattered. Following the usual morning clean-ups and inspections, the battalion took to the road down to the Pont-de-Briques railway station. There it received its first introduction to the famous military Pullmans, listed as 'Huit Cheveaux ou Quarante Hommes' (eight horses or forty men). It took time to get the whole unit to the station and assigned to the box-cars of the waiting train. Even after preliminary loading, the time of departure was still indefinite.

This provided an opportunity to stretch the military regulations a bit. The broke and hungry multitude quickly discovered that a suit of underwear or a pair of boots could be traded for several packets of violently strong French shag tobacco, cigarettes or perhaps a couple of big loaves of French bread. With luck, the trades included small quantities of the weak variety of French beer. This barter served two purposes. It gave temporary relief from a complete lack of essential supplies and at the same time slightly lightened the load on their tired backs.

It was late before the train got moving and after dark before it covered about fifty kilometres to a siding near the town of St Omer. The orders called for disembarkation and a march of several miles before halting for the night. Through some brilliant staff work at the battalion HQ level, the unit marched smartly off in the wrong direction. After several weary hours and becoming completely lost, a halt was called to wait for daylight and rescue from the wanderings. Meanwhile, brigade headquarters, which had been searching in all directions for its lost sheep, finally located them soon after daybreak. It was considered essential to recover position in the general scheme of movement. First, the distance back to the point of departure of the previous night had to be covered, then the correct mileage for that night made up. Finally, the march for the day was still before them. It was a sorry lot who came to rest in their proper place late that second night.

Another three days' marching completed the move to an open area just over the Belgian border outside the village of Locre. This was a few miles in advance of the Canadian general headquarters at Bailleul in France, of which more later. For the remainder of 1915 and until April 1916, Locre was the Fifth Brigade reserve billeting area. In certain respects it was the nearest thing to a home away from home the troops could hope for. When not in the trenches or in forward close support the battalion was frequently stationed in or near this village.

The brass band was broken up before leaving camp in England. Except for those retained as buglers, the performers were returned to regular company duty. Only the pipe band remained intact. It consisted of Pipe Major J. Carson, sixteen pipers, six snare drummers, one tenor drummer, one bass drummer, twenty-five men in all. During the several days' marching from St Omer to Locre their value was clearly established. Nothing could make such a journey easy but somehow the pipe music did help the men to get through in better shape. At least the whole battalion reached its destination intact, without any fallouts or men missing. Some of the other battalions were not so fortunate. It took several days for them to round up all their stragglers and regain full strength.

Shortly before leaving England the 25th received a draft of about forty men from another unit recruited in Quebec. These men were posted at least two to each of the sixteen platoons. The 25th men made the newcomers welcome. In a short time most of them were well established and popular. The idea was to have one or two men readily available to communicate where necessary with the civilians in France and Belgium. At the start this proved quite helpful but very quickly most men picked up enough army French to do their own communicating.

It had been customary to work slowly in preparing green troops for front-line duty. Because of plans already far advanced to open what later became known as the Battle of Loos, more rapid action was unavoidable. The day following arrival at Locre, groups of officers and NCOs were sent into the trenches in front of Kemmel Hill for prelimi-

nary instruction by the English regiment holding lines in that sector. On
the night of September 20th, half battalions of the 25th and 22nd moved
into the front lines. The trenches assigned to the 25th were held by the
5th Battalion of the King's Own Liverpool Regiment. For two days and
nights the English troops remained to give what small amount of training this brief period permitted to the new arrivals.

The 22nd on the left of the 25th received the same help from the English regiment in its sector. Then, on the night of September 22nd, just
eight days after leaving the camp in England, the other halves of the
battalions came in as the English regiments moved out. The 25th and
the 22nd were left on their own in the front lines, facing the German
trenches on the lower slope of the Wijtschate Ridge.

A diary of that period contains notes as follows:

Sept 16th: Brigade HQ at Wallon Cappell.
Sept 17th: Brigade HQ moved to Hazebrouck.
Sept 20th: Half battalions 22nd and 25th sent into trenches in front of
Kemmel Hill.
Sept 21st: Officers of 24th and 26th sent forward for instruction. First
casualties; one killed in 22nd and one in 25th.[25]
Sept 22nd: Balances of 22nd and 25th sent in. English troops of 83
Brigade withdrawn.
Sept 24th: Heavy rain. Trenches bad.
Sept 27th: Eight officers each from 24th and 26th sent in to learn trench
duties.
Sept 28th: 24th relieved 25th. 26th relieved 22nd. Very bad weather.
Relief completed 11:30 p.m.
Oct 4th: 22nd relieved 26th. 26th billeted La Clytte.
Oct 5th: 25th relieved 24th, 24th billeted at Locre.

The misfortunes and miseries of active service did not all come from
the hazards of combat action. Filthy toilets on the cross-channel ship,
plus common use of crude field arrangements quickly resulted in an
attack of body crabs. A very large number of the men were infected. The
outbreak developed fully just as the battalion moved into the front line

---

25 Clements's memory appears to be incorrect here. The first member of the 25th Battalion to be killed in action was William Small (b. 1882), on 3 October 1915. A native
of Tillcove Mines, Newfoundland, Small was a railway brakeman before enlisting in
the 25th at Halifax in December 1914.

for the first time. Medical services organized a counter-attack led by stretcher bearers supplied with suitable medication. The infection was gradually overcome after considerable discomfort by the unfortunate victims. Wet weather added to the joy of the occasion. A muddy trench on a rainy day was scarcely an ideal location for being stripped bare to received needed treatments.

The diary just mentioned speaks of heavy rain on September 24th, just two days after taking over from the Liverpool regiment. Again on the 28th very bad weather was recorded during the first relief of the 25th by the 24th Victoria Rifles of Montreal. The rains and mud of the Flanders battlefields are already a matter of historical record. Possibly it has not been made quite clear that the whole area is a solid mass of brown clay. There is not a natural stone as big as a small potato in a square mile. Even the paving blocks used to surface roads have to be quarried and imported from France. When the country was dry the clay could be cut with a shovel like cheese. It only needed a single day of heavy rain to saturate the ground completely. The result was a slimy grey-brown mixture almost impossible to control. It stuck to shovels like glue and caked all over boots and clothing.

As soon as the rainy season developed, trenches became drains filled with water. When the sides started to cave in the whole setup was a nightmare. In places, as a solution to prevent the total collapse of the trench sides, corrugated iron sheets or combinations of heavy wire and burlap secured by stout stakes gave temporary security of sorts. Latticed wooden walks known as trench mats elevated a foot or so above the trench bottoms provided footing in spots, allowing some water to run away underneath. In particularly swampy ground the only choice was to build sandbagged barricades on the surface, heavily plastered and banked with mud. Concealed as far as possible, they gave some shelter from direct rifle and machine-gun fire.

This soft ground did have one advantage, particularly with regard to shellfire from howitzers. Any shell dropping from a high angle tended to bury itself deep enough to lose much of its explosive force in the ground below the surface. Shells timed to explode in the air were more dangerous but any fragments of the shrapnel after hitting the ground seldom carried further.

Introduction to Reality

From the rear area near the Kemmel-Ypres road two roughly parallel communication trenches led forward to the sector of the front lines held by the 25th. The trench to the left followed the direction of a local country road which someone had christened the VC road. The right trench was shown on the maps as the Via Gellia. These two also served as communications for the 22nd Battalion on the left and the 28th Battalion of the Sixth Brigade next on the right.

On the first trip into the trenches one 25th man was killed by a German sniper's bullet. A few others were slightly wounded or injured. The main troubles were discomfort and difficulties due to the start of the wet weather season.

The second trip began with relief of the 24th by the 25th on the night of October 5th. For the next three days the weather was mixed. Regular trench routine became better organized and understood. Nights were spent bringing up food rations and water supplies. Defensive positions were repaired and improved. Small cover parties worked out in no man's land between the trenches and the German lines. Barbed wire fences and barricades were thickened and strengthened to guard against sudden attacks. Movement during daylight hours was risky and restricted. Where possible, light work was carried out in daylight where there was enough cover from enemy observation.

The trench routine known as 'stand to' required every man to be at his post in full fighting order from one hour before to one hour after sunrise. This was considered the most likely time for an attack to develop. In reverse, in the evening the time was one hour before to one hour after sundown. That was the situation on October 8th, 1915, as the evening light began to fade following what seemed to be just another day in the trenches. The inexperienced troops of the Second Division did not have any way of suspecting that in places where the lines had been static for several months and where opposing trenches were quite close that it was possible to dig tunnels underground and plant mines.

The Germans had succeeded in placing a heavy mine directly under one of the trenches held by the 25th. Two even heavier mines were under the Sixth Brigade sector on the right of the 25th. It has since been thought that underground listening posts detected the approach of British counter-mining near where these mines were located. If so, it could have been decided to blow them before they might be discovered and the troops above warned of their danger. Again, it might have been the fear of flooding from the wet weather season.

Whatever the reason, they were blown just before 'stand-down' on the evening of October 8th. When they went up the ground shook like an earthquake. At the same time a heavy barrage of shellfire plus sustained machine-gun fire covered the whole of these forward positions. The West Lancashire field artillery, then supporting the Canadian front, returned the fire until its limited supply of ammunition was used up. After that the Germans had it all their own way. For the next hour they poured a heavy concentration of shells into the area around the mine craters.

Where the mine blew under the 25th trench, half of one platoon simply disappeared. They were blown to pieces and never seen again. Another twenty men nearby were wounded more or less severely. The remainder in both the front and support lines did not know what to expect next. For a time they could only believe an attack would follow at any moment. To their everlasting credit, they held their ground, rescued and took care of the wounded men and stood ready to fight it out. The Sixth Brigade battalion on the right went through the same experience and stood up equally well. Unfortunately, their losses were heavier than those of the 25th.

Such a severe test would be enough for fully trained troops with long battle experience. In the years which followed, the 25th Battalion successfully faced many worse situations. On this occasion, hardly two weeks from their first entry into the trenches, the courage of these men was proven beyond doubt. They truly deserved much greater recognition than ever was given to them at the time or later.

The mine explosions and heavy shelling temporarily destroyed all communication between the forward trenches and the control headquarters of both the Fifth and Sixth Brigade units some distance further back. For a time, through lack of exact information some confusion developed. When the first shocks had been absorbed it slowly became clear that the front was being held. After an hour the German shelling tapered off.

As the hazards of movement diminished, contacts were restored. Then the work of clearing the wounded and surveying the damage began. Some heavy repairs were possible before daylight on October 9th. From then on until relieved by the 24th Battalion on the night of October 10th, every effort was made to rebuild the damaged trenches and to repair and strengthen the barbed wire out in front.

The Tunnelers

It is not quite clear if the organization of a Canadian tunneling company was a result of the German mine explosions on October 8th. It may have had something to do with it or at least hastened a decision. In one diary it was mentioned as early as October 11th and again on October 23rd. A natural source of manpower was from among the coal miners of Cape Breton and eastern Nova Scotia in the 25th Battalion.

One officer of the 25th who had been a mining engineer in civilian life was drafted to head the new group. He took with him about 100 men accustomed to working underground. They were replaced by a draft from reserve camps in England. The whole operation was very much hush-hush and further contact with this company was infrequent and limited. Their former comrades knew what they were trying to do but where and how was rarely mentioned. There must be an official record somewhere of this tunneling company. It continued to work in the Ypres area for the best part of the following three years.

Some evidence of their effective work was revealed when the entire German forward position along the crest of the Messines Ridge was blown open by the mines which they had placed. This cleared the way for a very successful British advance of considerable temporary importance. Part of the success was due to the use of experienced miners and their ability to work much deeper than formerly had been thought possible. Among their former comrades the word got around that frequently they tunneled far below the German counter-efforts. Some reports suggested detection of enemy works above which were blown from below with the German miners in them. This may have been just a cookhouse tale but it was current in the 25th Battalion during the winter of 1915–16.

One nasty bit did develop from all the mining and counter-mining activity. After a shaft had been established and galleries tunneled out to and parallel underneath the German lines, these had to be loaded with explosives before being sealed off, ready for use later when thought to be most effective. Several times during the winter the 25th Battalion was called upon to supply night carrying parties of from 100 up to 200 men. TNT in boxes weighing about forty pounds each would be brought up shortly after dark by the Corps of Engineers as far as horse-drawn transport could be safely used. These supplies were then taken over by the carrying parties.

Each man shouldered a forty-pound box and in the miserable dark rainy night, in single file at about one-yard intervals, they proceeded forward to the shaft head. There they handed the boxes to the miners, who quickly passed them along down to the lower levels. The whole job had to be done before daylight and the shaft head covered up and camouflaged to prevent detection by the enemy. At some points old country roads could be used. The stone-paved parts helped to give better footing and ease in keeping direction. At other times the route would be alongside or down in a slimy communication trench or in mud to the boot-tops or deeper across open fields.

It is a real ducky feeling to be out in the open on a filthy night with forty pounds of TNT on your shoulder. Every time an enemy gun is fired you hold your breath until you know where the shell went and how far from your track it landed. It is just as well not to think of what would happen if one struck close enough to your party to set off a box of the TNT. No one would ever credit the army with good management so it must have been good luck which prevented disaster to any of the parties from the 25th. One or two men did get wounded by stray bullets while near support line trenches. There is not any record of medals being given for that kind of service. It evidently was considered all in a night's work and part of the penalty for enlisting in the PBI in the first place.

Chapter Seven

Phooie – Il Pluie

On the good old firing line,
On the good old firing line,
When I fire at Heinie's head,
Fritzy fires at mine.

While you eat your chicken dinners,
On bully-beef I dine,
And I wish oh Lord, I'd fell overboard
On my way to the firing line.

Colonel Hilliam Takes Over

In the haste of organizing the Canadian overseas forces there was little clear understanding of the physical requirements for service in the combat areas. This had nothing to do with the risks of injury or death at the fighting front. It was entirely a matter of long weary days and nights without adequate sleep or rest after extended periods of being chilled and soaking wet, with poorly prepared food at irregular intervals.

The experience of the 25th Battalion was not any different from that of all the other units. In every battalion there were senior officers well beyond young middle age. They had worked long and sincerely to prepare themselves and the men under their command for the perils and hardships of active service. Rapid replacements by younger men physically able to meet the conditions of service in the forward areas had to be made. It must be clearly stated and repeated as many times as necessary that there never was any question of lack of courage involved.

Those older men tried to the limits of their physical strength to carry out their duties. They simply could not withstand the strains they were called upon to face and had to give way.

With the Second Division these changes came very quickly after the movement to France in September 1915. By mid-October, following a few weeks' exposure to the rain and mud of the Flanders battlefield, a number of the older officers were returned to England. Others moved back and down to base camps where the living conditions were enough better to enable them to continue in useful service for a time.

As these changes began to develop, Major Edward Hilliam[26] from the 10th Battalion of the First Canadian Division, promoted to the rank of lieutenant colonel, assumed command of the 25th Battalion. This fine officer already had a distinguished military career, first as a young man in the regular British army, later in Canada in the North West Mounted Police, followed by his service with the First Division. That included the second Battle of Ypres in April, then the actions in May at Festubert and in June at Givenchy. His strong character and broad previous experience quickly made itself felt. It was just what was needed to bring out and develop further the fine fighting qualities of the men under his leadership.

Before he again received promotion as a brigadier general to take command of the Tenth Brigade of the Fourth Division in January 1917, he led the 25th Battalion through St Eloi in April 1916, Sanctuary Wood and Maple Copse in June 1916, Courcelette on September 15th, 1916, and Regina Trench in October 1916. After the desperate casualties on the Somme, he rebuilt the battalion to its former strength and left it well prepared for the Vimy Ridge success a few months later in April 1917.

In Chapter Two a brief reference was made to the lamentable lack of any organized and effective publicity on behalf of the 25th Battalion. The people of Nova Scotia then and later heard very little about Colonel Hilliam personally. They never understood how much of the magnificent fighting record of the 25th resulted from his wise leadership and great ability to organize, control and inspire his men under the most

---

26 Edward Hilliam (b. 1862) was born in England and served with the 14th Lancers in the British army. He immigrated to Canada in 1893 and served in the North West Mounted Police and in the South African Constabulary during the South African war. He was a fruit farmer in Kamloops, British Columbia, when he signed up to go overseas in 1914 as adjutant of the 5th Battalion. He commanded the 25th Battalion from October 1915 to January 1917, then was promoted to brigadier general commanding the Tenth Brigade from January to November 1917, when he retired.

difficult conditions. It was from among the survivors of the younger
men whom he selected, trained and directed that the later strength of
the battalion was developed and maintained. Very few men who served
under him are alive today. In a few more years they will be gone. It is
hoped that these few brief words in tribute to a wonderful soldier and
a fine gentleman will at least prevent his name and record from being
completely forgotten in Nova Scotia in the years to come.

The General's Dishes

At the junction of the Via Gellia communication trench and the main
support line there was a control post manned by half a platoon in
charge of a sergeant. The nearby area contained a few trees and low
bushes. There was also quite a bit of long grass in the open fields to the
rear. With care, a few men could move about in daylight without drawing fire from the German field guns, although there were always stray
bullets floating about.

In a field back of the post was an abandoned farmhouse still in fairly
good condition. There were strict orders to keep away from it, particularly in daylight, to avoid drawing enemy fire into the area. Quite naturally, when soldiers are told not to do something, curiosity is aroused.
This frequently leads to taking a chance to investigate for their own
satisfaction, this on the basis of 'never believe anything you hear and
no more than half of what you find out for yourself.'

Early on before the foul weather set in completely there would be an
occasional fine dry day. On one such, the sergeant was persuaded by
some of his men to take a small party to visit the house. They crawled
through the long grass without being seen by either friend or foe and
reached the objective intact. On arrival, they were attacked by a large
pheasant, which naturally had to be shot in self-defence. Note: Among
other very definite orders was one prohibiting the shooting or otherwise taking of game birds or animals; this, according to army regulations, was a very serious offence.

The pheasant being the only casualty, the party worked around and
entered the house from the rear. The cellar and the main house were
empty of anything worth having. Others had been there before. There
was a closed hatch in an upstairs ceiling which seemed to invite inspection. The lightest member of the group, when hoisted up, managed to
open it and scramble through to a sort of attic. Light from a window at
one end revealed the place to be empty except for one fair-sized wicker

hamper. This evidently had been abandoned or overlooked when the original owners had fled to safety further back. When opened, the hamper was found to contain a full dinner set of excellent quality china.

The hamper was carefully lowered down but just at that time one curious soul stuck his head out a window opening to look around. The place must have been under close German observation. Right away whiz-bangs began to dust off the house and yard. In no time flat the party, along with the precious dishes, was down in the strong brick-covered cellar. There it stayed put until the Germans got tired of wasting ammunition and quit. The dishes could not be moved in daylight so were left while the finders crawled back to their proper post. They were quickly recovered and brought in after dark.

The following morning after stand-down, the usual trench breakfast and issue of rations for the day, the dishes were unpacked and laid out on a trench mat for further examination. They were certainly good quality and a rather attractive pattern. The question was what to do with them. By the time each man had dealt with his own personal load, including rifle and supply of ammunition, he did not have any spare space or capacity to carry around extra china dishes. The solution came suddenly from a most unexpected quarter.

While the survey was in progress and all the dishes were neatly sorted and laid out, the sentry at the intersection challenged a party coming up the Via Gellia from the rear. On arrival, it proved to be no less than the brigade commander with a small escort, intent on seeing for himself how the trenches were standing up and what his new troops were doing. The sergeant saluted and his men stood to attention awaiting further developments, which were not long in coming. The general could not possibly miss seeing the dishes so he walked around the display with considerable interest. He then turned to the sergeant and the conversation went somewhat as follows:

General: That is a good looking set of dishes.
Sergeant: Yes sir.
General: Where did you get them?
Sergeant: I found them.
General: What do you intend to do with them?
Sergeant: I have not decided.
General: Do you intend to carry them around with you?
Sergeant: No sir.
General: Would you consider selling them to me?

Sergeant: Yes sir.

General: How much do you want for them?

Sergeant: As much as I can get sir.

General: Would fifty francs be about right?

Sergeant: (nobly concealing his relief) Yes sir.

General: Very well. Here is your money. Pack them carefully in the hamper and I will send a carrying party for them after dark tonight.

Sergeant: Thank you sir. They will be ready when the party comes for them.

General: You seem to be fairly comfortable here.

Sergeant: Yes sir.

General: Any unusual activity?

Sergeant: Not much. The Jerries sometimes throw a few shells at that old house back there.

General: So I have heard. What are your instructions?

Sergeant: To keep away from it.

General: See that you do so.

Sergeant: Yes sir.

General: How far is it from the front line?

Sergeant: About 150 yards.

General: Is the trench passable?

Sergeant: It's a bit mucky but you can get through if you don't mind some mud on your boots.

The general then gathered up his party. Salutes were exchanged and they moved forward. The dishes were collected that evening and were reported to have given quite a touch of elegance to brigade HQ table settings for some time thereafter. The fifty francs provided the sergeant and his followers with tea and crumpets the first night out after the relief. At least, that is what they said they had when the story leaked out and they were questioned by some of their friends from other platoons.

The Wandering Wabbit of No Man's Land

Did you ever see a real live Belgian hare? This elongated creation has the anatomy of an ordinary rabbit, only more so: more bone and less meat, with longer legs like steel springs and great long ears. It is geared to travel at high speed and when on the move only needs a pair of wings to soar like a bird after each jump. Sometimes it even seems to soar without the help of wings at all.

One night toward the end of 1915, one of these stray residents in some way worked its way through the trenches and out between them into no man's land. No one will ever know whether it was a fugitive from German tyranny or in flight from the sporting fraternity in the Canadian Corps. There had been some fog and mist during the night but an hour or so after stand-down the air cleared enough to see about half way over to the German front line.

One of the bright boys in the 25th suddenly spotted Mr Wabbit sitting on the edge of a shell hole midway between the front lines. He quickly alerted several nearby associates and with visions of a possible rabbit stew they all took aim and opened up on the unexpected visitor. Alas for the collective marksmanship, they all missed but plowed the dirt up all around the lonesome beastie. It first went straight up in the air like a rocket, then took a couple of record jumps in a southerly direction and sat up again to resurvey the situation.

A second volley brought about a repeat performance but it did something else. It aroused the whole 25th Battalion front line and the Germans opposite. Both sides temporarily forgot their personal quarrels and concentrated on the intruder. This time the rabbit took off southbound, non-stop down the middle of no man's land. It was soon out of range of its original tormenters but as it continued its flight each unit on both sides took over as it passed. The shooting multiplied and the noise could be heard for miles. Distress flares started to pop, followed by artillery support from forward field batteries. This in turn pulled in some heavier howitzer counter-battery activity. Both sides seemed to think the other was getting ready to attack and reacted accordingly.

It took a couple of hours to convince the opposite brass that the whole thing was a false alarm and have proper orders issued to stop the waste of further precious artillery ammunition. Some time around noon the front returned to normal and settled down to another dreary, wet and miserable trench day. There is not any record of the rabbit ever being hit or where it finally went. It certainly stirred up four or five miles of front line during its rapid transit journey along no man's land. Even when the truth came out those in the rear found it almost impossible to believe that one forlorn small animal could be the cause of so much excitement. No one knows exactly what Colonel Hilliam thought. He could have been pardoned if he began to wonder what sort of a bunch of wild men he had undertaken to manage.

Siege Farm

After the shock of the German mine explosions on October 8th, the troops began to settle down to a more regular trench routine: six days in the front line followed by six days in brigade forward support positions, return for a second six days in the front lines, then the next six days a little further back in brigade reserve. The 25th worked in and out in exchange with the 24th Victoria Rifles from Montreal. The 26th New Brunswick unit did the same with the 22nd. With slight variations these arrangements continued throughout the rest of the war.

For most of the winter of 1915–16 one brigade forward support position was at a group of buildings near the Kemmel-Ypres road known as Siege Farm. Shelter for the troops was provided in the barns and out-buildings. In the centre of the group of buildings was the usual farm midden, full of wet and rotting refuse from the house and barns, all carefully preserved for use as fertilizer on the surrounding fields.

On dark nights when more than a normal amount of tanglefoot[27] had been absorbed, it was not unknown for some unfortunate to wander into the midden and emerge soaking wet, smelling anything but rosy. Any such were consigned to further misery by being denied entrance to inside shelter. They were compelled to spend the rest of the night outside, wherever they could find a soft spot to lie down in the rain. From then on until the worst of the perfume had evaporated, they were somewhat less than popular with their brethren. On one occasion a junior officer joined this unhappy band to the ill-concealed delight of his temporary inferiors.

The routine from Siege Farm involved nightly working parties up to the close support areas. Cleaning out blocked communication trenches, preparing reserve defence positions, carrying forward ammunition, water and rations, building barbed wire fences, and similar duties kept everyone busy. Parties were kept well forward, close at hand, until just before daylight in case of any sudden enemy assault action. Except for some occasional degree of comfort during daylight hours resting inside the barns, protected from the worst of the weather, the men very often preferred being in the front lines. If they had to be there every night, they were at least spared a couple of miles or more of walking each way in the dark and rain in coming up from Siege Farm and returning to it before daylight.

For a time, some of the Locre accommodation was in canvas tents. Ten or twelve men with all their equipment in a regulation army tent were not much better off than sardines in a can. If the floor boards were

---

27 'Tanglefoot' is slang for alcohol, especially whisky.

on a slant, as they nearly always were, the unfortunate at the lower side frequently woke up low man on the totem pole, underneath a pile of his friends from higher up. The wise and experienced avoided any position close to the door flap outlet. Those so placed were certain to be stepped on when the usual calls of nature demanded a hasty exit from anyone further inside the tent. The NCO in charge always swung his rank to pick the best possible position for his personal use. As the weather grew worse, the tent camps were gradually abandoned and better shelter requisitioned in barns and old houses around the town. Later again the prefab Nissan huts began to develop, providing shelter for complete battalions in selected areas.

Baths

For the rest of September and early October following arrival in France on September 15th there were occasional warm days. The country was spotted with old shell holes full of water. With care not to stir up the mud in the bottom, it was possible to skim off enough water to fill a bucket or an empty biscuit tin and have a sort of sponge bath in behind the nearest hedge. While at the job, underwear could be turned inside out and lighted matches used to follow the seams and burn out the live lice and nits. This would establish a kind of armistice for a few hours before collecting a fresh colony from the blankets or too close contact with infected fellow unfortunates in packed tents or dugouts.

On the first trip back to Locre there was an organized bath parade. The bath house was a hastily built rough board shack in two sections. The first, used as a changing room, provided space for twenty men to undress and hang their clothes on nails in the wall. On the other side were rough boxes and bags where dirty underwear, socks and top shirts were collected. In the second section, on a slatted wooden floor were ten wooden tubs made by sawing big beer barrels in two. The walls were thin and full of cracks, so that the cold air came through almost like a wind tunnel. Outside in the yard was a half-broken-down fire pot and boiler providing a very limited supply of hot water.

When completely bare the twenty men went into the wash room in pairs, two men per tub with one piece of yellow laundry soap. The bath crew put two buckets of cold water and one of hot into each tub. Then the pairs stood in the tubs and scrubbed each other as best they could. After a time limit of three minutes the victims were driven back to the dressing room and tubs emptied to make way for the next lot.

The now presumably clean group each received a towel on the way out. After drying, they went to a hole in the wall through which they were each given one set of underwear, one pair of socks and one top shirt. The garments passed out all had unidentified previous owners. They had been washed and disinfected to a tattle-tale grey shade with a strong creosote smell. At least for the moment they were free from lice and other similar pests.

As usual, the old army game of one man one shirt prevailed, compounded in fiendish delight by the sadistic attendant behind the wall. Naturally the heavyweights drew the small sizes and the midgets came up with enough to cover themselves twice over. Even much fast trading failed to completely sort out the problem. A man six feet tall squeezed into a small suit of Stanfield's (somewhat shrunk, in spite of the label to the contrary) with the legs ending at his knees and the sleeves at his elbows was at best a very sad sight, not an example in any way of well-managed public relations. In reverse, the comments of one 5' 6" draped in folds of fabric around his middle, with the legs turned up to his knees and sleeves doubled to his elbows, exhausted the normal army words of comfort and relief and added others previously unknown to contemporary English.

Any changes just had to be improvements. As time passed, the old shacks were replaced with better buildings. The wash rooms were fitted with shower equipment and enlarged to accommodate forty or fifty men at a time. When occupied, there was hot water under pressure fed from elevated tanks and kept on for two or three minutes. Then the whole soaking lot were driven back to the dressing room in a crushing rush by a change to ice cold water through the spray heads in the ceiling.

Replacement underclothing also improved as the months went by. First came issues of fresh new socks, but still reconditioned underwear and top shirts. Next came completely new underwear, and finally new top shirts as well, in addition to a fairly reasonable range and choice of sizes. Troops arriving by mid-summer 1916 and later only knew by hearsay the really rough bathing conditions experienced by the original men of the First and Second Divisions.

Clothing

On enlistment in Halifax in November 1914 each man was issued with one pair of trousers, one uniform jacket, and one greatcoat. For reasons or lack of reasons never completely clear to the lower ranks, the possibility of replacements ever being necessary did not appear to exist in the minds of the mighty. The men wore the same clothes for six months' training in Halifax, a further three and a half months' training in England, and for most of the fall and early winter of 1915–16, in and out of the filth and mud of the front lines in Flanders. It is difficult to clearly picture the condition of the clothing by January 1916, a full fifteen months from date of issue. Among other helpful developments, the length of the greatcoats added to the joy of nations.

When crawling and wading through mud and water knee-deep and sometimes deeper, the lower parts of the coats became so caked with muck that further movement was almost impossible. The natural cure was amputation of a foot or more off the coat-tails. This operation carried out through use of an army clasp knife produced some weird results. Some coats ended up short in front and longer in back, a general cutaway effect. Others in reverse had pointed sections in front with high back outlines. The canvas pockets were originally white and even when turned to something less than snowy still gave a curious ornamental effect when two or three inches hung down below the point of amputation of the coat-tails.

Finally, small quantities of replacements began to appear. With leave to England starting about the same time, some of the new garments were held back to refit such fortunates before departure for brief appearance in more civilized surroundings. More of this later. The general arrangement supplied each battalion with about thirty new sets of clothing at a time. Divided between four companies and the auxiliary details such as transport, QM Stores, HQ staff, etc, this meant about six sets per company at time of issue. Company commanders were notified to select their six most ragged men and parade them to the QM Stores for refit. At first the companies were called in rotation, starting with 'A' Company and working down through to 'D' Company, this of course after the HQ auxiliary details had received the pick in their allotment of six outfits.

Somehow that failed to work out exactly as intended. When 'A' Company turned up with its six men, care was taken to slip in another three who were expert thieves. In ways difficult to trace the total company take was nine complete outfits instead of six. With 'B' and 'C' Companies equally intent on furthering their interests to the limit, it developed that when 'D' Company came along the well was almost dry. They were lucky to find even three complete sets of clothing as their share and these were of odd sizes not easily adjusted to actual needs.

New caps when included came out short in much the same way with latecomers restricted to sizes 6 ½ or 7 3/8 with nothing in between. A small head encased in a 7 3/8 size with a large tuck in the back, held together by a heavy horse blanket safety pin somehow escaped the ideal of smart military style, even if it did hold a certain flair of artistic achievement.

For once, some rare military accident provided the new tunics with soft rolled collars and loose-fitting cut. That was a welcome replacement for the skin-tight originals with their stiff and high single collars. The new caps also were more sensible, being soft cloth without the stiff sides and crowns of the 1914 models. Gradually as 1916 progressed, between continuous issues of new clothing and better-clothed replacement personnel, the battalion became fit to be seen in public as a respectable military assembly.

Chapter Eight

What Next?

Siege Farm Potatoes

One of the barns was of solid heavy stone construction. At a point inside there was a very large bin of extra-thick hardwood, its door on thick iron hinges secured with an enormous padlock with the key kept by the farmer on a chain tied to his belt. To provide for ventilation there was an opening about eighteen inches square, high up in the outside wall, protected by iron bars leaded deeply into the stone. When first discovered by the always hungry troops, the bin was more than half full of good-looking potatoes. Probably the farmer was saving them for his own use and perhaps some for seed next spring. Whatever his reasons, he refused all offers from the men to buy some of them to add to their mostly slim and frequently missing army rations of fresh vegetables.

Review of the problem was not long in coming. A survey from all angles inside and outside the barn confirmed that direct personal entry was impossible. The level of the potatoes inside the bin was too far below the ventilating opening to bring any potatoes within arm's reach. Today, mention is frequently made of thinkers' meetings as being something new and very modern. Not so. Thinkers' meetings were common practice long ago, particularly in the Canadian army of World War I. The variety of problems solved accounts for the survival of many of its otherwise less deserving elements.

In this case the procedure was as follows:

Item No 1. Find wood to make a rough ladder long enough to reach the opening in the outside wall. Not easy. Wood scarce but scouting came up with the requirement at the first try.

Item No 2. Two bean poles about twelve feet long.

Item No 3. One piece of strong stuff wire. Easy. Plenty of barbed wire with the barbs removed.

Item No 4. Two sandbags. Again easy. Plenty on hand.

Item No 5. Nails for ladder and one big one extra.

Procedure. (a) Make ladder; (b) bend wire and attach to end of one bean pole to make a loop; (c) tie one sandbag to loop to make like a dip net; (d) cut head off big nail and set as spike in one end of other bean pole; (e) climb ladder to ventilating window, push wire loop with sandbag attached between bars, lower to top of the potato pile; (f) push second pole between bars, lower end to potatoes and spike one; (g) lift and transfer potato from spike to sandbag; (h) repeat until several potatoes in sandbag; (i) lift to bars, turn bag inside out and pour potatoes out between bars; repeat as often as desired to fill extra bags; (j) remove all equipment and hide securely until more potatoes desired; (k) be careful not to take too many in any one operation; share only with Thinkers' group.

For a short time the farmer was not aware of the shrinkage in his potato bin. At first he was only suspicious, but before long he knew definitely that something was very wrong. It was interesting to watch his efforts to solve the mystery. First he examined every detail of the construction inside and out. No answer there. Next, he developed a system of frequent visits at irregular intervals, evidently hoping to catch his tormenters at work. Still no luck. He even stayed up late and made visits at night before going to bed. No man can keep awake forever and with ten others watching for him he was beaten before he started. No doubt he has long since gone to his rest but he must have died still wondering how so many of those potatoes vanished without a trace.

Feet: The Care Of

The hazards of the Flanders campaign in the winter of 1915–16 did not all come from direct enemy action. At times the Germans were far less of a menace than the weather. It may seem tiresome to dwell on the vile climate and its effects on the men of the 25th and throughout the whole Canadian army. Even so, some details of existence during the months from September 1915 to May 1916 should not be forgotten. They are worth a few further comments at this time.

The winter season in that part of Europe is always extremely wet and dreary. The winds come in steadily from the east and northeast.

They bring with them almost continuous fog, drizzle and rain off the North Sea. Now and then there is a bit of wet snow for a day or two and perhaps a short period of freezing temperatures. Mainly it is rain, rain and more rain until the longing for even a flicker of sunlight becomes almost an obsession.

With the soil entirely of clay saturated with water, the resulting mud has to be seen to be believed. When wet it is like glue and when dry like cement. All the words which have been written or are likely to be recorded in the future cannot fully convey its effects on the men who had to try to live in it and with it.

Back in the reserve billets it was possible to dry out long enough to scrape off this mud and brush clothing fairly clean. Boots could be dried, greased and polished, buttons burnished and equipment including rifles thoroughly cleaned. Half an hour out in the rain on a night working party, or moving forward to take over front-line duty and everyone was soaked to the skin again and covered with sticky mud. Lacking any normal means of keeping dry, several unusual methods developed. To some limited degree the purely animal heat of several men huddled together in a dugout would evaporate the worst of the water from wet clothing. When that happened, the inner clothing would become almost dry even if the outer layers were still wet.

Another twist when any empty sandbags could be temporarily borrowed was to pull several over each foot and up the leg to tie above the knee. After a few hours under cover with layers of these sandbags on each leg the body heat would expel the moisture through the bags. The outer layers would be soaking wet but each successive inside layer would be drier. By the time they had all been peeled off, the permanent clothing would be practically dry. What that did to the legs and feet was something else again. Skin took on a puckered, bleached, parboiled texture. Often lacking clean dry socks, some small relief was possible by changing from one foot to the other to alter the set of the wool. The first hour of walking in hard wet boots was pure torture. The shock from a plunge into knee-deep mud and ice-cold water is impossible to describe.

Any idea of taking blankets into trenches was not worth a second thought. Beyond ordinary clothing and greatcoats, the only extras came from empty sandbags the men could collect from the trench supply brought in by working or ration parties. It soon became clear that effective action would need to be taken to protect the men from what became known as trench feet. In extreme cases after long periods without relief from the soaking-wet conditions, lack of blood circulation would result in something very much like gangrene. If not given attention, in time this could mean loss of one or more toes or even worse, loss of whole feet.

To combat this hazard, a rigid trench routine was established and maintained. Once every day, in small groups, each man was made to remove his boots and socks and massage his feet with whale oil from supplies brought into the trenches for that special purpose. No one was permitted to dodge this smelly task. The officers, or in their absence, the senior NCOs personally stood by and forced each man to protect his feet in spite of any protest. An attempt to overcome the problem through trench issues of long-legged rubber waders fell through. Once over the tops and soaked inside, it was not possible to dry them out and they rapidly became useless. The task of transferring these boots from outgoing to incoming reliefs proved completely unworkable. Finally the waders just lay around the trenches in soggy piles. They gradually disappeared in some unknown fashion and were never replaced.

Pay (Sometimes)

Soldiers on active service in France and Belgium were only allowed to draw a portion of their pay, the balance being kept to their credit at the central Canadian pay office in London. Pay was issued twice a month. Privates drew fifteen francs, lance corporals twenty, corporals twenty-five, and sergeants thirty each payday. Officers were paid through monthly credit to their accounts established in the Bank of Montreal, Waterloo Place, London. Against these they could cash three cheques per month in France of one hundred francs each, no more than one on any one day.

All such drawings were charged at the rate of five francs to the Canadian dollar. Balances accumulated in London were available for extra money when going on leave from the front to England. These rates do not sound very generous when compared with money values today, but until the arrival of the Americans some two years later the Canadians were by far the best paid soldiers in the allied forces.

It is not hard to understand why many people in England and Europe generally got the idea that all Canadians were wealthy. They directed their efforts toward separating them from their fortune as rapidly as possible. That was not too hard to do. Many soldiers exposed to front-line duty quickly developed some degree of fatalism. Here today and gone tomorrow became a working reality. Money was regarded as something to be used and enjoyed in any way to personal preference while still alive and able to spend it.

Christmas & New Year's 1915–16

For once, the luck was with the 25th. They were relieved from the front line by the 24th Battalion on Christmas Eve, December 24th, 1915, and moved back to billets in Locre. In the morning, following the usual efforts to clean clothing and equipment and get rid of the muck from the trenches, mail and parcels were given out at breakfast time. Somewhere in the background there must have been a special effort to hasten and complete delivery of both parcels and letters from home in Canada. Whoever was responsible did an outstanding job. Very few men were left without something from their families and friends.

Parades were held to a minimum. An extra pay issue was passed out and thankfully received. Brief church services were held by both Protestant and Catholic chaplains. At this late date the details of Christmas dinner are not very clear. Memories of quite a few other events of the day are somewhat hazy. A grand time was had by all present.

The next five days passed quickly. On the night of December 30th the battalion moved back into the front lines to relieve the 24th and give them their New Year's holiday back at Locre. Contrary to the rush of mail for Christmas, distribution in the front line for New Year's was limited. To the delight (?) of one ex-banker,[28] his total take for New Year's day consisted of a personal copy of the annual report of the Bank of Montreal complete with a few words of cheer from the president. Seated on the remains of a biscuit box, partly sheltered from the rain under a sheet of corrugated iron, it was a great comfort to note that the bank was still in business and doing nicely in a financial way in spite of the difficulties created by the loss of staff to the armed forces. After this inspiriting mental nourishment, the day's rations complemented by the last soggy remains of a Christmas pudding and a handful of walnuts completed a day of joy and a festive entry into the new year of 1916.

Life??? in the Front Line

The trench systems held by the Fifth Brigade faced what was known as

---

28 That is, the author himself.

the Wijtechate Ridge. The brigade held roughly one third of the Second Division front in the centre, between the Fourth Brigade on its left and the Sixth Brigade on its right. Trenches were identified by a combined lettering and numbering arrangement. For the balance of 1915 and early 1916 the 25th spent its front-line time holding the J, K, L and M sections.

The German trenches were on the higher slopes of the ridge. A general distance between the opposing lines was about 200 yards, but it varied quite a bit from one point to another. Being higher than the Canadians, the Germans during those rainy winter months drained the water out into no man's land and forward on top of the already soaking Fifth Brigade men in the swampy ground at the foot of the ridge.

There was one most unusual trench known as J3. It was quite short and was held by only one platoon. Directly in front there was a piece of woodland called the Petit Bois (Little Wood). In order to hold it the German trenches came forward in a rough half-circle so that at its extreme point the distance from J3 was about fifty yards. The ground in between was stacked with barbed-wire fences and barricades put out by both sides. In addition, dozens of coils of barbed wire had been uncoiled and left loose in great loops and piles. The entire space was a solid mass four or five feet high. Even a rat would have had a tough time passing through. For men there was no chance whatever. The distance was a little too far for either side to throw a potato masher or a Mills bomb.

This did not prevent a steady exchange of verbal insults directly contrary to standing orders. Strangely enough, the Canadians seemed to know more insults in German than the Germans did in English and usually won most of the shouting matches by default. The best part of the whole affair was that neither side dared to shell that sector. The lines were so close to each other that they could just as easily hit their own men as their enemies.

The troops somehow managed to keep the place drained fairly dry. Dugouts were roofed with heavy elephant-back iron sections covered with dirt and sods, safe from anything but a direct hit from a heavy shell. They were large enough for some degree of comfort. Hundreds of tins of bully beef had been set in the mud to pave the bottom of the trench and provide more solid footing. Altogether, when in the front lines J3 was by far the pick of the lot. It was not too easy getting in and out as the ground behind was nothing but a swamp. There were not any direct usable communications. Usually, movement meant side-slipping through J4 and J5 into the K series to find footing solid enough to navigate. That took longer and added to the hazards during reliefs.

Communications

Several methods were used to maintain contacts between the front lines and battalion headquarters some distance further back. Primarily this was the duty of the signal sections. Wires were laid on the ground from point to point to service the telegraph keys. These wires were often broken by enemy shellfire and needed frequent repair or replacement. During heavy enemy barrage fire, wire connections would be completely cut off. Efforts to make repairs at such times often resulted in bad casualties to signal sections. These men never did receive the recognition or credit they deserved for quiet devotion to duty under extremely difficult conditions.

Beyond the wire arrangements, each company kept one or two selected men called runners, ready to carry messages in times of emergency. This work often meant taking extreme risks. Only very exceptional men could be used for such duties.

During the first few months of front-line service by the Second Division there was another method of contact. This consisted of a carrier pigeon service. At selected forward points the signal sections maintained cages of pigeons so that in extreme emergencies, if the wires broke down pigeons would be released to carry attached messages back to their home bases. So that the birds would continue active and effective, they were only kept in the trenches for two or three days and then released. Replacements were brought in before the others were flown out. When the carrier pigeon idea was discontinued, reports circulated via the latrine gazette and the cookhouse chronicle that the 22nd Battalion had been turning the birds into trench squab on toast until the supply became exhausted. To be fair, it should be admitted that any guilt in that direction was probably not confined to the 22nd alone but the story sounded better that way. It was not necessary to be a French Canadian in order to appreciate the taste of squab in any form as an alternative to bully beef and cheese. Whatever the real reason, the use of carrier pigeons for communication purposes was not very common by the early part of 1916.

The Battle of Bailleul

Soon after the withdrawal from the Dardanelles[29] early in January 1916,

---

29 The ill-fated Allied assault on the Dardanelles, conceived and championed by Win-

rumours began to circulate concerning the movement of the Australian divisions to the western front in France and Belgium. The program
as understood by the usually well-informed lower ranks provided for
a handing over of existing lines to the incoming Anzacs. The Canadians would then sideslip further north, closer to the apex of the Ypres
salient. Up to that time the Canadian general headquarters had been
located at Bailleul. That was to be handed over to the Anzacs with the
future Canadian headquarters nearer to Ypres at Poperinge.

Quite a lot of planning and some progress toward that arrangement
appeared to have been made. While volumes have been written covering the battles of the war in great detail, as this tale proceeds it will be
quite easily understood why accounts of the doings at Bailleul were
never mentioned in any of the published records.

Canadians remained temporarily at Bailleul awaiting the arrival of
the advance elements of Australians prepared to start taking over. In
due time these advance parties turned up. During the first few hours,
while both sides were busy over official details, everything seemed to
go smoothly and some progress was made. As the evening got under
way, business was adjourned for further attention the next day. Naturally, with so much of more individual importance to discuss, unofficial
conferences opened up in the cafés and estaminets.

No record exists of the exact time and place where one Australian
was reported to have loudly proclaimed that he and his comrades had
been brought to France to clean up what the Canadians had started
and could not finish. The reported equally loudly voiced reply wanted
to know why the Australians had not successfully finished the work
at the Dardanelles before they came. After that the result was beyond
any doubt. First it was fists and feet, then bottles and glasses. In a very
short while any weapon readily available, including NCOs' side arms,
either used by the owners themselves or snatched from their scabbards
by other combatants, were involved in the fracas.

The riot spread quickly throughout the whole centre of the town.

---

ston Churchill, then first lord of the admiralty, had been launched in February 1915
in order to open the supply lines to Russia via the Mediterranean and Black Seas.
Australian and New Zealand troops were landed on Turkey's Gallipoli Peninsula in
April, and, as a result of indecisive leadership and an unexpectedly fierce resistance,
a bad situation only got worse over the course of the summer until the Allied forces
withdrew at the end of the year.

Both sides were about equal in numbers and advantage swayed from one to the other as the fighting spread. First efforts by senior authorities to control and separate the warriors were not at all successful. Finally the nearest regiment of English cavalry was brought in. By using their horses and the flats of their swords they restored a semblance of order and an uneasy truce. Next morning all further efforts to make the originally planned exchange were halted. During the day, minor clashes continued but by that time military police and control elements had been reinforced and any fighting was quickly subdued.

The casualty figures were never made public but throughout the Canadian Corps first-hand accounts from individuals who had been directly involved were gradually pieced together. These seemed to strongly suggest there had been some men from both sides actually killed. Probably another hundred had been taken to hospitals with severe injuries and all the remainder carried assorted bruises and contusions as a result of the evening's activities.

The major decision made at the highest level was to recognize the certainty of further and even more serious outbreaks if the two groups were left in any direct contact with each other. For the time being the Canadian headquarters would be left at Bailleul and the side movement northward delayed. The Australians would be put in the line further south and an entire British division positioned between them and the Canadians. The lines of communication from front to rear ran parallel but as far apart as possible. As a further precaution, the Australian rear bases along the channel coast were established around Le Havre. Those of the Canadians were left further north at Etaples.

Thereafter, there were only a few very rare occasions when Canadians and Australians were located side by side in the forward areas. When that did happen they were both kept so busy fighting the Germans that they could not spare the time or energy to fight with each other. Otherwise, the bad feeling which started at Bailleul continued for the rest of the war. Whenever elements from the two sides came in contact on leave in England or elsewhere, the danger of open conflict was never far away.

One other result was cancellation of the regulation for senior NCOs to carry side arms as part of their walking-out dress. The injuries during the Bailleul trouble made it very clear how dangerous these weapons could become in such violent circumstances.

It is certain that very few if any of the men directly involved are alive today. Many of them were killed in the Ypres salient a few months later at St Eloi and Sanctuary Wood or during the Somme battles in September and October. Those who replaced them inherited the feelings from the original groups and kept them alive throughout the following years of active service on the western front.

Chapter Nine

Waiting Time

Preparations for the Third Division

At the outbreak of the war in August 1914 Canada had only a very small force of regular professional soldiers. The Royal Canadian Regiment (RCRs) maintained detachments at Halifax, Nova Scotia, and London, Ontario. When the British regiment then on garrison duty in Bermuda was quickly recalled to England, it was arranged to send the RCRs from Halifax as a temporary replacement. On a short-term basis, the idea of a winter in Bermuda in exchange for Halifax had its attractions. Later developments extended the Bermuda duty much longer than originally expected.

As organization of the Third Division developed, a number of new battalions were brought out to France at intervals. The Princess Pats were recalled from service with a British brigade. The 42nd and 49th came along from England and the RCRs arrived from Bermuda. These four battalions formed the Seventh Brigade of the Third Division.

It was rather a shock to the regular professional soldiers of the RCRs when they were sent forward to their experienced amateur brothers in the 25th to be indoctrinated into the mysteries of actual combat service at the front. From December 1915 to late January 1916 hardly a week passed on trench duty without some detail from the Third Division being sent forward to the older units for instruction. Among others, quite a number of men in the CMR[30] regiments were given their first trench experience with the 25th.

---

30 Canadian Mounted Rifles.

Manpower

It was not very long before a shortage of replacement officers developed. Casualties could not be fully covered. For quite long periods companies were down to no more than one semi-senior company commander and one or at the most two junior officers. Platoon sergeants had to take over and assume officers' duties. They did not mind the extra responsibilities. Generally they carried on just as well or even better than those they were replacing. It always looked a bit unfair that any thought of extra pay for the increased load did not seem to be part of the bargain.

As the months from September 1915 to March 1916 on the Kemmel front moved along, there was a slow but steady drain of personnel. Mention has already been made of the draft of Cape Breton men sent away to one of the mining companies. There were others lost by sickness and accident. Considering the desperate conditions of front-line service, the number lost was surprisingly small. The inoculations against typhoid fever must have been nearly 100% effective. Casualties from that cause were extremely rare.

With long periods of exposure to cold and rain, sheltered only in wet holes in the ground or slimy ditches, it is a marvel that any human beings survived. The daily two-ounce ration of strong Demerara rum given out at stand-down every morning was a little help for a few brief moments. It had some effect as a morale builder but beyond a slight flicker of pleasant warmth on the way down, the results could not be noticed. In a way it did help through some long dreary nights as one small pleasure to be anticipated come morning.

Real combat casualties were something else. As the weeks passed the men learned a great deal about protecting themselves. The risks from stray bullets and bursts of machine-gun fire while moving in the open at night during reliefs and on forward working parties were always present. During that period the Germans had much more field artillery and supplies of ammunition than we did. They did not hesitate to use it. In spite of all precautions, there was always some toll in killed or wounded or both from every trip into the front-line zones.

In the enemy lines opposite the J, K, L and M trenches the Germans had several fantastically accurate snipers. They would try by faking various movements to get some curious and inexperienced Canadian to pop his head above the sandbag parapet for a quick better look. He rarely lived to take a second one. After several men had been killed that way, the rest learned to keep their heads down under cover and rely on trench periscopes to keep watch on the opposite trenches.

There was one sniper who, after lacking a better target, took some pleasure in shooting out the top glass of a Canadian periscope. It was quite a shock while watching through a periscope to suddenly and without warning lose your view and have the glass above your head crash and splinter with the crack of the bullet as it went through. This man was even known to oblige by knocking off a bully beef tin or an empty bean tin placed in his view on top of a parapet. This practice stopped very quickly when his several shots into a limited area were followed by a shower of whiz-bangs from an artillery battery, pumped into the same section of trench. Some distance back, off the side of the Kemmel-Ypres road in the beautiful military cemetery at La Clytte, there are graves of a number of the original 25th men who lost their lives in those first few dreary months in Flanders.

German Efficiency

Behind the German lines back of the Wijtschate Ridge there was a rail-road track which ran roughly parallel to the trench systems for several miles. The Germans had mounted some sort of a medium-heavy gun on a railroad truck so that it could be easily moved from point to point. The gun was probably a naval-type weapon. It was long-range and fired a high velocity shell on a low trajectory. A rough guess would place the shell in about the 6" class. The truck could not be seen from the Canadian lines and was out of range of our eighteen-pound field guns. It was still close enough so that with the prevailing wind from the east the sound of the engine could be easily heard as the gun on its mounting was moved along.

Because of its high velocity the report of the gun could not be heard until after the shell arrived. There was not any advance warning such as generally happened with the 5.9 howitzers. In the 25th those 5.9s were known as coal boxes because of the dense black smoke when the shells burst. With coal boxes the gun report came first and the flight could be anticipated by the sound of the shell in the air. This special railroad gun was a real menace, not only from the size and speed of the shell but also because it was fantastically accurate.

Where the Germans failed was through their insistence that everything had to be done on a rigid time schedule exactly to plan. Each day as the morning developed the gun could be heard starting several miles

to the south. There would be two or three shells, then a short pause and
then another lot. After each pause the following reports would be a little further north. Some time around midday with the wind in the right
direction, the gun on its mountings would be near enough to the 25th
trenches for the engine to be heard as it moved along the railroad track.

At 2:00 p.m. three shells would land in the Sixth Brigade trenches
just south of the 25th lines. Then the engine would be heard moving
the gun to its next position. At exactly 2:15 p.m., not one minute before
or after, the first of three shells would hit within six feet of an exact
spot near the centre of the 25th Battalion section. The two other shells
followed at brief intervals and then the gun moved again. The next lot
landed at exactly 2:30 p.m. a little further north into a trench held by
the 22nd Battalion. The moves continued until the sounds were lost in
the distance.

A day or two of that was enough for the Thinkers' conference to come
up with the right answer. Each day before 2:00 p.m., as the gun could
be heard moving up from the south with its three shells due to arrive
at 2:15 p.m., the 25th men in the danger zone were quietly moved back.
They took shelter in support trenches a safe distance away. The shells
always landed right on time and dead accurate. Daily, the same pieces
of trench were blown to bits and three great holes left where the parapets had been. The normal garrison was long gone elsewhere. They
waited long enough to hear the next lot of shells fall on the 22nd Battalion front, to be certain the gun had passed for the day. Then they moved
back into the undamaged parts on both sides of the holes and settled
down to wait for darkness.

With the trench in full view of the Germans not more than 200 yards
away, nothing could be done in daylight to make repairs. Also, the
enemy had machine guns trained on the openings. Any movement in
that area immediately drew a blast of fire. Even after dark there were
still a good many bullets flying about around the broken-down spots. A
method was soon developed to safely close the gaps by filling sandbags
under cover and then working them forward from the sides without
exposing the workers until a solid wall had been reestablished. After
that it was only a matter of reinforcing with more bags and a thick
banking cover of sods and earth.

Each day for weeks the Germans blew in that spot at exactly 2:15 p.m.
Each night the Canadians put it back to its original shape. During the
whole time not one Canadian was killed or wounded by that special
German effort. All they accomplished was to waste a lot of expensive

ammunition to no permanent advantage. The same routine developed all along the line as the timetable became known and recorded. This was just one of many cases where the German love for a carefully prepared and rigid plan completely defeated its purpose.

The Old and the Young

In spite of the age limits for recruits originally established, the regulations were sometimes bent a bit at both ends of the scale. A few young lads of large size for their ages managed to get by the recruiting authorities by rather vague recollections of their exact birthdays. Once accepted they were not likely to be further checked. At the other end of the scale, a military record from the South African war or some special knowledge or skill in short supply could open the door for a man a bit past the maximum age limit.

When the first efforts were being made in Halifax to organize Tommy Slater's brass band, the ability to blow a horn seemed important enough to forget some of the age requirements. One man definitely overage but with somewhat sketchy musical talents presented a couple of other claims for consideration and was accepted. He sported South African medal ribbons awarded during his term as a regular soldier, quite possibly in the regimental band in one of the older British regiments. Later, some said it was the Inniskillen Fusiliers from Ireland, while others identified his former unit as a Welsh regiment.

For purposes of this record he can be known as Herbie, which is not anywhere close to his real name. There must have been some truth behind his claims. He did receive a small quarterly pension from some military source. The pension had come to the attention of the Thinkers' group early on. The due dates were kept in mind to assist Herbie in the prompt disposal of the proceeds. These usually provided for one good night out for the host and his self-invited guests.

Events proceeded according to plan until the brass band was broken up when the battalion moved to France. Herbie, along with the rest of his companions, was then returned to ordinary company duty. He managed to stagger along somehow under full equipment for the first few weeks, helped over some of the rougher spots by the younger men. Finally, as the weather turned sour and the going got worse, it was evident that Herbie was just too old. Some other solution to his problem would have to be found.

After some thought it was decided to transfer Herbie to the battalion pioneer squad. He would be excused from trench duty and remain at the horse lines. There, with others of similar talents, he would be employed keeping things tidy and working at the quartermaster stores, preparing food, water and other supplies for issue to the men when back in camps or billets, or for transfer to the front lines by the regular ration parties.

This all happened at the height of the clothing shortages. The results in Herbie's case were nothing short of spectacular. During his brief tour of trench duty he had come upon the remains of a dead German soldier uncovered by a heavy shell explosion. The German's regulation high jackboots were still intact and far better than Herbie's badly worn Canadian issue. They were just his right size, so he promptly made the exchange and achieved a definite improvement in foot comfort.

Between failures of the fastenings and quite probably a few trades for short beers, all his buttons and badges had vanished. His jacket was kept closed by strings tied at the button-holes. He had lost his uniform cap. For a head covering he had created a most interesting sandbag arrangement. It was folded into a fore and aft design shaped like a regular winter fur hat. It had a drawstring to keep it firmly in place. Using an indelible lead pencil, he had done his best to draw duplications of the regimental cap badge on both sides of his bonnet. His overcoat was in tatters, minus all buttons. With so much of the lower part cut away, a couple of inches of dirty white pocket hung down below the cut-off on both sides.

None of this is intended to suggest that Herbie was not well adjusted to military life and survival. When faced with the need to account for his sins, he could quote numerous extracts from the King's Rules & Orders (KR & O) and the Manual of Military Law in defence of his actions. He was adept in separating the favourable parts from those less likely to establish his innocence.

His prize performance came about following receipt of one of his quarterly pension payments. The mail corporal had been carefully instructed to promptly advise the Thinkers on the arrival of the pension cheque. Herbie would not have a chance to conceal his temporary good fortune. They took special care to escort him to the paymaster to secure the proceeds and note the exact amount. He was kept under constant observation until all were dismissed from duty for the day. As soon as it was possible to leave the camp, the miniature parade departed for a conference at the nearest estaminet. As Herbie's ego expanded in reaction after the first couple of quick ones, his generosity to the escort was only governed by the limits of his purse. The funds lasted long enough to provide the group with a most satisfactory evening of merriment and song. When at last no further lubrication could be expected, the party regretfully adjourned and departed to return to the camp.

It was during this journey that Herbie's real trouble developed. While being supported and guided by two of his guests, delayed action took over. He got very sick indeed. What was worse, and not noticed at the time, he lost his upper plate. In the following morning, when the plate was discovered missing, no one could recall when and where it had happened. A delayed search was unsuccessful so Herbie was left without teeth to deal with stone-hard biscuits, tough meat and dry cheese. A liquid diet of army tea, flavoured with gasoline and chloride of lime, with small quantities of softer bread and jam was meagre comfort to the afflicted hero.

Parade to the regimental doctor finally brought the prospect of some relief for Herbie's distressing condition. He was given a special pass and instructed to report to the nearest army dental clinic, then located near Bailleul. Transportation was not provided. He would have to navigate the several miles from Locre on foot. He was permitted to draw a little money intended to take care of probable small expenses while away.

In spite of his strange appearance he managed to cross the border checkpoint at Locre from Belgium into France and finally reached the dental clinic. After some delay he was given the usual preparation for a new upper plate, then told to return a few days later to secure it. At that point Herbie felt the need to fortify himself in preparation for the long walk back to Locre. It was the German jackboots together with his total lack of any visible identification which brought about his downfall. When he stopped at an estaminet for a few quick ones, the owner spotted the German boots and called in a local French gendarme. Between them they felt quite elated at having captured a spy.

Herbie could not speak any French and the gendarme could not speak any English. An interview at the French police station made little useful progress. Herbie was deposited in the civic jail for later attention. When he failed to report back to the camp on time, he was posted as being absent without leave and listed for attention by the military police. The French investigation took several days. Finally, after interviews through an English-speaking interpreter, the military police were called in to properly identify poor Herbie and take him into their custody.

On word of his location reaching the battalion, a sergeant and two men were sent to Bailleul to spring him loose and escort him back to the camp. When his new teeth were ready he was taken back under escort to the dental clinic as it was not considered safe to let him wander alone that far away. Resulting from the publicity, Herbie was promptly relieved of his German boots and provided a new regulation issue. From the next lot of clothing received, he was fitted with a completely new outfit: pants, tunic, overcoat and cap.

This brought about an interesting change in his personality. He evidently considered his new clothing much too fine to be exposed to the indignities of the working pioneer detail. After locating safe places of refuge and relaxation at both ends of the camp, Herbie selected the lightest and neatest shovel he could find. He cleaned and polished the blade and scraped the handle smooth and white with a piece of broken glass. This made the shovel suitably in keeping with his new clothing. Then developed a carefully planned and timed routine. He would emerge undetected from one of his hiding places. Then he would walk through the camp carrying his nice clean shovel. Mostly he carried it on his shoulder at the slope. Now and then he used it more as a cane with quite a nice flourish.

It was obvious that anyone seeing a man walking smartly along carrying a shovel would draw one of two conclusions. Either he was just returning from a job of work or on his way to start one. Not so with Herbie. When he reached his haven at the other end of the camp he would retire in comfort for another hour or two. He was always on hand at meal times. His other timing was almost perfect in avoiding any degree of physical exertion. At rare intervals he was unable to completely escape from some form of menial labour. At the time he received the new clothing issue he kept his fancy sandbag hat. When trapped into actual work he always wore it as a form of silent protest against such unfair treatment.

The Thinkers' group watched his antics with quiet enjoyment and never let on that they knew what he was up to. He lasted throughout the summer of 1916 and went down to the Somme with the battalion in September. When the remnants of the unit moved back north in late October, Herbie was not with them. He may have been sent back sick or wounded or just plain worn out by age. Possibly he was killed when the desperate casualties at Courcelette forced the call to the fighting area of every man who could stand up and carry a rifle. Whatever his fate, he provided touches of gentle humour to many rough and weary days. Goodbye Herbie and God rest your soul, wherever you are.

Chapter Ten

Dear Old Blighty:
Diary of a Leave to England, January 1916

Day 1

Told to leave trench and report to horse lines to go on leave. No time lost in obeying order. Given fresh clothing. Drew from the paymaster fifteen French francs and a cheque for ten pounds against London pay office account.

Party going included one' company sergeant major and three other platoon sergeants. All given transport vouchers to their own choice of destinations in Britain. CSM going to Midlands to see family, one sergeant home to Belfast, Ireland, other three sergeants booked to London. All stayed at horse lines for the night.

Day 2

Ordered to carry rifles, ammunition and full equipment on leave and return. Left 4:00 a.m. to walk from Locre to Bailleul to railhead. Distance seven miles. Took train to Boulogne. Transferred to cross-channel steamer. Landed at Folkestone. Smooth crossing, about two hours. Took train for London. Arrived Victoria station 6:00 p.m.

All went to pay office at Millbank to cash cheques. CSM and sergeant for Belfast left at once to catch night trains for the north. Other three with battalion sergeant from pay office as guide made for nearest pub to remove travel dust from throats and plan further movements.

Half an hour later moved on to Lyons Corner House[31] at Charing

---

31 Lyons Corner Houses were popular restaurants operated by the Lyons tea company. Their opening hours were much less restricted than those of pubs and licensed res-

Cross near Strand. No place to hang rifles and equipment so piled
the lot in a corner on the floor behind table. One sergeant ordered a
whole roast chicken complete with extras and necessary carving knife
and fork. The others chose extra-large steaks and assorted vegetables.
Someone from a nearby table sent over a round of free drinks. Shortly
afterwards a bottle of champagne came from another table.

Before very long several tables joined together with the three Canadian guests of honour and a real party developed. No record of who
paid the check. Certainly not the weary travelers. Finally, completely
wined and dined and very happy, the three took a taxi to the Maple
Leaf Club, Berkeley Square. Parked all surplus equipment in lockers,
had a hot bath, clean pajamas and into a real bed with sheets and blankets. So ended Day No 2.

Day 3

Leave covered six full days in England, plus time in transit both ways.
In morning followed usual procedure. Lifted head off bed and retrieved
boots, one from each bed leg. Removed and checked cash from under
pillow. Had another hot bath. Given new clean underwear, top shirt and
socks. Had good breakfast. Total charges bed and breakfast one shilling
and sixpence. God bless Lady Drummond and all the other Canadian
ladies who made this possible.

Wandered down through Piccadilly Circus, Leicester Square, to Trafalgar Square and along Strand. Bought souvenirs and had picture
taken to send home. Went to see Westminster Abbey. Not very exciting.
In evening to Drury Lane Theatre to see English pantomime, *Puss in
Boots*. Back to Maple Leaf Club for another good night's rest.

Day 4

Sergeant No 3 gone elsewhere about his own business. Sergeant No 2
had date with girl who wanted to bring a friend. Maybe she did not
trust him alone. Agreed to blind date girl No 2 for evening supper and
a movie.

Claimed to be secretaries to bank officials. Rather doubtful. Both
ladies on lookout for rich Canadian husbands. Reception rather frosty

---

taurants. They were staffed by waitresses in black uniforms, and customers could
order just tea and cakes if they did not want a full meal. The first Lyons Corner
House opened in London in 1909.

when true financial status established. Incidentally, both had very big feet. Movie also not too fancy. Took girl home on bus. Taxi too expensive as she lived about a mile past King's Cross station.

By time returned to King's Cross station it was closed. Time was 1:00 a.m. Policeman suggested hurry to Euston station. Got there 1:40 a.m. Last bus inbound had left at 1:30 a.m.

Continued to walk. Fortunately night dry. Also self. Not too cold for January. Too late to go back to Maple Leaf Club. Headed for Union Jack Club. Further away but open all night. Walked miles along past Russell Square, down Southampton Row and the Kingsway, around Aldwych and across Waterloo Bridge.

Arrived Union Jack Club, Waterloo Road 4:00 a.m. No beds left. Many men sleeping on floor. Given two blankets and finally found empty spot under a billiard table. Rested (?) until turned out at 8:00 a.m. by cleaning-up staff. Had sketchy breakfast and made way back to Maple Leaf Club for shave and bath. Sergeant No 2 had better luck. Got rid of his girl soon enough to return to Berkeley Square before club closed.

Day 5

Swore off any more dates blind or otherwise. More fun seeing the animals at the zoo and visiting wax-works.[32] Spent some time listening to the nutty speakers in Hyde Park. In evening managed a less expensive seat and enjoyed musical show, *Tonight's the Night*, at the Gaiety Theatre. Going to Horsham tomorrow to see a friend from home in training at the artillery school.

Day 6

Discussed plans with Sergeant No 2. Trip to Horsham would last overnight. Arranged to meet on return to London late next afternoon. Reached Horsham by train about 12:00 noon. Located friend's camp and waited until he came off duty. Had supper with him and others. All then went out for evening at a nearby pub. Plenty of fun but spent too much from funds already sadly reduced from Days No 3, 4 and 5.

Day 7

Slept overnight at friend's barracks. After lunch, left to return to Lon-

---

32 Madame Tussaud's.

don. Had arranged to meet Sergeant No 2 at Trafalgar Square. He got wires crossed and waited at Leicester Square. After paying train-fare from Horsham left with exactly one shilling pending contact with Sergeant No 2, who was in better financial shape. Good for a temporary loan to cover remainder of leave.

Failed to find No 2. Walked to pay office at Millbank and put in request for five pounds. Pay book came back through the wicket marked in red ink, 'Account overdrawn, no further withdrawals.'

No amount of pleading could effect a change in that decision. Returned to Strand for further search for Sergeant No 2. No luck. Finally at 9:00 p.m. without any food since noon, walked to Maple Leaf Club and settled for bed for the night. Cost nine pence. Cash balance three pence. And so to bed.

Day 8

Stayed in bed as long as permitted in case might have to sleep in park next two nights. After shave and wash, no charge, again went looking for Sergeant No 2 as he had not returned to Maple Leaf Club the previous night.

Toward noon found a cheap restaurant on the Strand. Invested one penny for a mug of muddy coffee and a second penny for a large hard bun. Buns stale but chose very carefully to make sure to pick largest one on the plate. Cash balance one penny.

An hour later overjoyed to see Sergeant No 2 coming along Strand. Adjourned to nearest source of food and made up for lost time at his expense. Settled lack of success in meeting the previous night. Secured loan of three pounds and went together to investigate the London West End. The professional ladies of Leicester Square and Piccadilly Circus worthy of observation but somewhat shopworn. In any case they operated in financial brackets beyond current possibilities.

Any thought for search of an ardent amateur definitely too dangerous. Could end up just as expensive and easily lead to serious future complications. After experience evening of Day No 4, decided to leave the ladies to others possibly better fixed financially. Went to another show and back to club for the night. This time able to pay for breakfast as well as bed.

Day 9

Last day in London. Due on train early evening. Got equipment out of locker and made sure everything in order. Sergeant No 3 turned up at noon. Had been out in country visiting with a family he met while training at Sandling the previous summer. At least, that is what he said, although there were gaps in the story which left time unaccounted for.

In early afternoon took another walk around for a last look at West End. Visited a couple of pubs popular with Canadians on leave. After short wait met up with Sergeant No 4 returning from Belfast. Last to appear was the CSM back from his home in the Midlands.

Contrary to the reduced conditions of the four sergeants, the CSM was loaded down with extras. One package contained a large fruitcake and several generous-sized meat sandwiches. A leather pouch with three pounds of pipe tobacco was tied to his belt. In a wooden box with air holes in it he had a live ferret. Another package held two pounds of raw meat for its food. The idea evidently was to use the ferret in the trenches to combat the rats.

When the train for Folkestone was called the party with all its belongings including the CSM and his extras took over and completely filled one compartment. Under some pressure the CSM was persuaded to open up the sandwiches and cake. Strangely enough six bottles of beer also came to light among the other traveler's effects. By the time the trained reached Folkestone all available food had been consumed. The CSM still had his tobacco plus the ferret in its box and the raw meat for its survival. The party transferred from train to cross-channel steamer for Boulogne.

Day 10

Sailed from Folkestone after midnight. Crossing very rough. Most of party managed fairly well but CSM very very sick. Lost all his share of the sandwiches, cake and beer and reduced to a most wretched state. After arrival in Boulogne the others in the group had to carry ashore all his equipment plus the ferret and its meat. Also, practically carry the CSM himself along the lower town street to the nearest open hotel for temporary shelter.

After daybreak found early open restaurant and all went in to get breakfast. CSM not hungry but finally persuaded to try to eat something. Someone fed him Camembert cheese instead of butter. Awfully sick all over again. Sat on curb with feet in ditch holding head. Lost his upper plate three times. No more interest in food at any price. Journey to RR station delayed by need to help CSM along and carry his equipment, still including pipe tobacco, ferret in box beginning to smell very stinky, and its raw meat diet, also smelly. Train late leaving. Slow and dirty. Many stops to unload other troops and supplies. Reached Bailleul early morning Day No 11.

Day 11

Stayed at station until daylight. Found a place to get breakfast of sorts. Then slowly, held back by CSM still in very bad shape, made way back on foot seven miles to horse lines at Locre. Very glad to find battalion out of front line and in camp there. Had time to clean up and get a rest, as not due on duty until next morning.

The stupidity of forcing men going on leave to carry full equipment both ways, particularly rifles and ammunition, finally penetrated high enough up the scale of authority to have that practice ruled out. No doubt the action of several browned-off types at different times, sending five or ten rounds rapid fire through the glass roof of Victoria station in London hastened this more sensible arrangement.

PS: The Fate of the Ferret

The CSM was unable to personally care for it. Did not know how. He engaged another sergeant who in his younger days in England had experience in poaching game birds and animals from the landed gentry. Sergeant played with it for a couple of days, then traded it to some men in a Lancashire artillery battery in exchange for half a pickle bottle of army rum. He told the CSM he had put the ferret down a hole after a rat and it failed to come out again.

Spies

Spy stories of one sort or another began to circulate just as soon as the battalion reached the forward area. Many will recall the warning signs in the estaminets and other public places: 'Meffier Vous. Tessier Vous. Les oreilles des ennemies vous accouter,' meaning in English: keep quiet; do not talk; the enemy is listening.

One night shortly after the Second Division took over the Kemmel trenches, a man in the uniform of a British engineering lieutenant with correct badges and speaking excellent English came up to the front line through the communication trench. He explained to those in the trench that his engineering unit was responsible for work maintaining defensive structures, including the barbed-wire fences out in front. He stayed long enough to learn the numbers and identity of the holding troops, then said he would have a look at the barbed-wire defences. He went over the parapet and was seen for a few minutes out in the wire checking its condition. Then he simply disappeared. No doubt he went right across into the German lines and got clean away.

After that incident it was made mandatory that no officer or man should travel alone in the forward area. There was not to be any less than two together and one of these well-known and easily identified by the troops in each sector or location. One fairly senior officer from another unit thought he was important enough to disregard the rules. One night he entered alone a trench held by a platoon of the 25th. The sergeant in charge really knew who he was but pretended ignorance and marched him out at the point of a bayonet to turn him in to battalion headquarters. There was quite a row over the officer's indignant protest but in the end the sergeant was excused as having only done his duty and the officer was properly told off by higher authority. The story went around the Fifth Brigade to the delight of the lower ranks and no further incidents of that sort developed thereafter.

For some months after September 1915 there were quite a few civilians living on farms and in villages not many miles back from the trench locations. The village of Kemmel had people living in it when the Canadians took over. After several shellings and some casualties the civilians were finally moved out. People were allowed to stay in Locre. Food and other small stores continued to operate. The estaminets along with one or two eating places were open.

Roads from Kemmel in the direction of Ypres were used at times to bring supplies to farmers still living near them. Every day a man came along one road riding a box-like cart pulled by a team of dogs. He sold bread as he went along and every day made the same trip. The Canadians billeted around Siege Farm and other camps nearby sometimes bought bread from him. They paid little attention to his movements, presuming that if he was OK with the Belgian police it was not any concern of theirs.

There were several versions of what finally happened. The accepted report was that one day while he was selling bread to some Canadian soldiers, the dogs took fright. Their sudden dash upset the bread cart. The top of the cart with all the bread broke away. Underneath in a false bottom another man was hiding. Peep holes were discovered in the sides, evidently for observation and air supply as the cart moved along.

The soldiers held both men and turned them over to the Belgian police. While never confirmed to the troops, there was pretty good evidence that both men were convicted as spies and shot.

Not all the farmers in the forward areas were as friendly to the Allied armies as might have been expected. Some were downright hostile as far as they dared to be. All were considered possible German sympathizers. One had a number of cows, one of which was white and the rest black. He owned or at least controlled several fields near his house and barns. The cattle were moved about from one field to another almost daily. For some weeks it was quite clear that the Germans were getting accurate information on Canadian troop movements, particularly concerning reliefs to the front lines. They appeared to know just when to direct their night shelling to certain forward roads and communication trenches in order to catch the movements of the relief troops.

Possibly the farmer became suspect for other reasons. Under observation, someone suddenly noticed that on each relief day the white cow was always in a certain field all by itself. Otherwise it was pastured with the other cows as they moved about from day to day. While the field was too far back to be reached by shellfire, there were points on Messines Ridge held by the Germans from which it could be seen. Also, it could be watched from observation balloons and planes. Somewhere along the line the farmer must have slipped up. Then the movements of the white cow drew more attention to his operations. Shortly afterward he and his family were taken in by the police and the farm operation was closed down. The men of the 25th never heard what happened to him after that.

Chapter Eleven

You Can Have It

St Eloi March–April 1916

As the damp and dreary winter months slowly moved along, the drain from casualties continued. Each trip into the forward areas for night working parties or the six-day turns in the front lines resulted in some count of men wounded or killed in action. There were not many at any one time but there was hardly a day without some loss. To maintain strength, reinforcements continued to be brought from England. Several of the following units from the Maritime provinces were broken up after arrival in England to supply needed men: first the 40th Battalion, followed by the 64th and then the 112th.

A short break in the vile weather developed early in March. A few days and nights were clear and bright. The sun seemed warmer and the soggy ground showed signs of drying out. There is not any record indicating that this false spring influenced the thinking of those responsible for starting the battle of St Eloi on March 27th. It may have been so but the official accounts indicate that planning for this action had been under way for some time. In any event, some days before March 27th, the weather was back to its regular shocking state: nothing but rain, rain and more rain day and night. In many places along the front and around the remains of the village of St Eloi, trenches as such no longer existed. As fast as any digging was done, the holes caved in or filled with water up to ground level. The only protection for the forward troops was by sand-bagged barricades above the surface of the ground. Sometimes these were roofed with corrugated iron sheets. All were banked with extra mud to conceal them to some limited extent from full enemy observation.

During the winter a number of mines had been dug and loaded under parts of the German front lines. Several were under or near some slightly higher ground known as the mound. As the mount was held by the Germans, they could observe the British lines to great advantage. It was decided to blow six of the mines and in a following attack to push the enemy back far enough to make our positions more secure and effective.

The Canadian Second Division had been scheduled to sideslip north from the Kemmel front to take over at St Eloi to make the attack when these mines were blown. The plan was changed just shortly before March 27th, the date set for the action. Under the revised plan the Third British Division, already in position and much more familiar with the area of operation, would make the attack. After it had taken the objectives, the Second Canadian Division would relieve and consolidate.

No one has ever explained why those in command could be so consistently successful in picking the worst possible weather in which to begin their various enterprises. From the very start the conditions could not possibly have been worse than on March 27th, 1916, and in the following three weeks. Weather forecasting such as we know it today must have been unknown or completely ignored. As an item worth noting, there was quite a heavy and wet snowstorm on March 24th, just to make conditions that much more ducky for the attack due three days later.

As part of the general scheme the 25th was one of the Second Division units already withdrawn from the Kemmel trenches, having been relieved by the 24th Battalion during the night of March 26th and brought back to a reserve area near Locre.

At 4:15 a.m. on 27 March, when six mines were blown at St Eloi, the artillery barrage also opened. The shock of the explosions was distinctly felt even that far back. The noise of the shellfire was clear evidence that something unusual was up. It took the rest of the day before the lower ranks gathered a rough idea of what was going on. The first definite information came when a small group of German prisoners passed through Locre in charge of some men from the Gordon Highlanders. Many men from the 25th hurried to the roadsides to watch them go by and question the escort.

It seems very strange but is actually true that while the 25th, along with all the Second Division units, had been in action a full six months continually in and out of the trenches, most of them had never seen a German soldier close enough to know just what one looked like. Often they had spent days and nights not much more than 100 yards from the Germans opposite them. During that time many of the original 25th men and not a small number from the reinforcements had been wounded or killed. A few had very limited sights of small groups in German uniforms moving in the open long distances back from the front-line trenches but nothing of a close-up view. The next few days would see a drastic change in that experience.

In the attack area everything seemed to go wrong. Careless talk around the reserve areas and in the estaminets had alerted the German intelligence services. While they were not certain about the exact time and place, they knew enough to thin out the holding troops in their extreme front lines and to concentrate more heavily far enough back to be ready for rapid counter-action.

The enemy trenches directly over the mines simply disappeared, taking with them several hundred German soldiers and leaving great deep craters wide open to the pouring rain. The force of the explosion shook the whole nearby surrounding ground so badly that all existing trenches and barricades collapsed and rapidly became flooded with water, leaving the soldiers on both sides without shelter of any kind. The craters were so deep and close together that the attacking troops could not move straight forward to assault the intended objectives. Where men did get ahead through narrow gaps between the great holes, they were cut off from effective support. The craters quickly began to fill with water and the sides turned into slimy mud. Very soon the only way to reach or reinforce the men who had gone ahead was around the ends of the blown-out areas. To add to the confusion, fog along with the steady rain reduced visibility to nil. Aerial observation was impossible. No information from that source was available. One after another the battalions of the British division were completely exhausted and had to be withdrawn.

The Germans were not in much better shape. The whole combat area was one big sea of mud and water. Small groups from both sides blundered into each other and fought hand-to-hand without really knowing where they were or what to do about it. Prisoners were taken by both sides. Wounded men died in the mud or were drowned in shell-holes and by sliding helplessly down the slimy sides into the water-filled craters. That was the situation when the take-over by the Second Canadian Division was hastened. The gallantry of the British division was beyond praise. They had not been defeated by the Germans but entirely by most atrocious weather, far beyond the limits of human endurance.

On the night of April 4th the Sixth Canadian Brigade completed the takeover. The information available to it was very limited and misleading. There were not any forward communication trenches or firmly established battle locations. Relief involved taking over a few shallow ditches with many groups detached and partly isolated. This lack of adequate communication or clear knowledge of where or how strong the opposing German positions might be was critical.

A long section of the presumed front line was only held by a string of disconnected Lewis gun sections or bomber posts. Some of these were manned by men supplied by the Fifth Brigade battalions. Several Lewis gun sections were from the 25th. Fighting was continuous during the next three days. The Germans were more familiar with the ground and far better supplied with both light and heavy artillery, together with plenty of ammunition.

The Sixth Brigade casualties mounted rapidly. Men of the Fourth and Fifth Brigades plus extra troops from pioneer battalions were working day and night to reestablish communications, repair and enlarge defensive positions and carry forward ammunition. Special groups assisted in moving food and water ahead to the battle areas.

Early on the morning of April 6th, after a violent and concentrated barrage, the enemy mounted a counter-attack. Again, faulty communications and a relief in progress greatly hindered rapid movement, resulting in heavy casualties. Sixth Brigade forward positions were wiped out. Among these was one Lewis gun section of five men from the 25th. They fought as long as their ammunition held out. Finally, when surrounded and cut off with their Ross rifles completely useless, they had to surrender to be taken prisoner by the Germans. Note: aside from these five men who had been left in an impossible position, the 25th lost only three more men as prisoners in the following two-and-a-half years.

By the time the counter-attack was contained and halted, the Germans had occupied all the craters as far as mud and water would permit. The Canadian front line was back around the ground originally held before the mines were blown. Continuous fighting and floundering around in the mud and water without adequate food or sleep from April 4th to 7th temporarily finished the Sixth Brigade men. During the night of April 7/8th they were relieved by the Fourth Brigade and withdrawn for reorganization and essential rest.

From the 7th to the 11th attacks and counter-attacks bogged down in the mud. Both sides lost heavily without gaining any advantage. After four days the Fourth Brigade was done in and the Fifth Brigade took over. This relief took place on the night of April 11th. The 22nd Battalion relieved the 20th Battalion on the right of the front. In the centre the 25th relieved the 18th. The 26th relieved the 19th on the left. The 24th Battalion was temporarily held in reserve at Scottish Wood.

This was one time when there was more than enough hell and little of it merry. When ready to move in, each man carried the following load:

- one suit heavy wool underwear
- one top shirt
- one pair wool trousers
- wool socks in heavy boots with ironclad soles
- legs wrapped in wool puttees
- one service jacket
- one service greatcoat
- web equipment including full water bottle, haversack with the emergency rations, one bayonet in scabbard
- in ball pouches, 100 rounds .303" rifle ammunition
- two cloth gas masks in holders, slung across chest from shoulders
- two extra cloth bandoliers also slung across chest from shoulders, each bandolier containing fifty more rounds .303" ammunition, making a total of 200 rounds per man

Note: two loaded straps each way across the chest made it just peachy for easy breathing.

- on back, one equipment pack containing rubber sheet, spare socks, extra food, mess tin and other personal effects
- finally, the twelve to fourteen-pound Ross Rifle, and fifty men in each company wearing the newly issued steel helmets. The rest still wore their cloth caps.

Moving out of billets into pouring rain and fog, they first had to cover several miles over rough stone block-paved roads, as far forward as was considered safe in what passed for daylight. As soon as full darkness developed, they moved forward again, still on hard road for another mile or so. When they halted at a forward dump to pick up extra water in gasoline tins, each man was handed a shovel or a bundle of sand bags to add to his burden.

A short distance further on, they left the road, which at least had been solid footing, to take off across open fields. There was still more than a mile to go to reach the front lines. The only way to maintain direction was by following the outlines of old communication trenches full of water and unusable. In spots there was small help from sections of duckboard laid over the worst and deepest mud and water.

Stumbling and sliding, falling into old water-filled shell-holes and being pulled out by others, they moved for about ten minutes, then halted for a rest and to check to make sure everyone was keeping up and none were lost. Some guidance was provided by flares around the crater area, sent up by both sides. There were two hours or more of this slogging, frequently going flat, mud or not, to duck shell-fire and flying shrapnel or bursts of machine-gun bullets. Many stray bullets passed over and around, some too close for comfort, and several men were wounded. At one halt in the darkness, someone recited 'The Charge of the Light Brigade.' Further along, another started to whistle 'Soldiers of the Queen' until shut up by the sergeant on the ground of danger to security.

About midnight forward posts of the 18th Battalion were reached and the relief completed. As much as possible of the incoming loads were dropped off. A start was made at filling sandbags to build up barricades and shelters. Efforts continued to join together the separate posts. Listening posts were pushed out in front, with men lying in the mud on lookout to guard against surprise attacks.

At daybreak, the rum ration helped a little but not much. By then the outline of two craters could be seen a short distance out in front. There was no way of knowing which of the six they were or where or how many Germans were likely to be holding them. It quickly became clear that many of the barricades and shelters were wide open to rifle and shell-fire from the sides and rear. The curve of the salient enabled the Germans to fire on positions held by the 25th from behind as well as from the front.

Efforts made to extend shelters against this crossfire resulted in more men being hit. Some were wounded and several were killed trying to hasten the work in daylight. While the fog and rain kept visibility low, the Germans could still fire blind and rake the area steadily. Wherever small bits of ground even a foot or two above the low spots existed, attempts had to be made to dig shallow drains to take off the worst of the water.

On top of an old shelter about fifty feet to the rear there was the body of a very big Canadian soldier with the head missing. It was suicide to send anyone out in the open to investigate. A short time later a German 5.9" coal box made a direct hit. When the smoke cleared, the old shelter and the body had completely disappeared. The whole thing was blown to bits and never seen again.

The Germans had some sort of a spring-operated catapult a short distance behind their forward posts. It was set to throw an iron container about the size of a five-gallon oil drum filled with high explosive and fitted with a lighted fuse. The trench name for these was 'rum jars.' When the catapult let go it made a thumping noise which could be clearly heard in the Canadian posts. As it sailed through the air any good ball player could easily gauge where it was going to land and quickly arrange not to be there to meet it. Fortunately, the range was too short to fully reach the 25th barricades. Most of these rum jars landed in the craters out in front. The only effect was a colossal bang and a great shower of mud and water.

With many bodies from both sides in the craters, there were often pieces of dead men thrown up in the air by these explosions. This mess could reach the barricades to land on top of the defenders, adding further to their miserable condition. To be hit in the face with part of a dead man's leg is hardly a happy event but better than being killed or severely wounded.

The Ross Rifle

Every battalion in the Second Division had its own stories of rage and frustration over the failure of the Ross rifle as an effective trench weapon. Even when reasonably clean, a few shots, sometimes not more than three or four, were enough for the bolt to seize tight and make the rifle useless. Men could be seen cursing and frequently crying with rage as they tried in vain to kick or smash the bolts loose.

At times when under attack, they had only the help from a few Lewis guns until the Germans got close enough to be within bombing range or for hand-to-hand bayonet fighting. No one really knows how many men were shot down where they stood through failure of their Ross rifles and loss of any means of defending themselves. A few were lucky enough to salvage Lee Enfield weapons left around by casualties from the British regiments which had made the first attacks from March 27th to April 4th.

From April 8th to 11th the Fourth Brigade had made several attempts to improve the positions and recapture any sections of the craters still possible to occupy and defend. These had all bogged down in the mud without success and increased the already heavy casualty lists. Originally, it had been intended to have the Fifth Brigade continue the attacks. Following the relief on the night of the 11th all the information available from the Fourth and Sixth Brigades was reviewed. The higher command finally came to their senses and cancelled any thought of further futile and costly efforts. The task of the 25th and the other battalions of the Fifth Brigade became one of holding off several German counter-attacks while building whatever shelter the ground and weather would permit.

Support troops continued working all-out to open up communication and connecting routes from the rear to the forward lines. Up front it was cold food and little of it coupled with three full days (seventy-two hours plus) without any sleep. Fit men could not be risked to move wounded men out overland in daylight. These had to be tended by stretcher bearers and protected as much as possible until they could be sent out after dark. Where possible the bodies of men killed were taken out at night for proper burial in military cemeteries. The frightful condition of the ground and lack of men for carrying parties made this very difficult. Many men had to be buried near where they lay. With the ground continually churned up by exploding shells, all traces of many of the graves disappeared and were never found again.

On the night of the 14th, the 25th was relieved by the 24th, which took over at the crater barricades. Help was also sent to the 22nd and the 26th. Finally, the whole Fifth Brigade was replaced by the Sixth Brigade on the night of 18 April. The movement coming out was quite a bit easier than when going in. Weather was still foul but loads were lighter through leaving in the front posts all extra ammunition, shovels, sandbags, water tins and general trench supplies. Also, the efforts of the supporting troops were at last beginning to show. Some of the communication trenches had been cleared and fairly well drained, with duckboards set to walk on. Sides had been staked and supported with other boards and burlap-backed chicken wire.

After more than seventy-two hours without sleep, the men did not care what happened next. As usual, they moved back in small groups as their reliefs took over. As quickly as possible they made their way to the rallying points on the back roads. Once there, they lay right down and went to sleep, flat out on the ground in the rain. It took most of the next day to get all of them back and bedded down under better shelter. Even then, they were held in reserve on immediate call if needed. Only the fact

that these men were in superb condition enabled them to take such punishment and snap back to full duty after only twenty-four hours' rest.

The Second Division continued to hold the St Eloi crater front.
Gradually, as April passed the real spring and early summer weather
improved. With clear days and nights the sun and wind dried the
ground. Both sides dug in and were temporarily content to hold where
they were. There was the usual building of barbed-wire protection and
night patrol activity in no man's land. Harassing shell-fire and sniping
continued as the front settled down to routine trench warfare.

Out of the whole experience several things seemed clear, at least to
the men at battalion level who had personally gone through the actual
fighting. First, we could beat the weather or the Germans separately,
but not both of them at the same time. Second, the Ross rifle was hope-
less as a combat weapon. Note: it took another three months and further ghastly experience in June at Sanctuary Wood before the Canadian
high authorities would face the truth. It was not until the move down
south in August in preparation for the Somme battles that the Ross
rifles were called in and replaced by Lee Enfields. Third, we must have
greater artillery support with far larger quantities of shells of all sizes.
It was useless and little short of criminal to attempt to fight metal with
human flesh alone.

The rear reserve camps were still at Locre or alternatively Reningelst.
More forward support positions were in Dikkebus. Close support and
battalion headquarters while in the St Eloi front line took in what was
left of the village of Voormezele, including the remains of the convent
and the convent walls.

The 25th continued to take its turns of front-line duty at the craters,
where barricades were slowly transformed into trenches with more
comfortable dugouts and better communications. The three weeks
from March 27th to April 18th, 1916, passed into history. Very few of
the men who saw action there are alive today.

Ypres Salient 1915–16

If you think it crude to be rough and rude
    this tale is not for you.
There is nothing nice about rats and lice
    from any point of view.
Yes, the rats do roam and make their home
    In the fields where the dead men lie.

Yes, the lice do bite all day and night
    and never quit till you die.
Where the human moles from their stinking holes
    crawl up through the muck and slime,
to hide all day, then work all night
    till there is no sense to time.
The great shells roar through the leaden skies
    as their targets crouch in the drains,
then burst with a roar and the shrapnel flies,
    and it rains and rains and rains.
On a dirty night when your nerves draw tight
    and you rouse to the gas alarms,
in a dank shellhole you'd sell your soul
    for a night in a woman's arms.
When a grey green mass of chlorine gas
    drifts down from the eastern sky,
you choke and spit as your lungs are split
    and you see your best friends die.
In the stink and stench of a rotten trench
    mid the swarms of filthy flies,
some men got caught so their bodies rot,
    and the maggots eat their eyes.
There tattered bums from city slums
    with pampered sons of the rich
all lie with God on that sodden sod
    and you can't tell which is which.
In that sea of mud you can feel your blood
    grow cold as you shake with fright.
Then among the dead you raise your head
    to stand to your post to fight.
So a few survive and are still alive
    when at last relief breaks through,
and the press reports 'all quiet'
    as they bury the lads they knew.
Theirs was the fate of German hate,
    its greed and mistaken pride.
From far-off days a soldier prays,
    forget not why they died.

Chapter Twelve

In the Good Old Summer Time

May 1st, 1916: A Cold Night

According to army regulations, summer started officially on May 1st. Blankets at camps and billets were no longer considered necessary. They were collected at Quartermaster Stores and turned over to the Army Service Corps for cleaning and storage. Unfortunately, the weather man did not always cooperate. On May 1st, 1916, the temperature was almost down to frost level. The camps were colder than charity. The 25th had just come back from the crater trenches and were under canvas near Reningelst.

Nearly every army problem has a solution if given the right approach. In this case the answer was readily to hand. Within easy reach in a nearby field was an engineering storage dump. Among other items was a mountainous pile of new sandbags neatly tied in bundles of fifty, just a nice size and weight for carrying. The men wasted little time in raiding the bag storage for supplies. Estimates placed the quantities taken in excess of 50,000 bags, somewhere between fifty and 100 bags per man. A thick layer underneath made a fine soft bed to sleep on. Others tied together formed very comfortable top blankets for protection against the cold night wind. The whole 25th Battalion went to bed more comfortable than they had been for a long time, actually even more so than under the usually restricted supply of wool blankets.

The reaction of the senior engineering officer in control of the supply depot was as expected. When he learned the next morning of his loss, he came charging over to the 25th headquarters to cut the whole outfit into little bits. An hour and four or five stiff drinks later, there was not any difficulty in arranging a satisfactory compromise. It was agreed that the 25th men could keep the bags for the week they would be there.

On the last day the bags would be carefully counted, tied neatly into bundles of fifty and put back on the pile where they had come from. The battalion kept its promise so everyone was happy when they headed back toward the front line. Shortly afterward, the weather decided to cooperate. With warmer nights the need for extra cover was no longer a problem.

The 25th Battalion vs Sam Hughes and Company

Forward of the Voormezele convent wall with the road to St Eloi nearby was a cushy one-company rear support position. The ground falling back from St Eloi dropped away sharply, forming a bank eight to ten feet high. The series of shelters and dugouts built into it were warm and dry. They also provided almost completely safe protection from enemy shellfire. Pieces of any shells bursting out in front passed harmlessly overhead into fields further back. Other shells going over carried on for some distance to the rear and were equally harmless.

The post was used as a forward storage dump for working tools and supplies. Such things as shovels, pick-axes, trench boards, barbed wire and sandbags were stored for use as needed. On quiet nights, horse-drawn transport sometimes ventured that far forward to bring in wagon-loads of these items. Being near the extreme right of the Second Division sector, the dump was also available for supplies for the English division alongside.

Just before full darkness one evening, while a company of the 25th was holding this position, a working party of three officers and 100 men from a regular battalion of the Yorkshire Regiment arrived to pick up shovels. Partly, no doubt, for the benefit of the rough and unruly Canadians, they put on quite a nice little exercise. Lining up in formation on flat ground close behind the bank, they went through the ceremony of piling arms by numbers. After making sure their nice clean Lee Enfield rifles stacked in threes were in perfect line and arrangement, the work party moved forward with shovels at the slope, to get on with the trench work further ahead. A corporal and two men were left behind to guard the rifles, pending return of the main party, due some hours later.

Another Opportunity for the Thinkers' Group

The first item of business was to pull the guard away from the rifles. After full darkness a cordial invitation was extended to the corporal and his two men to join the 25th in a friendly cup of hot tea in one of the most comfortable dugouts as far away from the rifles as possible. In preparation for this play, a supply of sweet biscuits and several tins of canned peaches had been located and commandeered from their protesting owners. From those strange sources which always seem to develop in real emergencies, something approaching a trench feast was organized, including a fair quantity of army rum. It did not take much effort to entice the Yorkshire guard to join the celebration, particularly with arrangements for some 25th men to temporarily assume their duties.

The real action then got under way. One hundred Lee Enfield rifles were transformed as if by magic into an equal number of Ross rifles, all carefully stacked by threes in proper military array. Good food, comfortable quarters and a liberal dosage of rum in their hot tea served to keep the guard content and at ease for the next few hours.

It is always sad when such happy moments have to end. When the working party returned just before daylight, the roof really blew off. The howl that went up when the Yorkshiremen discovered they had been rearmed with Canadian Ross rifles cannot be properly recorded. Their officers and NCOs stormed into the 25th posts accusing them of almost every crime known to the army.

The 25th Battalion company commander and his two platoon officers denied any knowledge of the affair. In this they were entirely correct. Their headquarters was at the other end of the position, fully 150 yards away from where the rifles had been exchanged. Combined search parties went through every shelter and dugout looking for Lee Enfield rifles without finding a single one. Through swift exchanges in the dark, every 25th man when checked was found in full possession of a standard Ross weapon.

The row raged from one end of the place to the other. Somehow, complete violence was avoided, often by a very narrow margin. It ended temporarily because the Yorkshire party had to get out of the area in safety before full daylight to avoid German observation. They departed grudgingly, carrying the Ross rifles, with loud threats of dire vengeance, swearing by all the gods to get even fast and hard.

The next reaction came quickly. As soon as the Yorkshire party reported to their own headquarters, sparks began to fly in all directions. The 25th company commander and his officers were summoned to battalion headquarters and severely questioned about the whole matter. The Thinkers' group was also busy. The Lee Enfields hastily hidden the night before were even more securely concealed.

Quiet contacts with other 25th companies enabled them to borrow

100 Ross rifles. When an official joint inspection by senior officers from the two battalions involved took place that evening, the company turned out, lined up behind the shelter of the bank, every man properly equipped with a Ross and not a Lee Enfield in sight.

It should be noted here that the 25th company commander and his two platoon officers were veterans of the fighting at the St Eloi craters a few weeks earlier. They knew from their own bitter experience just how useless the Ross rifle had been. Somehow, when relieved later in the week, they found it impossible in the dark to observe 100 of their own joyfully carrying Lee Enfields instead of their regulation arms.

There were further developments due next day, but through their spies at headquarters the Thinkers' group was well informed before the relief took place. Plans were being laid for a complete muster parade and inspection of the entire battalion, to be sprung on the men as early as possible the morning after the relief and without prior notice. Every man would be checked out in the open in daylight in order to discover any not carrying standard Ross rifles. At the same time, the camps and billets would be thoroughly searched by an official party including HQ military police, to winkle out any concealed Lee Enfield rifles.

'Forewarned Is Forearmed'

Through devious channels unknown to authority, the group started counter-action without delay. They had two days left. The first night, some time after dark a wagon quietly left the horse lines carrying a driver and the battalion armorer sergeant. Around midnight it returned, carrying a full load of Ross rifles obtained through personal connections at an equipment depot further back. In the barn of a friendly farmer (in this case suitably subsidized and threatened), some distance up the road toward the front line, the wagon was unloaded by a trusted working party and the rifles concealed deep underneath the hay. At the support post several groups were organized, each under a leader, from among the 100 Lee Enfield carriers.

The relief then proceeded as usual. An hour after arrival at the reserve camp area, when the officers had retired for the night in their own quarters, one party after another moved quietly to the barn to exchange Lee Enfields for Ross rifles. A check had already been made while still in the trenches with friends in other companies. There were a few in each who had come by Lee Enfields one way or another. They were also located and re-equipped before morning.

Thus, the stage was all set when the surprise party was sprung on the troops and the muster parade took place. It was really quite a show. For the first time in months all ranks were on display, including cooks, storemen, HQ clerks, grooms and transport drivers. The inspection party was reinforced by several red-tabbed officers from brigade and divisional headquarters. The men were exceptionally clean and well-behaved with their Ross rifles shined to perfection and correctly displayed with just the right suggestion of silent insolence.

Perfection is rarely achieved but for once the players batted 100%. There was not one Lee Enfield either on parade or found in any part of the camp during a most searching inspection. For the entire time in reserve the battalion was under constant surveillance. When due to return to the front line, a last-minute check of each company still failed to reveal anything but Ross rifles.

By a strange coincidence, an advance party from the company most involved left the camp quietly some time ahead of the main group. Other unexplained incidents delayed the departure until late in the day, so that it was quite dark as the company approached the barn. When halted for a regular ten-minute rest break, they were spot on the barn door. Minutes later they took to the road reinforced by the advance party. In the interval, 100 Ross rifles had mysteriously vanished and been replaced by Lee Enfields. The officers at company level developed a curious inability to see the difference between the two models. Everyone was happy as they moved forward toward the front line. The armorer sergeant and his men collected the equipment from the barn a night or two later and returned it to the original suppliers.

From then on, it became just a question of how long one stubborn man with any financially interested parties who might be supporting him could hold out. No matter how many times Lee Enfields were discovered and taken away from Canadian soldiers, they continued to pick up others at every opportunity. Finally, the Third Division at Sanctuary Wood in June repeated the desperate experience of the Second Division at St Eloi in April. After that, resistance collapsed. The whole Canadian Corps was re-equipped with Lee Enfields before moving south in August in preparation for action on the Somme in September 1916.

Sanctuary Wood, June 1916

The First Canadian Division had its baptism of fire at the second battle of Ypres. The Second Division went through the wringer at the St Eloi craters. In June 1916 it was the turn of the Third Division. The Germans really turned it on them, starting on June 2nd further up in the salient around Sanctuary Wood. The details of that engagement have already been recorded in the official histories and special accounts. They need not be repeated here. To the extent that they were involved, the Second Division played a secondary role in the fighting, which raged from June 2nd to 14th. It had only partly recovered from fighting the Germans and the vile weather a few weeks earlier at the St Eloi craters. Two battalions of the Sixth Brigade did become heavily engaged and were badly cut up near Hooge on June 6th. Otherwise, the Second Division was mainly used in a holding operation until the First and Third Divisions could regroup from their earlier heavy losses and carry out the successful counter-attacks on June 13th.

On the morning of June 2nd the 25th, as part of the Second Division, was still in the St Eloi crater trench area, a little further northeast and just off the side of Hill 60. The German barrage opened about 6:00 a.m. It was concentrated directly on the Third Division troops and also heavily at Hill 60, then being held by First Division battalions. Some of the shells did fall around the 25th positions but not enough to cause any great damage or casualties.

Momentarily it almost seemed as if the 25th was being treated to a grandstand seat. Even at that distance, the ground shook and the air vibrated from the roar and crash of the German barrage. It was the heaviest concentration of shellfire on a limited objective of the war up to that time. The skyline was filled with the flashes of explosions and smoke as the violent shelling continued. Before long, orders came through from brigade headquarters to prepare for relief that night. Soon after dark units from an English division came in to take over.

Immediately the battalion was assembled in the supporting area, it started a long forced night march toward Ypres, to pull into reserve behind the fighting front. The whole Second Division moved in the same way. By morning it was in position, ready for action wherever needed. Part of the Sixth Brigade was used before June 6th. The Fifth Brigade went into action a day or two later. The 25th was put in to hold trenches near the south side of Observation Ridge, including Square Wood. By continued digging, the position was improved and made more secure. A little barbed wire was set out but it was too risky to do much work above ground in daylight. From the start there was a steady toll of casualties. Wounded men could not be taken out in daylight. Some were wounded a second time or even a third time before it as possible to get them back after dark to the forward dressing station.

While the German shelling varied in intensity, it never stopped completely. At one time they were throwing salvoes of eight 5.9" coal boxes at a time into Square Wood, where the 25th trenches and shelters cut through. The whole place was one boiling inferno of smoke and crashing shell explosions. Trees twenty feet tall and a foot or more thick went down like pins in a bowling alley. The flying shell fragments were so thick that anyone above ground was certain to be killed or severely wounded. A few shelters were strong enough to resist flying shrapnel but any direct hit wiped out all unfortunate enough to be inside.

In a way the trees were a blessing. They caught and exploded many shells in the air before they reached the ground. That, at least, helped to protect the men lying in the bottoms of hastily dug trenches or under the thinly banked roofs of shelters. For long periods no one dared to move. They could only lie still and hope for good luck to keep alive and unwounded. Dead and wounded were cleared each night and vital supplies of food and water brought in.

On the night of June 12th orders confirmed that a counter-attack by troops of the First Division would go in the following morning. They would form up during the night in the open behind the 25th and adjacent trenches. At jump-off the attack would come up overland to pass through the Canadian front. In its own sector the 25th would move out and back as the attack went through to reform in support positions, prepared for further orders. Following the success of the counter-attack the 25th was moved further back to reserve. After the front became re-established they left about June 16th to return and again take over at the St Eloi craters.

The whole operation from June 2nd to 13th was made even more miserable by frequent heavy rains. The 25th part of the fight lacked any element of glamor or particular glory. It was not directly attacked or itself engaged in attacking. It just had the very dirty job of holding on grimly for several days and nights with slender protection against intense shelling and machine-gun fire. During those two weeks casualties were heavy. The records indicate something like 8,000 Canadians killed or wounded, with the German Wurttemberg troops who started the battle equally badly cut up.

The Wurttembergers were reported to have said in advance that after they got through, the Canadian Corps would never again be an effective fighting force. When the fighting ended, both sides were back almost where they had started. The Canadians had certainly suffered heavily but had shown that they could take anything the Germans had to offer and give it back to them with compound interest.

It is truly significant that for the following two and a half years to the end of the war, it was the Canadians who always did the attacking. The Germans never again made a direct assault on ground held by Canadian troops. After Sanctuary Wood they picked their shots elsewhere, avoiding any attempt to penetrate Canadian-held positions.

Summer Interval

It has never been clear what effect the heavy casualties in the Canadian Corps at St Eloi in April and Sanctuary Wood in June may have had on arrangements and the timing of the Canadian entry into the fighting on the Somme, which began on July 1st, 1916. At that time three Canadian divisions were fully organized but the Fourth Division was only just rounding into shape. Possibly, any original plans for an early movement to the Somme area may have needed some change.

The 25th had returned to the St Eloi crater trenches after the fighting around Sanctuary Wood quieted down in mid-June. The weather was much better so that even when it rained, which it still did quite frequently, the summer heat made conditions easier to take. The trenches were much stronger and provided increased protection.

The routine usually led to tours of six days in the front lines. The next six days in support involved working parties every night: communication trenches needed extension, barbed wire and other materials had to be carried forward, and signal cables located. These parties were usually required to remain close by until after daylight for immediate action in case of sudden enemy attack. Finally, six days in reserve were used for refitting and replacing equipment, receiving reinforcements and preparation for the next tour in the front lines. When possible, part of the time in reserve was kept open for personal relaxation.

When weather and other conditions would permit, sports were encouraged. That summer the battalion developed a baseball team which established an unbeaten record throughout the whole Second Division. In boxing and track they did fairly well but without outstanding success.

One ball game with the 26th Battalion had a real Frank Merriwell finish.[33] Going into the last of the ninth inning, the 25th was trailing 2

---

33 Frank Merriwell was the popular fictional hero of a series of stories published in the *Tip Top Weekly*, a bi-weekly American magazine that described itself as 'an ideal publication for American youth.' First introduced to readers in 1896, Merriwell was

to 3. Word came to the bench that the colonel had a heavy bet on the game, with the promise that there would be a full barrel of beer for the ball team if it could pull off a win. The first three batters managed to scramble onto the bases one way or another. Then the clean-up man came through a home run. Result: 25th Battalion 6, 26th Battalion 3.

The colonel won his bet and kept his word. The team with a few selected friends held its party behind a hedge at the back of the camp, partaking exceedingly well if not too wisely. The following day being Sunday, the padre at the church parade preached quite a sermon on the evils of alcoholic beverages. By Monday night the battalion was missing one padre. Somehow the colonel did not seem unduly disturbed, displaying a look of innocence not quite in keeping with his usual temper. In due course another padre turned up with less extreme views on several controversial subjects.

July passed quickly. All interest was centered on the progress of the Somme battles. In the back areas there were scattered contacts with men from the shattered remnants of English regiments which had taken part in the early attacks. On one occasion some men from the 25th met what appeared to be a badly under-strength battalion moving northward along a road. In response to the usual 'Who are you?' the reply came back 'Yorkshire Regiment.' To the second question, 'What battalion?' the almost unbelievable answer was 'seven battalions.' The whole column, officers included, could not have numbered more than two hundred and fifty men.

The word 'zombie' is of more recent origin but it could easily have applied to many of those men that day. Their faces showed it. They looked so drained of physical and mental resistance that their response to direction was little more than automatic reaction to their intensive military training and tradition. They simply kept going because they lacked the will to stop. Stopping might mean thinking and that they desperately wanted to avoid as long as possible.

It was strange to find that the further forward men were sent the less they knew of the broader action of which they were a vital part. What personal knowledge they might have of the conduct and progress of

---

the creation of writer Gilbert Patten and embodied a new type of dime-novel hero, one who relied as much upon mental as physical prowess. His academic and athletic exploits formed the subject of many *Tip Top Weekly* stories over two decades, with elements of romance and humour thrown in for good measure. The series continued in cheap novels and on radio until the late 1940s.

the war did not extend much beyond the limits of their own eyesight.
Often it was several days before they heard of events taking place a mile
or two away. Frequently, when they would hear the noise and see the
smoke of shellfire at a distance, they could not tell exactly where it was
or who was engaged. On the war in general the front-line soldier got
his news and information several days late from the London newspapers, when and if they could be obtained and brought forward to him.
Anything learned by personal contacts was usually a week or more out
of date. Civilians in Canada generally knew more of what happened
than the soldiers who were doing the fighting in the front lines.

Trench Fever

Discussions in the trenches often coupled pleasant wenches
    with attempts to learn the language of the land.
Life could be very merry, with a sleeping dictionary
    to pass the time and get to understand.
They could talk among their pals of dodging lovely gals
    who had gently tried to trap them into marriage.
They were good at fast romance but shuddered at the chance
    of being nailed to push a baby carriage.
To improve the army diet they would snatch a hen and fry it
    with potatoes which they also got for free.
There was bully beef and cheese, which could be flogged with
        ease
    for more tasteful liquid products than their tea.
When they tangled wiv a limey, e was quick to oller blimey,
    as they bashed is blinking ed against a wall.
Why would any blooming gent foster further discontent
    by more gentle ways to quell a free for all.
When a message from on high urged them forth to do or die,
    there was little they could to except to cuss,
and among themselves to wonder how to dodge this latest
        blunder
    while the senders held a five-mile start on us.
For the language of the forces never came from college courses,
    or resulted from intensive foreign studies.
It was fractured, it was bent, it was borrowed, it was lent,
    but they never brought themselves to swallow 'Buddies.'
In times of sudden stress, it was anybody's guess
    how the wicked always managed to survive

while their more deserving brothers, along with all the others
    had to scratch and scramble just to stay alive.
When fighting chores were done, they manufactured fun,
    avoiding ways to harm their precious skins.
Without damage to the nation they would take a short vacation
    and risk a call to answer for their sins.
So before you turn aside, remember this with pride:
    In the game of war they played the cards they drew.
You will never understand how they loved their native land
    but they proved it as they lived and died for you.

Chapter Thirteen

Notes from the Observers

One Mystery of Many

Shortly after the fighting at St Eloi craters had quieted down, part of a 25th company was holding a support trench about a mile back from the front line. There was good dry shelter with the right of the position resting on a country road leading forward toward the ruins of St Eloi village. As usual, two men were posted on watch in the trench at the roadside. During the night, when the front was quiet it was regular practice for one man to stand guard and keep alert while his companion rested close by. In good weather the men usually changed places at one or two-hour intervals.

On this particular night, everything went along normally until midnight, when one man stepped down and the other took his place. Up to then they had not heard or seen anything unusual. They reported all quiet when the platoon sergeant on his rounds checked with them a few minutes later. The man off post sat down to rest a few feet from the sentry and took the chance to catch a few minutes' sleep. This was not in any way a breach of duty. He was on call close enough for immediate action if needed.

In his later story he said he did not know just what woke him. He could not recall having heard noise of any kind, but he definitely had a queer feeling and sensed something was very wrong. His companion was not in sight and failed to answer when called. On looking further he found the sentry half leaning against the side of the road. For a brief moment he thought his friend had fallen asleep. When he moved over to wake him, the horror of what he saw sent him running back through the trench yelling for the sergeant to hurry to his aid. The man was so shaken that at first no one could quite understand what he wanted.

As evidently something was serious wrong, the sergeant hurried to the post to investigate. There he found the sentry's body, dropped where he had been standing, completely without any head. It was just as if it had been cut clean off with a guillotine. The strangest part of the affair began to unfold as the sergeant investigated further. The off-post man had not been more than ten feet away from the sentry at any time. He had not seen anyone else or heard a sound of any kind. The post on the other side of the road was held by another battalion. It was some fifty feet away and their men had not heard or seen anything unusual. The same was true of several other sentries who had been on watch at intervals along the 25th trench section.

A search almost inch by inch all over the ground within a radius of 100 yards failed to turn up the missing head or any part of it, including the man's uniform cap, which was also missing. The poor lad's headless body was taken out before daylight and given a decent military burial by the battalion padre in the cemetery at La Clytte. Further intensive search still failed to locate the missing head and it was never found.

Double precautions were taken to always keep two men awake at each post. It was felt that, having happened once it could happen again. No one had ever heard of or suspected headhunters loose in the area. Old military tales from Indian Army days told of Gurkha troops carrying heavy curved knives to cut off the heads of their enemies. There was not any evidence of as much as one Gurkha or men of similar origin anywhere in Belgium or northern France at that time.

The closest guess – and it was only a guess – pointed to a possible high-velocity shell fired from a long distance. If the wind was wrong the gun report might not be heard. A nearly spent shell could be almost silent as it came near the end of its flight. If, further, the shell was a dud it could have landed and buried itself in the soft ground almost anywhere, leaving not much of any trace. A direct hit right under the chin might be the answer to the missing head. The mystery was never solved. There does not seem to be any record of a similar incident during the remainder of the war.

Robert the Bruce

Accounts differ about just where and how the pipe band acquired the goat which became the battalion mascot. Some claimed the pipe major had paid a farmer for it. Prices quoted varied from two to five francs. Some unkind friends expressed doubt because the pipe band had never been known to pay for anything which could be had in other ways for nothing. The truth really does not matter. The goat was picked up in Belgium very soon after arrival at Locre in the fall of 1915. It was only a few days old and for some weeks fed from a bottle. When it was christened Robert the Bruce is also not too clear.

The animal was never particularly handsome or fully comparable in looks or dignity with the prize stock usually selected for military regimental mascots. It was more the general commercial Belgian variety. Its head was a bit on the small side, horns adequate as goats go but hardly ornamental. Its hair was a nondescript colour and lacking the full growth of show-stock selections. On the other hand, what it might lack in looks it made up in intelligence. It grew up to be one of the smartest of its kind. As soon as it was large enough and sufficiently strong on its feet, the bandsmen started to train it to march in front of them. At first it had to be led, but it caught on quickly. Before long it could be trusted to lead off by itself when desired.

When moving along the roads in battalion formation, the order of march placed the goat in the lead, followed by the pipe band. The colonel followed, mounted on his horse with the adjutant next in line. After them was the lead company with its commander also mounted. Colonel Hilliam nearly always carried a wooden staff, cavalry fashion, probably a reminder of his early days in an English cavalry regiment. It was interesting to watch the goat when he reached a crossroad. Without prompting, he would stop, turn around and look back. With his staff the colonel would signal a right or left turn or straight ahead. The goat never failed to take the correct direction.

Somewhere along the line Robert developed a taste for beer. Until controlled, he became a regular beer bum, whenever he could get loose and locate the nearest estaminet. More than once he had to be carried back and sobered up before being put on parade again. This once nearly led the goat to the same fate as one of the transport mules. This mule got loose and blundered onto a pile of old hops and suds thrown out when some beer barrels were being emptied and cleaned. After one taste of the delicious mixture, it did not know when to stop. It was later discovered bloated to enormous size, definitely and completely dead. Robert the Bruce made a similar discovery one day and started on the same track. Fortunately, he got drunk first and also was found before he had gone completely over the bend. He was awfully sick for several days but like all goats he had a strong constitution and was back on duty in a short time as good as ever.

As time passed, he grew to full size and began to feel the need for suitable female company. He could not do anything about his problem as long as he was securely tied near the pipe band billets when off duty. Unfortunately, when loose on his own leading the battalion he failed to control his ambitions. Passing through villages and towns he started pushing around any female who might be standing on the roadside watching the troops go by. As such actions could not be tolerated, the doctor was consulted and poor Robert the Bruce underwent surgery. After necessary convalescence, he resumed his usual duties. He never forgave the doctor who had ruined his joie de vivre and always turned back and walked away whenever his personal enemy came into view.

One of the highlights of his career developed during a very special event. Under favourable summer conditions a plan was made to hold a great parade of all the pipe bands in the Canadian Corps, in a salute to Sir Douglas Haig.[34] The record is not quite clear on the number of bands on parade that day but they were all there. Assembled on a clean piece of meadowland, they formed up at the bottom of the field in parallel lines. Each band was headed by its pipe major, followed by the pipers and then the drummers. The program called for the formal reception of Sir Douglas on arrival. Then the official party would take a review position at the top of the field, ready for the music and the marching to begin. Robert the Bruce was being held under tight leash by one of the drummers, ready to be led beside the pipe major at the head of the 25th Battalion column. It had been overlooked that several other bands had their own mascot goats ready for the same purpose.

The general idea was to start the music of the massed bands and march forward to the reviewing stand. They would then counter-march back to the start and repeat several times, finally halting in position for inspection and congratulations by Sir Douglas. After that they would play a farewell salute as the visitors retired. For a short while everything went according to plan. Sir Douglas arrived on time, was received, and took his place surrounded by a swarm of high brass at the reviewing point. The bands played and the march began. Robert led off proudly in charge of his keeper, but so did the other goats. Then the real

---

34 Douglas Haig (1861–1928) was born in Scotland, a member of the distilling family. He pursued a military career and served in India, South Africa, and at the War Office. In 1914 he was promoted to lieutenant general commanding the 1st Army Corps. In December 1915 he was promoted to full general and given command of the entire British Expeditionary Force. After the war, he was commander-in-chief of home forces from 1919 to 1921 and was elevated to the peerage as Earl Haig.

crisis developed. It came so quickly that no one could later recall which goat started first. With a quick jump Robert broke free. At the same second another nearby mascot did the same. Goat fashion, they charged toward each other, scattering the ranks of the pipers in between. Extra men had to help restrain the other goats from joining the picnic.

The first head-on collision set Robert and his enemy back several feet but only long enough to take aim and return to the attack. By this time the whole parade was in a mess. The music became a dismal wail with disorganized banging of drums and then ceased entirely. It took several men from each band to grab and subdue the furious animals. In the end they were carried bodily to opposite sides of the meadow and lashed securely to heavy trees. All the other goats were removed from the parade and kept apart under strong escorts. After this pleasant and entertaining interval, the whole parade reformed and started all over again. The final performance made a brave show much enjoyed by Sir Douglas and all others present. Robert at least proved that he was all goat, ready to take on any other of his kind, with or without notice or choice of grounds.

In time, a silver plate showing the regimental battle honours became part of his parade equipment. Fastened to a chain collar, it was worn on most special occasions. He carried it when returning to Halifax with the battalion in May 1919. It can still be seen on display in the military museum at Citadel Hill in Halifax. After demobilization Robert was taken to Cape Breton and died several years later on a farm of one of the battalion veterans.[35]

The Wreckage of the Spinster's Dreams

The hazards of the Ypres salient in 1915 and 1916 were many and varied. Not the least was the ability of the enemy to fly its captive observation balloons directly over our front lines. With the wind usually from the east, these balloons were spotted all along the front, directly overhead and too high to be damaged by our ineffective ground-fire. On a clear day it was possible to count as many as sixty or seventy within sight from any point in the salient.

---

35 He retired to the farm of Guy MacLean Matheson (1892–1981), who had enlisted in the 25th as a sergeant in November 1914 and rose to the rank of lieutenant colonel, having earned the Military Medal, Military Cross, and Distinguished Service Order.

With the salient a rough horseshoe shape, many of these balloons actually could observe sections of our trenches from behind. During daylight the slightest movement was followed by a couple of whiz-bangs dusting off your tail. It was not safe even to take care of the duties of nature until after dark. The old-timers had early learned to keep away from cookhouses and latrines any time the balloons were up in daylight. Getting wounded with your pants down was particularly sad.

Until the early summer of 1916 all attempts to deal with these pests had failed. They were kept too high to be reached by rifle or machine-gun fire from the ground. The few anti-aircraft guns at the front were too far away and their shells too small to do severe damage even when they burst near a balloon. Machine-gun fire from any of our planes which could get close to one was almost useless as these balloons were of cellular construction. They could stay up safely even when a number of cells were cut open by the ordinary machine-gun bullets. At the time, the Germans also had an edge in the air with better fighter planes, which they could use when needed to protect their observers. A telephone connection down the flight cable enabled the men in the hanging baskets to quickly direct their ground fire on any suitable target they could spot.

The solution came when a way to make incendiary tracer bullets was discovered. The gas used in the balloons was highly inflammable. Even one incendiary bullet properly placed would turn a balloon into a flaming ruin in a second. Whoever planned the operation did an outstanding job. It had to wait for a fine clear morning, with every detail just right and exactly timed. Fighter aircraft were assembled and stationed, with certain planes allotted to each balloon. The Germans had to be first given time to get all their balloons in the air in their usual places. By 10:00 a.m. one fine morning, everything was set up just right.

Men holding the trenches could hear the noise and see more than the usual number of planes over our back areas. Suddenly, by a pre-arranged signal the waves of British planes came roaring in for the kill. In full sight of the thousands of troops manning the trenches, they poured their bursts of incendiary bullets into the German balloons. The result was almost beyond belief. As far as could be seen in both directions, the sky was filled with flaming wreckage. At that time few if any of the observers in the hanging baskets had parachutes. As the burning balloons fell in flames, those in the baskets underneath plunged down to certain death. Within minutes there was not one single German balloon to be seen anywhere along the whole front.

It must have been a terrible shock to the German command. For several days the sky was completely clear. Then, cautiously, and far behind their front lines a few new balloons were put up. While in the air, each balloon was being protected by two or three German fighter planes. As time went by they did occasionally try to edge one or two a bit closer but never again anywhere near enough to our lines to menace our men as before. For the men in the still muddy wet trenches, the sight of all those balloons going down in flames was a wonderful lift to morale after all the hardships of the previous winter and early spring.

Fun and Games

As the summer of 1916 came along, the warmer dry weather proved a welcome relief from the desperately cold wet winter. By June it was possible to get along comfortably without much extra clothing. Most of the men completely discarded their heavy winter underwear. As one cheerful soul declared as he heaved his lousy undergarments over the parapet into no man's land, 'I stand while thousands fall.'

When down to the limit, a well-dressed soldier was covered only by tunic, pants and socks, plus boots and with regulation puttees around the legs. Three scouts whose reports of the condition of the German defences were held in doubt by a starchy officer hung their dirty underwear on the enemy barbed wire one dark night as positive evidence in support of their statements.

One advantage was simpler louse control. The numbers and extent of the breeding areas were reduced and easier to get at. When on the march, it was customary to get off the road at midday for an hour to rest and be fed before continuing the journey. It was quite a sight to see a whole battalion in company formation stripped to the waist and completely naked, sitting on their packs in an open field, all busy chasing the lice out of their garments.

The most effective attack was by lighted matches run up and down the seams. This not only disposed of the live population but also destroyed a large proportion of the nits due to hatch a day or two later. With any kind of luck, several hours of comparative comfort and relief could be achieved before the onset of another invasion.

This condition continued until late fall, after which those few lucky enough to have survived Courcelette and Regina Trench on the Somme picked up fresh underwear for the coming winter at their next bath parade.

Hidden Treasure

In contrast to some of the worst camp and billet conditions, there were odd places which actually contained real fireplaces. Men lucky enough to draw one of these soon learned to carefully clean out all dead ashes before starting a new fire. Evil-minded jokers had a habit of slyly burying a cloth bandolier of live rifle ammunition under the cold remains of their fires before leaving for other parts.

One event of that kind had a very strange ending. Half a platoon of the 25th inherited such a set-up. Through lack of previous experience, they set out to gather all the fuel they could come by. This was piled quickly on the hearth, disregarding the burned-out trash left by the previous tenants. The fire was lit and the lads gathered close around to fully enjoy the welcome heat from the burning mixture of broken biscuit boxes, charcoal and coke, sparked by a handful of sugar, with a few hard biscuits added for extra combustion.

The door was an old stable-type design, divided into two crosswise instead of up and down. The top section was left open to let in some fresh air, while the bottom part had a bolt on it, which was thrown shut. In a few brief moments things started to happen fast. As soon as the fire got nicely going, the heat reached the ammunition underneath the ashes. The explosions sent bullets and pieces of brass cartridge shells flying in all directions.

Fortunately, the walls and floor were stone and brick and the men had not unrolled their blankets. This helped to prevent any quick hazard from the burning parts of the fire being blown about. No one was hurt by bullet or shell pieces, although several were hit. The stampede to get out piled up against the bolted lower half of the door. It took a series of high dives through the open-top door section to clear the place in a hurry. When the action died down so that it was safe to re-enter, a rapid clean-up extinguished the scattered embers. The fireplace was properly cleaned and materials re-gathered. After a new fire was lit, the place gradually settled down for the night.

It was not noticed that the explosions had loosened a couple of bricks on one side of the opening. The next morning the man detailed to clean the billet took out a loose brick to replace it properly. When he did, he realized it had been loose on purpose and covered a hiding place behind. By removing the second brick, he was able to pull out an old tin box. The box was quite heavy and, being alone, the man hastily hid it in his pack before putting the bricks back in place. He did not tell anyone, waiting for a chance to break open the box where no one could see him. He found nearly fifty gold coins, none of recent date and some over 100 years old.

To keep his find hidden he bought a cloth money belt and lashed the treasure around his middle next to his skin. Fortune favoured him further because he got leave to England soon afterward. The coins, when sold to a dealer in London, provided the funds for one of the outstanding six-day celebrations of the century. Somehow the news finally leaked out, whereupon other eager hands tore apart every fireplace and chimney bottom in the area, unfortunately without any reported similar success. For centuries one army after another has fought in or through Flanders. Under such circumstances it is easy to understand why local residents would hoard gold and hide it from invaders.

No doubt in some cases the original owners were killed or later died without having revealed what they had done with their money. Additional to the foregoing account, there were rumours at times of finds by men in other Canadian units. The only other discovery by men of the 25th which became known occurred when four men were digging out a drain in a farmyard beside a boundary hedge. Near several large oak trees they unearthed an oak chest which contained old gold coins dating back before the battle of Waterloo. The secret could not be kept. In the end the coins were sold in London and the proceeds divided among the finders. Today no record exists of what they did with the money. It probably went the way of all windfalls in the hands of soldiers on active service.

Chapter Fourteen

The Birth of the Battalion Canteen

Problem

Relief while still five days away
   already had been planned.
A move to camp in close reserve,
   the men held tight in hand.
With several miles to the nearest pub
   no wonder the colonel worried.
If his men took off as they surely would,
   their return would be far from hurried.
The huts in the place were fairly dry,
   exceptional for the season,
but to hold his troops in a bone-dry camp
   was beyond the bounds of reason.
The problem when put to the RSM,
   that source of all wisdom and action,
quite quickly suggested a suitable scheme
   most likely to give satisfaction.
It would not seem hard to cover the need
   and satisfy everyone; when:
if the men cannot go the pubs themselves,
   you can bring a pub to them.
Aside from the trouble which bothered him now,
   the colonel had always been keen
to set up a service for all of his lads
   through a well stocked and active canteen.

But lacking an office fit for the job,
    what next could the poor colonel do?
The RSM settled the matter once more
    by suggesting a sergeant he knew.

Plan

The sergeant selected was up in a trench
    near a crater and wet to his hide,
when a message got through with an order for him
    to go back to HQ with the guide.
No mention was made of the matter in hand
    but the sergeant obeyed without worry.
He did not waste time for a better excuse
    to get to hell out in a hurry.
The RSM met him and gave him the gen
    of what all the stir was about,
then took him to see the Old Man himself,
    saying: see me again coming out.
Said the sergeant when questioned concerning his past
    and current inferior rank,
for twelve months or more I worked in a store,
    then slaved for three years in a bank.
Still rather in doubt of the candidate's worth,
    the colonel was licked in advance.
With time running out he could not delay
    and ended by taking a chance.
The sergeant was ordered forthwith to proceed
    to the horse lines and there to connect
with a drive together with limber and team
    and stock for the canteen collect.
He would draw for his need from the paymaster's funds,
    then hasten the project in hand
by the purchase of all of the various goods
    to establish the canteen as planned.

Procedure

Then as he withdrew from the dugout HQ
    the RSM checked his return,

and together they plotted the best way to cope
   with a detail of utmost concern.
They were quick to agree, the powers that be
   had diluted the strength of the beer
to a point where its action gave no satisfaction
   and need for a change was quite clear.
The brewer at Locre was a very smart broker
   whose clients were easily led.
Both he and his daughter would sell you brown water
   with just enough suds for a head.
But down in his cellar, not easy to find,
   he carried some stock of a far different kind,
with choice of an issue from back of that wall
   being just what was needed to gratify all.
The two men agreed the best way to proceed
   was to gather the groceries first,
then make a dead set to copper the bet
   with a brew fit to conquer a thirst.
Then away went the sergeant and gave full attention
   to picking up stacks of the proper supplies,
all piled in his wagon for transport to camp
   and arranged in a hut of a suitable size.

   He had cigarettes and chocolate bars,
   milk in tins and jam in jars,
   fish in cans and biscuits sweet,
   glasses filled with potted meat,
   pickles, cans of fruit and cakes,
   strong cigars of sundry makes,
   also after several trades,
   shaving soap and razor blades,
   all fine stock and nothing phony.
   He even found some real baloney.

While thus he was busy, two scouts who were sent
   to find out what they could discover,
returned with the news that the brewer had stacked
   ten puncheons of stout under cover.
The brewer well knew that the staff at HQ
   would respond with delight to such excellent brew

so, needless to mention, he had no intention
    of selling it off to a lower rank crew.
Thus the sergeant was faced with a difficult task.
    It was no use to beg, it was less use to ask.
He had plenty of money and made it quite clear,
    he could pay for the stout and he did not want beer.
He had to play poker with the brewery joker
    to scare him fair out of his tweeds,
with threats that the troops would run loose through his
        shop
    if they found he refused them their needs.
The sight of real bills beat the conflict of wills
    and the brewer's resistance broke down.
He agreed to deliver his stout to the camp
    without charge for the trip out of town.
I wonder how many alive to this day
    will remember the shape of that brewery dray?
It was high in the bow and low in the stern,
    not handsome, but still a most useful concern.
A horse and a pony were hitched as a pair,
    with a mule in the lead to complete the affair.
The barrels were rolled up the incline for hauling
    with pegs in the timbers to keep them from falling.
The whole of next day and evening was spent
    in placing the stock for the coming event.
Enough shelves for the groceries somehow erected
    and a separate hut for the stout was selected.
The wet goods produced from the brewery trade
    were carefully sampled before he was paid.
Then all of the puncheons when anchored in line
    made a sight to behold and a prospect divine.

Prelude

That night in the rain the relief was quite late
    and the mud made it tough getting out,
but the weather was bad for the Jerries as well
    so there wasn't much shelling about.
Small groups gathered first at the rallying points,
    then by companies got under way

with two drums and a piper to help each along
    and avoid any cause for delay.
It was well after midnight ere all had arrived
    and were safe in their huts for the night,
without thought of sorrow or care for the morrow
    as long as not called on to fight.
Next morning at dawn the pipe band turned out
    to play through the camp at full blast.
They were showered with boots and insulted by hoots
    but they roused all the lot as they passed.
There was PT at first and everyone cursed,
    then breakfast just slightly delayed,
with an hour which followed to get themselves clean
    and prepare for the muster parade.
When all had been counted and properly checked,
    replacement of clothing and extras came next.
Then parades to the baths were rapidly made
    with return to their quarters in time to get paid.
Meanwhile at the canteen the sergeant was busy
    arranging his staff for the coming event.
When all ranks are nervous they need to have service
    and it takes careful planning to keep them content.
The set-up of groceries did not disturb him.
    Four men at the counters could handle the trade.
It was rather the process of serving the stout
    and just how to govern that thirsty parade.
The news of the stout was already about
    and the thirst of the troops was intense,
so as soon as the work of the day was complete
    the business was set to commence.

Performance

That hut was too small to accommodate all,
    so the troops were set out in small groups on the
        ground.
Then two from each group advanced in a line
    and brought back from the barmen enough for a round.
At one franc a quart no man need go short,
    so the early arrangements worked fine,

but the strength of the brew slowly made itself felt
   and good order began to decline.
Before very long there were bursts of rough song,
   with words both expressive and snappy,
though with all of the clatter it did not much matter
   as long as the singers were happy.
Effect of the cheer on Pipe MacFear
   caused his later admission of guilt.
He had laid a left hook on the jaw of a cook
   who had questioned the set of his kilt.
Then Private MacFall hooked with Lance Corporal Hall
   and tore off the stripe from his jacket
because he felt grieved at not being relieved
   in time to get in on the racket.
It is fair to explain that Willy MacLean
   did not mean any harm or destruction
when he picked up a board which he used as a sword
   in a quarrel with Sergeant MacCutcheon.
Two Smiths and a Doyle waylaid Walter O'Boyle
   and accused him of stealing their lunches
but O'Boyle was no pigeon and won the decision
   when he flattened the lot with three punches.
All efforts to master the mounting disaster
   were beaten before they got started.
The provost patrol when called to control
   simply took one quick look and departed.
The two brothers Hirst, while successful at first
   in a contest with Archibald Murphy,
both ended forlorn, badly tattered and torn
   when he called in his friend Harry Durfey.
An officer's batman who told on his friends
   when chased by a Lewis gun section
was rescued before he completely collapsed
   and put under guard for protection.
Between five and ten, some eight hundred men
   put away those ten puncheons of stout.
The resulting effect was not hard to detect
   and beyond any reason for doubt.
The sergeant called time and the canteen closed down
   but the mood of the men was still evil.

Though lights-out was sounded, confusion abounded
    with further continued upheaval.
When the colonel returned from a call at HQ
    he found the whole camp in a terrible stew.
To control the commotion he doubled the guard,
    then started to crack down both quickly and hard.
The news travelled fast that the party was over
    and many returned to their huts to take cover,
while others still feeling effects of the drink
    were torn from their quarrels and rammed in the clink.
But a fire once started is hard to put out,
    so before all the tumult was stilled
it was well after midnight ere peace was restored
    and both of the guard rooms were filled.

Pay-Off

Alas for the wicked the morning comes fast,
    with thoughts of their sins most unpleasant.
It was useless to point to an excellent past
    while concerned with the crimes of the present.
The company offices opened at nine,
    when multiple charges were laid.
It took all the others to escort their brothers,
    which cancelled all thoughts for parade.
The charges severe and the evidence clear
    went beyond any captain's commission,
so all of the lot without further delay
    were remanded for colonel's decision.
At eleven o'clock when the colonel sat down
    with the adjutant's list of infractions,
the whole of the unit was mustered outside,
    awaiting his views on their actions.
He first of all questioned the officers present,
    who agreed with his thoughts to a man,
so the colonel prepared to administer justice
    and then the procession began.
The first to appear was a soldier named Gear
    who when then charged with starting a fire
denied that he did but failed in his bid

to prove his accuser a liar.
There was evidence strong that Private Dulong
   had taken some ham from the kitchen
and used it to further a dubious scheme
   intended to bring a young bitch in.
It was claimed that O'Malley assisted by Kelly
   had roughed up a batman named Clark
but the case was ruled out on a question of doubt:
   it had all taken place in the dark.
The colonel's own cook, Corporal Dickens,
   when commissioned to purchase some chickens,
spent the money on stout, then proceeded
   to steal from a farm what he needed.
But alas for the corporal's endeavour,
   which he tried while still feeling his jag.
It was rather more daring than clever;
   he was caught with the hand in a bag.
After more than a score had passed through the door,
   with case after case much the same,
it was plain to be seen by all present,
   there was only one party to blame.
Thus a call was sent out for the sergeant,
   who already was stationed nearby
prepared to face up to the colonel
   to explain what had happened and why.
No doubt at the start some expected
   the sergeant to be ill at ease,
but he faced the Old Man without flinching
   and made no special effort to please.
When called to account for his actions,
   which they claimed were the cause of the riot,
he accepted the blame without question
   and made no attempt to deny it.
He had taken his orders as given
   and carefully carried them out,
but he had made an error in judgment
   when he purchased supplies of the stout.
His action while lacking all evil intent
   and received at the start with delight,
was never intended to cause discontent

or end in a free-for-all fight.
Now it's easy enough to punish one man
    or a dozen or even a score,
but how do you deal with eight hundred
    when the whole lot are outside your door?
The colonel thought hard, then considered again
    and finally reached a decision.
He pardoned both old and beginners
    but laid down one further provision.
The canteen henceforth would operate dry
    without wet goods of any description.
The sergeant returned to his former platoon
    and an officer would take the position.
But the colonel had more than a notion
    there was still some small surplus about.
So, supplied by the sinner, that night with his dinner,
    he enjoyed a full quart of that stout.
Then he made very sure for the rest of the tour
    that his men spent their nights in the ditches.
They had to dig trenches, mend barbed-wire fences
    and sleep on the march in their breeches.
So the infant thus born in disaster
    and christened in lashings of stout,
we are bound to confess became a success
    and the best of its kind thereabout.
In the weeks and the months that came after,
    it grew and established its store,
extending its trade to the whole Fifth Brigade,
    then it closed with the end of the war.

PS

But the ghosts who roam that distant scene
    still met around the old canteen,
for none of them will ere forget
    that one big night it was really wet.

Why???

South to the Somme

Trench routine continued around the St Eloi sector for most of August. As late as August 20th the 25th Battalion relieved the 24th in the crater trenches. That tour was short. A few days later they handed over to incoming English troops. The whole Fifth Brigade, marching in brigade formation for the first time since arrival in France, left the Ypres salient on August 26th, moving back to army reserve near St Omer. The next eight days were spent in an intensive training and refitting program. All equipment was carefully checked and put in first-class shape. A small number of reinforcements brought the battalion up to full strength. On August 26th, to the great delight of all ranks, the long heavy Ross rifles were at last discarded and replaced with Lee Enfields.

At that time the battalion numbered about fifty officers and 1,000 other ranks. There was the solid hard core of the original unit, already veterans of ten months of intensive training followed by twelve months of front-line service. Reinforcements had replaced casualties from the previous winter and the vicious battles of St Eloi and Sanctuary Wood. Most of these came from the selected and finely trained men of the 40th, 64th, 106th and 112th Battalions, recruited in Nova Scotia and New Brunswick following the departure of the original 25th for overseas service. In magnificent physical condition, superbly organized and equipped, they were led by experienced officers with courage and devotion already firmly established and tested under fire.

Movement was resumed on September 4th by a march through St Omer to entrain for transfer south to another billeting area a few miles west of the small city of Albert. Another five days of intensive battle training followed. On September 9th identification flashes were first issued. These were more readily known as battle patches and, as worn by the 25th at the tunic shoulders, carried the Second Division dark blue rectangular cloth base topped by a red triangle representing the third battalion in the Fifth Brigade. While here, rumours began to spread of a new weapon – very hush hush – being made ready to spring on the Germans.

Infantry battalions such as the 25th were placed side by side in order of numbers. Companies were set in lines from front to rear, with field kitchens at the end of each company. Battalion headquarters with transport and quartermaster stores and horse lines were placed behind the rear company. There was just enough room between battalions for the necessary movement of men and supplies. The troops had to bed down on the open ground. There were no shelters of any kind. Couples laced rubber ground sheets together to make pup tents just big enough for the two of them to crawl under. They didn't provide much comfort but a small bit of protection from the wind and rain. Artillery batteries had come without their usual guns, prepared to take over from other divisions the guns already in positions.

The Brick Fields were far enough back from the fighting fronts to be out of range of enemy shellfire and free from direct observation. An equally fortunate blessing was the temporary superior strength of the allied air forces. For a few days this concentrated air cover was completely effective. There does not seem to be any record of casualties from German aerial bombing or strafing. The Germans must have known what was going on. Their intelligence service was certainly good enough for that. Any similar concentration under modern conditions would result in the most frightful slaughter from aerial attack.

During earlier fighting before the Germans had been driven back, parts of the nearby small city had been badly damaged. By September, some civilians had returned and a few estaminets, small stores and eating places were open. For a short time after making camp on the Brick Fields, men not on special duty were given passes for brief visits into Albert. One unusual sight was the cathedral tower facing the city square. Some time earlier on, a German shell had made a direct hit at the base of the great statue on top of the central spire. The explosion broke some of the iron rods supporting the figure but the remainder only bent and then held. The result was that it overhung the square in a horizontal position. Viewed from below, it seemed as if it was ready to let go and fall with a crash at any minute.

Possibly, after the original smash, some extra lashings had been hastily installed to prevent it from coming down. As the weeks and months
passed a superstition grew that when the figure finally let go and fell
the war would end. True or false, it was later reported to have crashed
late in 1918, just a few weeks before the armistice on November 11th.
Every Canadian alive today who passed through Albert during the
Somme battles will clearly remember the figure hanging out over the
square from the cathedral tower.   .

Introduction to Destiny

After one night on the Brick Fields, serious work started next day. A
party 500 strong was detailed for special duty. The column moved
through Albert, up the Bapaume road for several miles. It picked up
picks and shovels before turning off to the left into open fields just
beyond Pozières. Directed by engineers, the men were spaced six feet
apart in a long line to dig a trench six feet deep. It was intended to lay
and protect a special telegraph cable to the forward area.

It was not realized that the whole project as set up, in daylight came
under clear view from several enemy positions. Just as the job was
nicely under way, the Germans let go with everything they could bring
to bear on the exposed working party. The only place anywhere close
enough to give quick cover was an old communication trench about
100 yards away known as Dead Man's Trench. It was full of bodies of
dead Germans who had been caught during a relief by accurate and
concentrated British barrage fire some three weeks before.

The working party had no other choice. It was either pile into Dead
Man's Trench among the rotten bodies or stay above ground and get
killed. These were all tough experienced men who had been through
all kinds of dirty combat conditions, yet within minutes every man had
lost his last three meals and begun to wonder how much longer he
could stand the strain.

It was clear that work on the cable job could not be carried further in
daylight. With the party hidden from direct view, the Germans got tired
of pumping costly shells into vacant fields and their fire slackened. It
then became possible for men to crawl back several hundred feet to
where the trench came closer to the Bapaume road. From there, in small
groups they dashed over to the roadside ditches and worked back to
safety, out of range of the enemy guns.

A few men who had been killed had to be left for body recovery after dark. Wounded were assisted or carried out by the others and taken back to the medical post further down the road. When the whole group had been withdrawn, they formed column and marched back to the Brick Fields, arriving there about 4:00 p.m. Those who felt able to eat were fed. They did their best to remove the mud and filth from equipment and clothing, expecting to be given time to rest and recover from the day's events. After fourteen miles of marching (seven miles each way) and being shelled and chased into a trench full of dead bodies, they felt they had done enough for one day.

Not so. At 6:00 p.m. the same party, reinforced to replace those killed and wounded, was turned out again. Marching as far as was safe in daylight and the rest after dark, they once more covered seven miles, then worked all night to do the job they had not been able to do the first time. The trench was dug, cable laid by engineers, trench refilled and work completed shortly before daylight. The return seven miles to the Brick Fields was covered by mid-morning. Only then, after a total of twenty-eight miles of marching plus nearly eight hours of pick and shovel work, were these men able to have another meal and turn in for a few hours of sleep and rest, flat out on the hard ground of the camping area.

Such actions did not carry any elements of military glamour or news value. There were not any decorations or medals in the ration bags in recognition of that kind of activity. It was just another weary and dirty job completed and then forgotten with scarcely a word of thanks or encouragement from on high. A few unlucky had been killed and others severely wounded. The luckiest of the lot were those just wounded badly enough to require their return to England for complete recovery after a few weeks in the hospital. At least they were temporarily safe from the risks of front-line service and often able to tie into some set-up at a reserve camp for a further period of escape from the fighting front.

After one lesson on the hazards of working in daylight too close to the fighting lines, that mistake was not repeated. There were other working parties during the nights of September 12th and 13th, mostly to extend and improve communication trenches and move needed materials to the forward areas. Meanwhile, the old-timers could fairly smell all the signs of something big rapidly coming along. Earlier rumours became more definite in revealing sketchy details of the new tanks and their expected value, particularly to make breaks in the German barbed-wire defences.

The next move on September 14th took the 25th, along with the other Fifth Brigade battalions, through Albert and forward to what was known as the Sausage Valley. There they were stationed in a series of old broken-down trenches and chalk pits south of the Bapaume road, not far from the ruins of the village of Pozières.

Courcellette

By September 15th, 1916, the war which had started in August 1914 was already over two years old. With the exception of the early start of the Princess Pats under special circumstances, Canadian troops had entered the battle zones when the First Division moved to France in February 1915, followed by the Second Division in September of the same year. The Third Division was gradually assembled at the front in Flanders during the winter months of 1915–16. The Fourth Division was still in that area in the last stages of its organization and not yet quite ready for use as a complete unit. It was not moved to the Somme until around October 2/3rd. Prior to movement to the Somme, except for counter-attacks, the three operative Canadian divisions had been largely committed to defensive actions. Now, for the first time after a year or more of taking everything the Germans could throw at them, they were at last going over to the attack.

Official accounts of the battle which opened at 6:20 a.m. on September 15th seem to indicate that at the start the town of Courcelette was not included in the list of primary objectives. The battle plan of the British armies extended across a front of several miles. The Canadian Corps, as part of the reserve army, was placed to attack at the left flank on a front of about one mile astride the Bapaume road. The morning assault was made by the Fourth Brigade astride the road, with the Sixth Brigade on its left and then the Eighth Brigade of the Third Division at the extreme left flank of the Canadian part of the operation.

Out of a total of about fifty tanks available to the armies, six were allotted to the Canadian front. The attack moved forward quickly. By 8:00 a.m. the two brigades of the Second Division had successfully captured all their objectives. At the road, the Fourth Brigade had taken the heavily fortified sugar refinery in front of Courcelette. In the centre, the Sixth Brigade had captured Sugar and Candy trenches. The Eighth Brigade on the extreme left, while successful to a large extent, was not quite able to complete its intended advance. It had to dig in short of its final objectives.

This was the situation under rapid review by 11:00 a.m. A quick check through large numbers of prisoners indicated a decided shock to their morale from the use of the tanks, even if our own people realized they had been much less effective than originally expected. Up to that time the standard procedure by both sides had been to assemble attacking forces under cover of darkness, to start major offensives at dawn. This gave full daylight to complete the operation before risking extra confusion after dark, with the night providing cover for consolidation of the captured areas.

After the early and effective success of the morning attacks, a quick decision was reached to attempt a further gain that afternoon while the Germans might still be shaken and discouraged. It was thought that this would catch them by surprise and enable the Canadian troops to extend the morning advance by the capture of further German defences in Courcelette town and on the higher ground beyond. Without advance notice or any opportunity to examine the intended area of operation, the Fifth Brigade was summoned from its reserve positions. The only information given to them was from army maps with markings indicating the general locations of the forward posts held by the Fourth and Sixth Brigades after their morning advance.

Contrary to all established experience up to that time, the orders called for attack assembly out in open country in daylight, in clear view of enemy defences. They were to move up to positions in old trenches and shell-holes some 800 yards behind the Fourth Brigade. When the barrage opened at 6:00 p.m, the advance would be in lines in open order formation, passing through the Fourth Brigade posts to attack and capture Courcelette town and dig in along a light railroad some distance beyond. At the same time, the Seventh Brigade of the Third Division was set to move forward through the Sixth Brigade to advance the left flank enough to maintain contact along the complete frontage.

The Fifth Brigade attack was planned using the 22nd Battalion on the right and the 25th on the left, with the 26th following close to mop up, and the 24th kept in reserve. There was a street which split Courcelette equally down the middle, so the 22nd was given the right half of the town and the 25th the left-hand half. Except for the relatively few casualties from working parties, the 25th was up to the full strength brought down from Flanders. After allowing for transport and quartermaster stores details, this left a total of between 800 and 900 all other ranks available for an attacking force.

It was never sound practice to commit an entire battalion to the first stages of any action. Some portion had to be held in reserve for quick reinforcements and as a framework on which to reorganize and rebuild.

For the attack on Courcelette the four companies with the battalion headquarters totaled twenty-six officers and 650 other ranks, leaving a reserve of about twelve officers and some 200 other ranks temporarily held back at the Sausage Valley. On the way into the jumping-off positions there were a few casualties. Considering the risks of moving large numbers of men out in the open under enemy observation, these preliminary losses were light. They did not provide any real warning or indication of what was to follow a very short time later when the full attack went forward.

The forces assembled and stopped briefly about half a mile behind the advanced posts of the Fourth Brigade, using whatever shelter they could find. Promptly at 6:00 p.m. the Fifth Brigade moved forward. The supporting barrage on the German positions was of some help but by no means fully effective. It did not in any way prevent the enemy from pouring a concentration of everything they had into the advancing infantry. The Light Brigade at Balaclava at least had horses for reasonably fast movement. The unfortunates at Courcelette had to traverse that frightful field of slaughter yard by yard on foot. It was the longest and bloodiest half mile those men would ever see. As bad as the later battles of 1917 and 1918 turned out to be, none of them at their worst could fully compare with what happened to the Canadian troops on the Somme in September and October of 1916.

Many were killed outright and others were severely wounded even before they reached the Fourth Brigade posts. There they paused just long enough to regroup and move on again. Somehow, still losing more men every foot of the way, enough survived to enter Courcelette. Using rifles, pistols, bombs and bayonets they stormed and fought their way house to house right through the town and out beyond to their objective on higher ground along the light railroad track. Several hundred Germans quit. These were picked up by the 26th men and hurried back to the 24th for transfer to prisoner-of-war cages.

Others kept up some resistance in isolated houses and cellars. It took the 26th until next morning to subdue and collect all that lot. The 25th reached the final objective in just one hour, between 6:00 and 7:00 p.m. Five minutes later the 22nd burst through their half of the town and joined up alongside on the right. Less than thirty minutes later the first of fourteen German counter-attacks developed from the direction of Regina and Kenora Trenches. There were seven of these before next morning. Until relief by the First Division on the night of 17/18 September, the Germans were driven back again and again by fierce hand-to-hand fighting, using bombs or bayonets at close quarters with covering fire from rifles and Lewis guns. As usual, the weather failed to cooperate. It started to rain shortly after the advance through Courcelette. The troops continued to fight mud and water as well as the Germans.

As soon as messages could be relayed back, reinforcements from reserves at the Sausage Valley horse lines were rushed forward to replace the losses. During the next two days many of these in turn became casualties, adding to the frightful lists from the starting attack force. The relief, when it did take place, was not the usual orderly movement. Groups of First Division men struggled in over broken ground through mud and water to take over the ditches and old shell-holes forming the front lines.

The weary 25th men were all without rest and little if any sleep for three days and nights. Many were bearing slight wounds but refusing to quit. They worked back slowly to the Sausage Valley in small groups. Those who felt like eating were given all the hot food they could take. The kitchens were kept going and any Canadian soldier regardless of his unit was assisted and fed.

Through the quartermaster stores rum rations for three days at full battalion strength had accumulated. With less than half the battalion left, the exhausted men were free to take as much as they could carry. For the rest of the day and night they lay down on the open ground to sleep. When they gradually woke up after lying on the chalky ground in the rain, most of them looked as if they had been dunked in a whitewash barrel. It took another half-day for more food to arrive and to get rid of the worst of the dirt. As soon as possible a muster parade was held to count the losses. Finally, the battalion, after a few hours' stop at Brick Fields, was moved further back to the village of Toutencourt for a six-day rest and refit.

The Achievement and the Price

To avoid all possible misunderstanding, it is here put on record that the successful capture of the town of Courcelette on September 15th, 1916, resulted from the courage and devotion to duty of the whole Second Canadian Division and most of the Third Division. More than twenty battalions took part in one way or another. As was already described, the final attack between 6:00 and 7:00 p.m. that evening was made by two battalions, the 22nd and the 25th, backed by the 26th and the 24th. Without doubt it was one of the toughest parts of the whole operation.

It should also be remembered that very severe fighting continued in advance of Courcelette through the rest of September and all of October. The battle just did not end on September 15th. Far from it. This was and always has been clearly understood by all the men who took part in the battles on the Somme front and who were lucky enough to survive that and later operations and finally return safely to Canada.

Unfortunately, by September 1916, some two years after the start of the war, a lot of the early glamour had worn off. The realities of active service were more clearly understood and voluntary recruiting in Canada for vitally needed reinforcements was falling off. Already at home the elements of the conscription issue were forming. Quebec in particular was not producing its full share of new men.[36] Somewhere, somehow, probably partly by accident and certainly to some extent by intention, all the press and other news media were encouraged or instructed to feature in their reports the achievements of the 22nd Battalion in the capture of Courcelette. No doubt it was felt that this very special public acknowledgment would in some way help recruiting among their relatives and friends at home.

The result then and in later years has been to associate the name of Courcelette almost entirely with the 22nd Battalion from Quebec. No one in his right mind would for one moment attempt to discount or reduce the honours the 22nd men so gloriously earned at frightful cost that evening of September 15th, 1916. They deserved every possible credit given them then and since. Too long neglected and in need of correction before it is too late is the plain truth that the 22nd took only half of the town and the 25th the other fully equal and difficult half. It also cannot be overlooked that the closely following 26th and 24th Battalions had an equally dirty job and did it just as well.

---

36 By 1916 recruitment had become a problem, which only grew worse with the passage of time and the continuing slaughter on the western front. It was widely believed in English Canada that it was being bled of its manpower while Québécois men were shirking their obligation to Canada and Britain. In fact, 70 per cent of the 30,000 volunteers of the first contingent in 1914 were recent British immigrants; native-born Canadians provided only 9,000 men, of whom 1,000 were Québécois. While it is certainly true that Québécois enlistments were and remained lower than those in English Canada, the disparity between native-born anglophones and francophones was not as significant as was popularly believed. There were many reasons for the disparity, not least of which was the government's stubborn resistance to the creation of francophone battalions. Eventually, the government imposed conscription in August 1917. Cf. J.L. Granatstein and J.M. Hitsman, *Broken Promises: A History of Conscription in Canada* (Toronto, 1977).

There has been some confusion concerning the number of casualties from September 15th to 18th. One account gives them as 22nd Battalion 207, 25th Battalion 222 and 26th Battalion 224. Something is missing here. In the 25th Battalion alone, of the twenty-six officers who led the first attack only four came out fit for immediate further service: one captain, two lieutenants and Colonel Hilliam, who had been shot through his arm but still remained on duty. There were 650 men in the original attack. These were reinforced by another 200 between the 15th and the 18th. Out of this total only 400 were left available for duty on September 19th. The other 450 had either been killed outright or severely wounded. Of the twenty-two officers lost, all the company commanders had been killed and more than half of their juniors. The remaining junior officers lost were all severely wounded and with few exceptions were unable ever to return to full active duty.

This was the price the people of Nova Scotia, through their senior battalion on active service, paid for half a broken-down small French town and a few acres of muddy clay. Call it glory if you like. Some of those who were there and managed to survive had other words for it and for those higher up who had sent them and their wonderful young friends head-on into that deadly trap.

Commissions

When war broke out the officers of the hastily organized Canadian forces were drawn from the tiny permanent force, with a few others who had previously held commissions in the imperial forces. There were also some from the South African war still considered young enough for further service. Beyond these, the larger number came from men with a small amount of training in militia regiments. These sources had their limits. As the army expanded, likely young candidates were taken on. After brief preliminary training they were granted temporary commissions and posted to newly forming reinforcement units. In time, as the Canadians went into action, officer replacements for the inevitable losses came from these later recruits.

The first indications of change began to show early in 1916. In various battalions, including the 25th, one or two young NCOs of exceptional ability were raised to commission rank in the field. Several others requested recognition and when approved were sent back to England to a specially developed training school. There, if able to qualify, they were commissioned and returned to their original units as reinforcements. This procedure was known as commission *from* the field, as distinguished from commission *on* the field. This was the situation when the Canadians moved to the Somme in September 1916. The senior officers in all units were veterans surviving from 2nd Ypres, Festubert, Givenchy, St Eloi and Sanctuary Wood. Most of them had been promoted from original junior rank. Many of the juniors also had considerable trench and combat experience.

The few short and bloody days of fighting in and around Courcelette temporarily put an end to this comfortable routine throughout the whole Canadian Corps. In the 25th Colonel Hilliam was left with only one other senior officer. All four of his company commanders had been killed. Most of his fully trained junior officers had either been killed or severely wounded. There was still a pool of untried officers in England but even with the best of luck it would take too long to sort them out and bring them over to join the battalion. The only solution left was to draw enough candidates to fill the worst gaps from among the surviving veteran NCOs.

Following hasty consultations at brigade and divisional headquarters, fourteen were selected and prepared for promotion. After Courcelette clothing and equipment was pretty well wrecked but they did their best to make a respectable showing. The ceremony the next day was dramatic in its simplicity. In its way it was one of the highest honours any soldier can ever receive. The fourteen were drawn up in a single line at attention in front of battalion headquarters. General R.E.W. Turner VC,[37] commander of the Second Division, with a member of his staff and accompanied by Colonel Hilliam, came forward and very briefly inspected the tiny parade.

He then said that Colonel Hilliam had recommended advancement to commissioned rank and asked one simple question. 'Are you ready to assume the duties and responsibilities of commissioned officers?' As soon as they answered 'Yes sir,' he replied in five words, '*Very well,*

---

37 Born in Quebec City, Richard Turner (1871–1961) worked in his family's wholesale grocery and lumber business and was active in the Canadian militia. He was awarded the Victoria Cross while serving with the Royal Canadian Dragoons in South Africa. As brigadier general he commanded the Third Brigade until May 1915, when he was promoted to major general in command of the Second Division. He was not a success in the field, however, and was returned to England in December 1916 to command Canadian troops there. Nevertheless, he was knighted and promoted to lieutenant general in June 1917.

gentlemen. Fall out.'[38] There was a brief handshake all around and the parade ended, with the new officers *raised in the field* by simple word of mouth departing to their new duties. The appointments were officially confirmed in the *London Gazette* a few days later. Temporarily lacking any suitable clothing, they could only mark their new rank with cloth stars sewn to the shoulder straps of their field tunics. Within hours three of them were posted as company commanders preparing for the next trip into the front line three days later. The others were spread out through the companies as platoon commanders.

Regina Trench, Encore, Encore et Encore

Reorganized and rested as far as the brief six days at Toutencourt made possible, the battalion, now less than half its original strength, moved back to Albert on September 26th. Meanwhile, other Canadian battalions in a series of supplementary attacks in advance of Courcelette had made some further progress. On the night of September 27/28th the 25th relieved part of the Sixth Brigade in hastily dug shallow trenches facing strong German positions in Kenora and Regina Trenches. There was a slight rise and ridge in between which restricted observation and clear view of the location and strength of the wire covering the German lines.

Early on September 28th the 26th Battalion on the Brigade's right, in two unsuccessful attempts to enter and hold part of Regina Trench, lost so heavily that it had to be temporarily withdrawn to reserve and replaced by the 22nd Battalion. The same afternoon the 24th and 25th attacked together on the left and centre. Unable to penetrate the uncut barbed wire covering Regina and Kenora Trenches, they suffered severe losses and had to retire to their original lines. It was first intended to renew action the next day, September 29th, but the proposed attacks were held over for the two following days while attempts were made to break down the uncut German wire by concentrated heavy artillery fire. Through confusion at some gun pits, one battery of our 6" guns was given incorrect range and target information.

On September 30th its shells, instead of destroying German wire defences, began to fall short directly into trenches held by the 25th and 22nd Battalions. It was bad enough to face everything the enemy could

---

38 Clements does not mention the fact, but he was one of the fourteen men promoted to lieutenant at this time.

throw but getting killed by their own shells was just too much. Green
officers might not have been able to meet the situation. Not so with
the young officers in charge and only commissioned a week before.
They had not survived that far by any mistake. They wasted no time
in gathering up their men with others of the nearby 22nd. All quickly
withdrew to take cover in a deep sunken road about 100 yards to the
rear. From that point they could watch in safety as the 6" shells ripped
and tore the trenches they had just left. While this was going on there
was not any danger of the Germans coming that way. The main result
was the waste of many heavy shells intended for the German wire.
Contact with a forward artillery observation post finally located the
off-target battery. The shelling was stopped and the men moved back
to their former positions. It took quite a lot of pick-and-shovel work to
put things right again but that was much better than being killed by
accident.

That night the men with mules bringing up rations and water lost
their way in the dark. Somehow they missed the front line and went
through a gap between two posts and out into no man's land. They
almost reached the German barbed wire before the quartermaster sergeant in charge realized something was wrong. The party held onto the
mules and managed to keep all quiet to avoid discovery while the sergeant scouted around. Luckily, he made contact with his own trenches
and brought all his party back to safety. As soon as they delivered their
loads they wasted no further time and cleared out fast to security at the
Sausage Valley horse lines.

The climax came on October 1st. As usual, the weather failed to cooperate. A mixture of rain and drizzle increased the misery of the impossible task handed to what was left of the Fifth Brigade. The attack was
organized to start at 3:15 p.m. The 24th was to capture Regina Trench at
its junction with Kenora, the 25th and 22nd to overrun Kenora and continue to connect in Regina on the right of the 24th. The limited advance
observation failed to reveal that the Germans had managed to repair all
gaps in their wire made by our artillery fire on the previous two days.
Poor observation also limited the effectiveness of the covering barrage.
Weakened by the casualties of the 28th and 30th of September, what
was left of the three battalions started forward at the zero hour.

As soon as they came over the slight ridge into full view of the enemy
lines, they were met with a hail of machine-gun and counter-barrage
fire. Further casualties came fast but the survivors pressed ahead until
they came up against great rolls of barbed concertina wire rolled out by

the Germans to plug gaps in their defences. There was not any way of getting through and not enough men left to be really effective. All they could do was to try to rescue their wounded and by keeping low work back to their former trenches. Within an hour fresh ideas developed and orders came up to try a surprise attack without barrage protection.

Again the 25th men left their trenches to go forward. This time they only got over the crest of the ridge. Progress through the German barrage was impossible. Veterans always believed that, no matter how concentrated the shelling might be, no two shells ever fell in exactly the same spot. To survive when caught under heavy shelling the best chance was to lie flat, watch for a nearby shell-burst, then dive for the still-smoking hole and wait until the shelling stopped. This was just what the men did when the advance halted. Some were unlucky and were killed or wounded before they could reach even that much insecure shelter. After an interval, the German fire gradually died away. Then heads began to pop up from shell holes all over the place. There was not anything funny about it but they did look almost like a field full of gophers.

Again, the few young officers and NCOs who remained set about collecting the wounded and working their men back to the starting points. By this time the transport and quartermaster stores had been skinned of every man strong enough to carry a rifle who could be spared for front-line duty. There were not any further battalion reserves to draw on. By 5:00 p.m. on October 1st losses had reduced the 25th Battalion to less than 200 all ranks. The other battalions in the Fifth Brigade were just as badly off.

Then for the third time that dreadful day, without rest or relief, they were ordered over the top again in another attempt to take the original objectives. This time they had a little help from another protective barrage. No one really knows how these pitifully small forces made as much progress as they did. The Germans had withdrawn from part of Kenora Trench to set up a killing ground. Heavy machine guns from Regina Trench were positioned and trained to sweep the parapet about a foot above the level. If they did not get the men the first time while they were trying to get into the trench they caught them in the head or chest when they tried to climb out to continue their advance towards Regina Trench.

There they took shelter in shell holes until after dark before working back to Kenora Trench again, where another small group still held on. These had blocked a section of the trench to repel counter-attacking

German bombing parties. When their supply of British Mills bombs ran out, one corporal risked his life several times by climbing over the block to a cache of German potato-masher hand grenades. He carried them back by the armful so that his men could use them to beat off their original owners. They were not as effective as Mills bombs but made more noise and smoke when they exploded. The Germans were more frightened of their own kind than of ours. The 22nd men on the right got fairly close to the uncut wire in front of their section of Regina Trench. By then they were too reduced in strength to attempt further progress. All they could do was try to save what was left and get back somehow to the starting points.

As night fell it was sadly clear that the whole three-attack operation had been a dismal costly failure. Under cover of darkness, the 24th and 25th groups had to be pulled back from the small sections of Kenora Trench where they had held out. The next day and night the Sixth Brigade took over. Finally, when reassembled in camp near Albert the effective strength of the 25th Battalion, aside from greatly reduced transport and stores sections, counted just eighty-nine all ranks. In just short of three weeks the great battalion of over 1,000 finely trained wonderful Nova Scotians had temporarily ceased to exist. Loaded into six motor lorries, the brave little band was quietly carried away to the village of Bertincourt.

Immediately, the task of rebuilding got under way. The first draft of reinforcements, about 200 in all, had been gathered from the base camp at Etaples. It included lightly wounded men released from base hospitals and casualty clearing stations. The value of these was twofold. They were all well and strong former members of the battalion. They did not need any breaking-in and provided a solid core of experience to steady newer men due from the reserves in England over the next few weeks. After six days at Bertincourt the 25th, now back to about 400 overall strength, moved back north and, based on Bully Grenay near Lens, took over an established trench structure from troops of an English division.

Chapter Sixteen

The Corps Comes of Age

Winter Interval 1916–17

Coming up from the Somme to move into the trench system in front of Bully Grenay, the 25th found the area was temporarily fairly quiet. The cold rainy weather of late fall and early winter had already set in. For a change, the support and reserve billets in dry cellars and old houses were welcome improvements over previous winters in tents, ditches and holes in the ground. Even the front-line trenches were drier and better organized than those further north around the Ypres salient in the Flanders mud. It seemed the Germans opposite had been glad to avoid any aggressive action. They were using that sector to rebuild their own shattered regiments and not anxious to stir up any trouble.

As they departed after the interchange, the English troops were heard to mutter, 'Here we go again. Those bloody Canadians. They'll stir up the blinking Huns and all hell will break loose. Goodbye to a nice cushy setup. Let's get away from here fast and as far as God will let us.' As it turned out, a few weeks later the Limeys were not too far wrong. For the first few weeks efforts were concentrated in rebuilding the battalion to full strength. Heavy reinforcements of officers and men from reserves in England were received. As quickly as possible after the commissions awarded on the field at the Somme had been officially confirmed in the *London Gazette*, these officers were given leave to London to secure suitable clothing and related officers' equipment.

The allowance for this purpose was $250.00, equivalent to £50.0.0, not enough to cover all needed items, so they had to make up the difference out of their own money. All the men who had survived the Somme battles were also given leave to England as rapidly as they could be spared. Many had received well-deserved recognition by being promoted to non-commissioned ranks.

The first few turns in trench duty were used to improve shelters and communications. After dark, enemy wire and trench systems were quietly scouted. Then the fireworks started. A couple of well-planned ambushes put an end to all German patrol activities between the trenches in no man's land. A series of raids were carried out successfully by all the Fifth Brigade battalions in turn. Advance parties first had to cut a path through the barbed wire. Then, a quick surprise rush and stop inside just long enough to pour bombs down all nearby dug-out entrances, while eliminating or snatching all sentries found above ground. In no more than three minutes and frequently less, the job would be done and the raiding party with its prisoners was on its way back to its own lines. The trick was to do the job and get back again before the Jerry defences could light up the area with flares and bring their machine guns into action.

Quite naturally, German action including field artillery response was not long in coming. If not quick enough, the raiders sometimes had to take cover halfway back in shell-holes and ditches of no man's land. This might mean waiting out most of the night before the firing died down and the homeward journey could be completed. Through the prisoners taken, intelligence gathered valuable identification on the German troops in that area. Before the Canadians took over, the enemy forward trenches were very thinly held. The raids forced them to bring in many more men and gave them a decided case of the jitters. For several nights after each raid enemy flares kept no man's land lit up like a circus. Frequently they imagined movements which did not exist. These caused bursts of heavy machine-gun fire, often accompanied by a shower or two of whiz-bangs. They also took to changing their front-line regiments every few days. Prisoners taken were never from the same units as the previous lot.

The most notable raid of the 25th Battalion series took place on Christmas Eve 1916. Perhaps it was a bit of a dirty trick to go at them that particular night. Certainly they were not looking for it just then. Our men got through the wire and into their trench before they knew what had hit them. The raid was a complete success. A good section of the trench was wrecked and prisoners taken. A suspicion also developed that several Christmas parcels were included in the miscellaneous collection of souvenirs brought back. Christmas Day was mainly spent dodging and keeping clear of German shelling in retaliation for our raid on the previous night.

Two nights later the 24th came in to take over and the 25th went out to spend New Year's Day in the billets at Bully Grenay. Mail and parcels from home, extra pay and a fine special dinner with all the trimmings made the day a grand success for all ranks, in spite of the usual dismal weather. On January 15th the whole brigade was withdrawn to undergo a much-needed period of rest and reorganization. They spent the next twenty-six days in comfortable billets based on the large town of Bruay. Selected junior officers and NCOs were sent to army schools for short courses of instruction to prepare them for further advancement.

All clothing, kit and equipment was overhauled, repaired and where necessary replaced. By that time the battalion was back at full strength. The disastrous casualties on the Somme had been overcome. New officers and men received from England late in October and early November had settled down well. The veterans of longer experience were able to mix in with the newcomers to bring the whole battalion back to its former highly efficient fighting standards.

Private Simpson's Medal

The sky was wet and gloomy,
    the country now't but muck.
The soldiers from the trenches
    were completely out of luck.
Now the army never reasons,
    never takes a second look.
It enlists a fine pro boxer
    and he ends up as a cook.
The cook named Charlie Jenkins
    was all set to make a stew
but the meat was mostly skin and bones
    and the vegetables were few.
The water smelled of chlorine
    with a touch of gasoline,
and whoever soaped the dixie
    forgot to rinse it clean.
The rusty old field kitchen
    was shrouded by the smoke
from burning in the fire pot
    French coal and English coke.
At last the stew was finished
    and the bugler blew the call.

Come to the cookhouse door boys
   with mess tins one and all.
The cook called to the soldiers,
   'If you want your dinner hot,
pull up your socks and help me
   to lift this blinking pot.'
The troops lined up in single file
   with mess tins at the port.
The cook took up his ladle
   and the ladle held a quart.
Each soldier as he passed the cook
   received his share of stew,
enough to fill his mess tin
   with the dismal-tasting brew.
When Private Simpson took his turn
   and Jenkins made his scoop,
the total take was one big bone
   and half a cup of soup.
In vain poor Simpson voiced his wrath
   in words both hot and hasty,
which did not make that nasty bone
   the slightest bit more tasty.
And adding fuel to the fire,
   which clearly was his right,
he called the cook some vulgar names
   and challenged him to fight.
Now there was something vital
   which Simpson didn't know,
that Jenkins was a boxer
   and a tough and working pro.
He took him on behind the barn
   and much to his surprise,
he landed flat upon his back
   with shiners on his eyes.
Just then the bugle called again.
   This time a German putsch.
The unit called to reinforce
   moved forward in a rush.
But Simpson still was hungry
   and as he strode along,

his thoughts were strong on vengeance
  to the men who did him wrong.
Now seven of the enemy
  who thought that they could win
had occupied a piece of trench
  and were busy digging in.
When Simpson came upon them
  with violence still in mind,
he met the situation
  by action most unkind.
He shot the first one through the chest,
  the next one through the head.
The other five surrendered
  and to the rear were led.
When a further day of action
  secured the front once more,
the unit went back to the camp
  where it had been before.
The colonel phoned to GHQ,
  which thereupon decreed
a Military Medal
  for Private Simpson's deed.
Meanwhile, cook Charlie Jenkins
  set out to make amends
for roughing up the hero
  when by rights they should be friends.
He liberated lard and flour
  from sources he could trust.
While defaulters peeled potatoes,
  Jenkins mixed a batch of crust.
The butcher, old Bill Nadeau,
  produced some fancy steak,
together with four kidneys,
  a first-class pie to make.
When the pie was baked and ready
  it was quite a sight to see,
and the CSM donated
  a full quart of SRD.[39]

---

39 Standard rum issue?

Then Simpson and a few close friends
   who could no longer wait,
sat down around the kitchen
   and, just ate and ate and ate.
Some several hours later
   when the SRD was dead,
the bugler sounded lights out
   and the party went to bed,
to rest until the morning,
   released from all alarms,
with happy Private Simpson
   dead asleep in Jenkins' arms.
Now many years have passed away
   since those eventful days
and all the men who shared them
   have gone their separate ways.
Mrs Simpson's grocery orders
   come from Jenkins to her door
while all the Jenkins family
   buy their shoes at Simpson's store.
Each year upon a certain date,
   no matter what the weather,
the families gather for the day
   and have a meal together.
A Military Medal hangs in a frame
   upon the wall
and a great steak and kidney pie
   is shared by one and all.
Then after all have eaten,
   the two old men retire
to share a quiet toddy
   together by the fire,
to dream a while in fancy
   of days long since gone by
when Simpson won a medal
   and Jenkins baked a pie.

Preparations for Vimy

In mid-February the rest period near Bruay ended. Moving again to the forward area, the battalion got its first clear look at Vimy Ridge. They took over in the La Folie sector, slightly to the left and in front of the ruined village of Neuville St Vaast and a wooded spot known as Bois d'Allou. The reserve camp was located about three miles back near the village of Mont St Eloi.

The houses of Neuville St Vaast had originally been made entirely from blocks of chalk quarried from under Vimy Ridge. Very central to the extensive coal mining district, it had been known in prewar days as 'the white city,' the coal miners' Monte Carlo. Canadians were told of the wide-open gambling casino and female entertainment for those so inclined. By February 1917 there was not anything left of that haven of synthetic rest. The houses were just piles of shattered chalk but many of the cellars remained. These provided quite strong shelter from anything except a direct hit by an exceptionally heavy shell. They served as excellent points of close support to the forward trench system.

The entire Canadian Corps was getting into position and making intensive preparations for the forthcoming assault. While the exact date had not been fixed, the whole back country was jumping with activity. In the front lines work was continuous, preparing the trenches for the assembly and jump-off. Connections had to be improved and extended in all directions. In several places telephone cables were laid. For maximum security these were buried in trenches seven feet deep. It took plenty of pick-and-shovel work to get down that deep through solid chalk and flint. In reserve, except for the first day out, for clean-up, bath and pay parades, the night working parties never stopped. Tons of supplies and materials had to be carried forward and distributed. The usual vile winter weather did not help. Soaking-wet chalk is as slimy and slippery as axle grease.

About the same time in February that the 25th was coming forward from the rest at Bruay, an opening was being made in the Twelfth Brigade of the Fourth Division for a second complete Nova Scotia battalion. This was the 85th, a part of a Highland brigade recruited in the province in 1916. Originally, it had been expected to use the whole brigade as part of a fifth division. The severe casualties in the four divisions already in France during the two years from February 1915 to February 1917 and the need for adequate supporting reserves made a fifth division more than Canadian manpower could support.

Reluctantly, it was finally admitted that with the exception of two battalions, one of which was the 85th, all the others would have to be broken up and the personnel used to reinforce and maintain the existing Canadian Corps. The 85th arrived just in time to be thrown into the Vimy Ridge attack after a very few brief weeks of front-line training. In its very first major engagement it fully upheld the fine Nova Scotian traditions under which it had been organized and trained.

The veterans in the 25th Battalion already had memories of some eighteen months' campaigning in Flanders and on the Somme. They looked forward with mixed feelings toward another bash at strongly fortified German positions. This time they could only hope there would not be any repeat of the slaughters at Courcelette and Regina Trench or the frustrations of the St Eloi craters and at Sanctuary Wood.

As February gave way to March it became very clear that the lessons of Flanders and the Somme had not been overlooked. Every possible detail of the German defences was examined over and over again. At one point or another along the front between Arras and the Souchez Valley there were raids almost every night. These increased in strength and depth of penetration as time passed. When not in the front lines or on working parties, all troops in reserve were constantly rehearsed over tapes laid on the ground to represent German positions. Battalions, companies, platoons and sections were trained until every unit and every man knew exactly what he would be expected to do. By April the preparations were complete and finally the date was set for April 9th.

The Capture of Vimy Ridge, April 1917

The plan of attack placed the Fifth Brigade in the centre of the Second Division sector, directly in front of the ruins of Neuville St Vaast. The 24th and 26th were in the front line on a frontage of about 300 yards each, the 25th in close support and the 22nd detailed in reserve for mopping up captured ground, bringing forward supplies and rounding up German prisoners for transfer to the rear.

At zero hour the 24th and 26th would overrun the enemy front line and their frontage on the German Zwischen Stellung, a second-line trench system about 700 yards ahead. The 25th would follow close behind and after a thirty-minute pause to regroup would pass through the 24th and 26th to continue the advance another 1,000 yards to capture and occupy the German reserve position known as the Turko-Graben. Meanwhile, the 24th, 26th and 22nd would continue to clean up the captured ground, round up prisoners, open communications and bring forward supplies. As soon as the 25th had completed its assignment, the 24th would move forward to close support, ready to assist if needed against any counter-attacks which might develop.

Due to the formation of the ground and direction of the advance, the length of the frontage at that point began to widen rapidly. With the Sixth Brigade due to overrun the village of Thelus on the right front, it had been arranged to use two battalions of the Thirteenth British Brigade to pass through the 25th and complete that part of the action by the capture of Hill 135, after which the Fifth Brigade would again move forward and occupy this ground as the final objective for the day.

From notes made at the time, the following shows the timing of the barrage and advances:

Zero Hour, 5:30 a.m., April 9th, 1917
- At zero barrage will open and troops will advance to the assault
- At zero plus three minutes barrage will lift from German front line
- At zero plus eight minutes barrage will lift from German support line
- At zero plus thirty-two minutes barrage will lift from Black Line
- At zero plus seventy-five minutes infantry will advance from the Black Line
- At zero plus 103 minutes barrage will lift from the Red Line
- At zero plus 245 minutes infantry will advance from the Red Line
Note: prisoners were to be sent to the divisional cage at Aux Reitz Corner.

The weather on April 8th looked quite good. Frosty nights had dried and hardened the muddy ground, making the going easier and more favourable. As soon as it was dark enough, the forward movements began. For a short time there was a bright moon but the sky soon clouded over. With zero hour set for 5:30 a.m., all units were in their positions by 4:00 o'clock. In many places from the extreme front lines the leading groups were already out in no man's land and halfway across, lying flat in shell-holes and shallow ditches.

Just before daylight the weather took its usual filthy turn. There was thick wet snow and sleet, driven by a heavy northwest wind. This had at least one temporary advantage in lessening the possibility of early detection by the Germans of the approaching assault. Otherwise, it simply added to the misery of thousands of men lying unprotected out in the open waiting for zero hour.

The barrage which opened at 5:30 a.m. was a honey, the heaviest and most accurate seen up to that time. In many places German trenches and strong points badly damaged by continuous pounding during previous weeks were completely wiped out. The first lines of assault, already on the ground halfway over, largely escaped what counter-barrage the Germans were able to mount against Canadian trenches. When the barrage lifted at zero plus three minutes, the leading waves of the 24th and 26th were over and into their first objectives in seconds, before any living Germans could get out of any deep dugouts not completely destroyed.

It may seem strange but in fact, in an attack planned that way, there was a brief period when the safest spots were in the leading waves. They were out of their own trenches and clear of the early counter-barrage. Then, following closely their own rolling barrage, they were on top of the enemy in force before any real resistance could develop. Unfortunately, this brief advantage did not last long. In spite of the most violent and concentrated use of artillery in history up to that time, the German support and forward reserve trenches were not completely destroyed. The advancing troops had to face and overrun resolutely defended concrete machine-gun emplacements and surviving trench systems in places still partly protected by heavy bands of barbed wire.

Over ground torn beyond recognition by shell-fire and slimy from snow and sleet, the men of the Canadian Corps drove forward. As always, the price in casualties was very high but in spite of every obstruction they reached their first objectives right on time. Complete success at the Black Line Zwischen Stellung was reported by 6:15 a.m. and fully confirmed by 6:25 a.m. Other brigades on both sides of the Fifth were equally successful and the whole First and Second Division frontage had been secured.

The 25th assault force coming up behind the 24th and 26th lacked the advantage of early position. It had to face and pass through the German counter-barrage as it crossed the original front lines and former no man's land. There was another half-mile of shell and machine-gun-swept broken ground to cover before reaching brigade position in the captured Zwischen Stellung. There was not any way of avoiding casualties. These mounted rapidly as the Nova Scotians pressed forward.

Following the established plan of action, they made their advance and reached the Black Line right on time. The pause was brief. At 6:45 the 25th passed through the 24th and 26th to take over the leading lines of attack. In the next hour, using rifles, bayonets and bombs, it fought forward another 1,000 yards to its Red Line objective in the Turko-Graben trench system. On the way, eight heavy machine guns and two field artillery pieces were silenced and captured and, helped by mop-up parties from the 22nd, close to 400 prisoners were subdued and rounded up. By 8:00 a.m. the job was done with the Red Line secured along the whole of the First, Second and Third Division frontages.

While the work of cleaning up and consolidating went rapidly ahead, the next waves of fresh troops were moving into position. At 9:30 a.m. two battalions of the English Thirteenth Brigade passed through the 25th Battalion. By 11:00 a.m. they had completed the last part of the advance on that frontage. This cleared a group of woods on the back side of the ridge overlooking Vimy village. Again, men of the Fifth Brigade, including the 25th companies, moved up in close support ready to help repel counter-attacks and fully secure the captured ground. At the same time, the Sixth Brigade on the right had taken the ruined village of Thelus and was busy preparing for the last stage of the day's operation. About 12:00 noon they moved forward again to penetrate beyond the village of Farbus. By 2:00 p.m. the final Brown Line, including Farbus, was secured from right to left by the First, Second and Third Divisions and the two English battalions which had temporarily been attached to the Canadian Corps.

As this is essentially a story of the 25th Battalion, there follows only a brief mention of the difficulties which the Fourth Division on the extreme left met in carrying out its assignments. Hill 145 on its front with the ground around it was the highest point on the ridge. More heavily fortified and strongly garrisoned, it was laced with tunnels, deep dugouts, concrete machine-gun posts and heavy trenches. The attacks on April 9th were only partly successful. It took all of the next day of April 10th before the Germans were completely driven out and this last section of Vimy Ridge placed securely in Canadian hands. In this process the newly arrived 85th Nova Scotia Battalion suffered heavy casualties in its gallant and successful part in the final attack.

The immense task of clearing the broken ground on the ridge to establish a sound base for further advance was greatly hampered and delayed by the continued vile weather. Strong winds with sleet and wet snow delayed a supplementary operation for another two days. When mules hauling field guns forward became completely bogged down in the slimy mud and unable to move further, some guns were actually picked up and carried into position by the gun crews. Over large areas no form of transport could move. All supplies had to be carried by manpower or done without.

On April 12th Brigadier General Hilliam's Tenth Brigade drove forward again to capture a position north of the ridge facing Givenchy and locally known as the Pimple. At the same time English troops on its left cleaned out the last German hold at a spur of the Notre Dame de Lorette Ridge to completely free the passage through the Souchez and Zouave Valleys. By the afternoon of April 12th the German High Command had given up any further thought of counter-attacks or attempts to recapture Vimy Ridge. During the night it carried out a disengaging withdrawal across the flat ground of the Douai Plain, in some places as far as two or three miles. Its new and more favourable positions still covered the city of Lens and several nearby villages. Because of the terrible conditions already mentioned, it took the Canadians several days to move forward enough to resume contact, establish new lines of communication and safely hold the occupied ground.

In the two days of April 9th and 10th the 25th Battalion suffered casualties totaling nearly 250 officers and men. This was about average throughout the Fifth Brigade. Some other brigades very temporarily got away slightly better but many others lost even more heavily. While this was by no means as bad as Courcelette and Regina Trench a few months earlier, it still clearly showed the dreadful price in human lives and severe injuries which had been paid for the victory at Vimy Ridge.

For the next few days the usual trench routine could not continue. There were brief periods, just long enough for essential food and rest, with time to clean off the worst of the mud and filth from clothing and equipment. Otherwise, the work went on day and night. In a few places wooden plank roads over the mud enabled horse-drawn transport to be used to bring supplies and materials some distance forward. From there on it was pack mules or manpower the rest of the way.

In several places out on the flatlands beyond the ridge, further attacks advanced the lines and consolidated additional ground. This type of fighting went on for the rest of April through May and June. The 25th had another crack at it on April 23rd. It was put in to secure the left flank of a First Division attack to capture the village of Arleux. Uncut wire and misleading information on the exact location of its objective delayed the battalion advance but after a brief pause before an unmarked sunken road it completed its assignment and held on until relieved.

In that engagement casualties were much lighter than on the 9th and 10th but again a price had to be paid and accepted. Shortly after the 9th a first draft of replacements came up from the base at Etaples. Later in April another large draft of officers and men from the reserve camp at Bramshott in England brought the unit back again to its full strength.

Chapter Seventeen

In Again Out Again

In Between

With the capture of Vimy Ridge a tremendous amount of work was needed to improve communications over the ridge itself and down on the other side across the flatland toward Lens. Existing roads were rebuilt and widened. Many new tracks and trails were developed and established at more convenient points. When on the Méricourt frontage, the Fifth Brigade used a good camp at Mont St Eloi for reserve billets. In support, troops were quartered in dry cellars on top of the ridge at Neuville St Vaast. Another reserve camp sometimes used while working north of Lens was in heavy woods at the back end of the Notre Dame de Lorette Ridge.

This ridge extended from the camp to the forward spur at the Souchez Valley. In one of the earlier battles the French had lost heavily in retaking it from the Germans. Between the camp and the Souchez Valley, a distance of several miles, the ridge was quite heavily wooded and crossed with old trenches and dugouts, overgrown with thick weeds and coarse underbrush. Once away from the camp among the old trenches and dugouts, all sorts of battle debris could be found: broken rifles and bayonets, water bottles, scraps of uniforms including buttons and badges, brass shell cases, rusty cartridges, and in some places there were human bones and skeletons. There were also stories of men having found money and other valuables such as watches, rings, pistols and field glasses. If any of those tales were true, the men involved kept the details strictly to themselves. It was a weird and unhappy place at best and on a dark wet and dreary day particularly depressing. Men in the 25th at the time will remember being there a couple of times but never with any desire to return once they were clear of it.

During one trip while the 25th was in support at the cellars of Neuville St Vaast, a small party was seen coming up from the back country.
Coming closer, it was seen to consist of three French civilians (two men
and a woman) escorted by a French gendarme and a Canadian officer.
On entering the ruins of the village they spent a little time before locating the remains of one building. The party went down into the cellar
and after a further search one of the men picked a spot and removed a
couple of the chalk blocks. From a cavity behind the wall he recovered
several large-mouthed glass jars, which were seen to contain gold coins,
paper money and what looked like stock certificates and bonds. After a
further look around the party made its way to safety in the back country. The reaction of the troops was immediate and entirely as expected.
Reasoning that if there had been one hidden hoard of wealth there
could be others, they set to work with picks and shovels to tear open
every cellar wall in the town. All their extra work was without reward.
If there was any further hidden treasure none of them found it. A day or
two later they had to move along. By the time they made another stop
at Neuville St Vaast, other troops had completed the search. There was
not any use wasting further effort on such a wild goose chase.

Prelude to Hill 70

In the early summer months following Vimy Ridge there was continuous activity. The captured ground had to be cleared and consolidated.
There were supplementary attacks at different points along the frontage
held by the Canadian Corps and the English divisions on both flanks.
In between tours of trench duty, mainly in the Arleux-Méricourt-Avion
sector, there were rest periods in the reserve areas. In the 25th these
were used to complete reorganization in preparation for forthcoming
action at Hill 70 on the northern outskirts of Lens. Junior officers and
senior NCOs were given advanced instruction by three-week courses at
a corps school established near Pernes.

In early June the corps bade farewell to General Sir Julian Byng, who
had been its commander since the spring of 1916.[40] Under his guid-

---

40 Sir Julian Byng (1862–1935) commanded the cavalry in the British Expeditionary
   Force, then the Ninth Army Corps in the Dardanelles campaign, and in November
   1916 was given command of the Canadian Corps. He subsequently commanded the
   British Third Army until the end of the war. In 1919 he was raised to the peerage
   as Baron Byng and during 1921-6 was governor general of Canada. He finished his
   career as commissioner of the London Metropolitan Police from 1928 to 1931, and
   was promoted to field marshal in 1932.

ance the corps had expanded to its full four divisional strength. There is no doubt whatever that the success at Vimy Ridge was a tribute to his qualities as a soldier and a first-class leader. The men liked him personally and had great respect for his military judgment. General Currie, the commander of the First Canadian Division, was promoted to replace General Byng as corps commander.[41]

During one of the rest periods brigade sports were held on June 20th at Chateau de la Haie, followed by Second Division sports on June 23rd at Hersin Coupigny. The 25th had entries in most of the events but did not make any great showing. The baseball team had been smashed on the Somme in 1916 and never really did get going again. Later in June, following the rest period and the sporting events, the battalion returned to trench duty.

This took them into some badly disorganized unconsolidated ground between the town of Liévin and the city of Lens. There had not been any opportunity to scout out the position in advance and very little clear information was available. As it turned out, the place was a mess. To make matters worse, the relief of a sadly under-strength English battalion took place in a thick night fog. The incoming two forward 25th companies had great trouble finding and relieving scattered small outposts. That was bad enough but even more serious was the lack of any contact with other Canadian troops coming in on either flank.

As soon as the English battalion had thankfully departed, the only course open was to dig in and hope for better visibility after daylight. Digging noises out in front were at first thought to be coming from a German working party. The company commander took a small scouting party to probe cautiously forward. As they crawled closer he was greatly relieved to suddenly hear a good stout Cape Breton curse. It proved to be the other forward company, also lost and busy digging shelter at a better position behind a high hedge of a sunken field. As daylight was near, any further movement was too dangerous. Both

---

41 Born in Strathroy, Ontario, Arthur Currie (1875–1933) moved to Vancouver, where he was an insurance broker. He was also active in the militia and in September 1914 was appointed commander of the Second Brigade of the Canadian Expeditionary Force. He was promoted in September 1915 to command the First Division and in June 1917 succeeded Byng as commander of the Canadian Corps. He was knighted in 1917. After the war, he served briefly as inspector general of the Canadian militia during 1919–20, then as principal of McGill University from 1920 to 1933. Despite his lack of post-secondary education, he proved to be extraordinarily successful as a university administrator.

companies stayed where they were and managed to establish continuous trench sections, one behind the other, about 200 feet apart.

A short time after daylight the fog began to lift. It was then clear that the two companies were on downhill ground with the road from Liévin to Lens close by on the left and a section of railway embankment parallel on the right. The nearest houses in Liévin looked to be about half a mile up the hill to the rear. The first rows of miners' brick cottages in Lens were not more than 200 yards from the forward outpost of the two companies.

The Germans must have had a pretty good idea where these outposts were located. During the night they had frequently whipped the road and nearby hillside with bursts of machine-gun fire. They also sent over showers of pineapple-shaped trench mortar bombs. These were particularly vicious as they only made a slight whispering noise in flight. At night they were impossible to anticipate or dodge. Most of them landed much too close for comfort. Several men were badly wounded by flying bomb fragments. At these exposed forward points movement above ground during daylight was impossible. Further back, the whole situation could be better determined. It was discovered that the 22nd Battalion had also been lost in the fog. It had dug in north of the Liévin-Lens road about 500 yards further back than the two 25th companies.

Lack of any contact on the right was due to the railway embankment. There was another Canadian battalion level with the 25th on the other side. Contact at that point was established soon after dark. Orders were issued for the forward 25th company to establish its position as the new front line and to maintain connection over the railway embankment. Interchange of frequent patrols would be carried out while a trench connection was being cut through.

Immediately after dark the second company would cross the road and move forward far enough to connect with the new front line. At this point it was to dig in within 200 feet of the first rows of houses in Lens. The whole movement was carried out quickly, without being detected by the Germans. At the same time, scouts from the 25th guided the 22nd into position to close the gap and connect with the next battalion on its left. By morning, all companies were in their new places, holding one continuous fairly secure front line close to the nearest rows of houses in Lens.

Further back, one support company was relocated about halfway toward Liévin and the reserve company along with battalion headquarters was in strong houses and cellars at the forward edge of the town. Everyone had been busy all night, with a lot of help from the 24th and 26th Battalions holding close-up reserve positions. Rations, water, ammunition and barbed-wire supplies had been brought ahead and the whole situation was under good control.

One advantage of the new front-line location was its closeness to the German-held houses in Lens. They could not operate against the 25th with any normal open field of fire or risk shelling for fear of hitting their own men. Certainly the Germans could clearly see where the Fifth Brigade trenches had been established but they were not quite ready to do anything about it.

The second day passed quietly. During the third night the 25th and 22nd managed to string out some preliminary barbed wire as protection against a surprise attack. Parties from the rear worked all night to further improve communications and second-line defences. After daylight and stand-down the men relaxed, expecting another quiet day, but they were in for an unusual surprise. During both previous nights Germans had been heard working inside the nearest rows of houses directly in front of the 25th position. They must have placed several tons of dynamite or TNT. Just about 9:00 a.m. there was one colossal explosion. The entire two nearest lines of houses simply disintegrated in a great cloud of plaster and brick dust. The air was full of falling bricks and timbers, with dust so thick that nothing was visible for a long distance in any direction.

The heavy stuff came down all over the place with quite a lot falling into the 25th trenches. Fortunately, no one was badly hurt although several men did get bumped by various bits and pieces. A slight breeze from the east drifted the dust over toward the Canadian lines. Nothing could be seen and the troops quietly prepared to meet any German attack which might develop. Except for bursts of machine-gun fire and several showers of pineapples, no direct action developed. An hour or so later, as the air cleared gradually, the outlines of a strong enemy defence could be seen a short distance behind where the houses had been. The houses were reduced to mounds of rubble but it later turned out that the cellars were intact.

Under cover of the dust clouds they had been occupied by small advance elements of the German forces. The removal of the houses gave a clear view of our positions and an open field of fire for German artillery. For the next few nights both sides kept busy building further defences. By the time the 24th Battalion took over on the night of July 6th, the situation had settled down to normal trench warfare with that

part of the front firmly consolidated. Considering the dirty job, the casualties had been very light but the 25th men were more than glad to
get back to dry comfortable shelter in reserve at the back end of Liévin.

One Way to Stay Alive

The survivors of the original Thinkers' group, now mostly commissioned officers and several already company commanders, still held
their private sessions at convenient times and places. As preparations
developed for another tour in front of Liévin to relieve the 24th, certain
intelligence contacts began to spark. Big brass was roughing out plans
for a raid in force on the German lines facing the trenches to be taken
over by the 25th.

It was the standard idea: concentrated shelling, hopefully to break
enemy wire enough for quick passage, anticipated but not guaranteed.
Then a box barrage including indirect fire from heavy machine guns to
seal off a selected area would be followed by a rush at two-company
strength to storm the enemy trenches, grab a few prisoners, wipe out
as many others as possible. After a preset number of minutes, the men
would rush back to their original positions.

The official reason for the raid was the need to secure prisoners for
identification and questioning by intelligence. The side-effects: one or
two DSOs for senior planners observing the operation from a distance
through field glasses, Military Crosses for company commanders if
they were lucky enough to survive, a DCM or two for senior NCOs
and some Military Medals for the lower ranks. One other item: letters
of condolence to the relatives of the 10% of the attacking force it was
estimated would be killed in the process.

The members of the Thinkers' group had never failed to face duty
as they saw it. They had all taken desperate chances many times when
there was some hope of useful results. On the other hand, they resented
very strongly the idea of acting as sacrificial pigeons to satisfy the aspi-
rations of one in particular of their seniors toward securing a DSO for
himself at their peril. The plan had not quite matured when they went
in to relieve the 24th. The urgent question was how to stop this suicidal
venture and protect themselves and the men who respected them and
trusted them with their lives.

An immediate and careful study of the opposite position revealed
two things. First, the old cellars in front were very lightly held. During
the day the Germans mostly hid underground with only one or two
men outside on watch. Secondly, the ditch alongside the road leading

through the German lines was very deep and overgrown with long grass. Against the road on the German side was a cellar and what seemed to be an isolated sentry post. The whole set-up looked ideal for a snatch raid. After a further cautious survey the two platoon officers in the front line decided to try it. They first sneaked out a covering party of one corporal and two men with a Lewis gun. These were settled in the long grass of the roadside ditch about halfway across. Then the two officers, along with a sergeant and two other men, slowly worked their way forward.

Luck stayed with them all the way. The German sentry was not at his post and the little party slid in without being detected. A quick look located two Germans comfortably asleep in the cellar. When they woke they were both facing the muzzles of .45 Colt automatics right between the eyes. Without alerting any other nearby Germans, the party withdrew as quickly as they had entered, forcing the prisoners to crawl back through the ditch with them. On the return journey they collected the Lewis gun covering party. The whole job was done in about twenty minutes without firing a shot or the loss of a single man. Both the prisoners were very young and at the start badly frightened. Neither could speak any English or French. They acted as if they expected to be shot at any moment. A heavy drink of army rum at the company headquarters dugout helped to loosen them up. Without loss of time they were rushed back under escort to battalion headquarters. Within an hour they were in the hands of intelligence officers at divisional headquarters.

The capture of these two prisoners largely eliminated the official reasons which had been pressed to justify plans for the big raid. Before the promoters could get going again the 25th's tour of trench duty ran out and the 24th took over. The idea failed entirely a few days later with the movement over in front of Hill 70 as part of the preparations for the attack at that point. Incidentally, the expectant promoter of the original idea did not get his DSO but he saw to it that neither of the officers or any members of their little party received official recognition for the chances they took to protect themselves and their men against his personal ambitions.

Hill 70 – 15 August 1917

Several plans had been considered for the possible capture of the city of Lens. It was finally decided that the first step would have to be possession of high ground known as Hill 70, which overlooked Lens from the northwest.

Moving from Liévin to take over from English regiments badly reduced in strength, the 25th found lines facing the Lens suburb of Cité St Laurent anything but a bargain. In many places there was not any real continuous front line at all. A collection of old trenches ran from our position straight toward the German lines. In these, blocks had been set up, held by small isolated groups of men.

There was not any recognized no man's land or exact knowledge of where the German forces were strongly dug in. While small 25th scouting parties were checking house ruins and cellars, work went rapidly ahead digging a complete new line, connecting the separate posts into one continuous system. A close support line was also extended and strengthened with some of the old ditches deepened to provide better connections between the two lines.

In one case, while an officer and two men from the 25th were checking the back of a house in the dark, a heavy German patrol went down the old street on the front side. By the time the 24th Battalion came in six days later for their turn, the outlines of an effective trench system were well established.

On July 22nd the whole Fifth Brigade was withdrawn to reserve to start training over the tapes for the assault on Hill 70, due the following month. Bad weather delayed the date originally set for the action. Finally, August 15th was selected and plans went forward accordingly. The 22nd and 25th Battalions, side by side left to right, would lead the Fifth Brigade part of the attack. They would smash the German front line and advance another 700 yards through the ruins of Cité St Edouard to capture the enemy second line on the crest of the ridge. As soon as this position could be secured, the 26th and 24th following close behind would pass through to press forward the advance another 800 yards. That would carry them through a part of Cité St Emile to take and hold the German third line, known as Nun's Alley, on the lower reverse slope of the hill facing the outskirts of Lens at Cité St Auguste.

As darkness fell on the evening of August 14th, the Canadian battalions selected for the first phase of the attack moved smoothly and quietly into their assault positions. The Fifth Brigade was stationed at right centre connecting on its left with the Second Brigade of the First Canadian Division and on its right with its own Fourth Brigade. By 4:00 a.m. everything was set. The usual morning rum ration had been passed out: two ounces per man, no more, no less, just enough to kill the night chill and break some of the tension. Last-minute checks were completed and confirmed to battalion headquarters. Watches were coordinated and the men waited quietly as the minutes ticked off toward zero hour, set for 4:25 a.m. Officers and senior NCOs moved about with a quiet word of reassurance or a brief last-minute order.

The storybook idea of going forward into battle under one great surge of emotion with the cry of death or glory ringing in their ears was just so much baloney. The newer recruits were under more strain. They could not be sure how they would react when facing their first severe test. The older vets who had been through this sort of thing several times before mostly looked upon it as just one more dirty job. They were nearly all fatalists. While hoping for the best, they were prepared as far as humans can be for bad luck if they were due for it, should some shell or bullet have their number on it.

Five minutes before zero the front-line men crawled silently over the parapets out into no man's land and assembled, lying flat on the ground about 100 feet from the remnants of the German barbed wire. The second wave also moved up over the parapets at a set distance behind the first. The 26th and 24th slipped forward to replace them in the main trench areas. Right on the dot of zero at 4:25 a.m. the sky in the rear flared out into a great burst of light. Light travels faster than sound so it was a split second before the roar and crack from the guns and the rush of shells overhead reached the ears of the men waiting on the ground and in the jumping-off trenches. As the barrage descended, all hell broke loose over the whole enemy front-line area. Our eighteen-pounders were concentrated largely on the forward trenches and connecting sections. Heavy machine guns poured a steady stream of bullets into advance positions. The 4.5" and 6" howitzers took care of reserve trenches and by counter-battery fire silenced many of the nearest German guns.

For the first three minutes the advance lines of the 25th and other battalions lay where they were in no man's land. The barrage was a real wizard, right on target all the way along. Shells passed over our men by not more than three feet to explode less than 100 feet ahead, spot on the German trenches. The storm of machine-gun bullets was not much higher but still not any danger to the men waiting on the ground. Bursting shells always carry forward; while deadly to anything unprotected in front of them, they are of little danger to those they pass over. It is a little sticky to have shells passing with two or three feet overhead but it can be tolerated and accepted after the first few minutes of tension.

In this attack the elements of complete surprise were lacking. The Germans knew the date but were not quite sure exactly where or how strong it would be. To some extent they had expected and prepared for it a little further south on the other side of Lens. Even so, their counter-barrage began to hit the Canadian trenches within two or three minutes. Here, the 25th men were temporarily in the best spot: far enough out to avoid the German fire and safe underneath the umbrella of their own shells. At 4:28 a.m. (zero plus three minutes), the barrage lifted 100 yards. With a quick rush the 25th men were into the enemy front line before any of the defenders still alive could think of resistance. They had previously thinned out that line and withdrawn their main forces to shelter further back. Very few remained alive to be taken prisoner in that first rush.

After the heavy pounding of the previous several days, the final barrage had completed the job. The whole trench was a shambles of torn earth, dead bodies and ruined dugouts. A second quick rush took the attackers forward again as close as was safe to the new barrage line. Following lifts at three-minute intervals, the 22nd and 25th reached and captured their objectives in the German support line. A few pockets of resistance which developed were quickly subdued with the defenders either killed or taken prisoner. Most of them were glad enough to give in quickly without a fight. There were a few sticky spots which had to be overcome to secure the entire line. By zero plus twenty minutes at 4:45 a.m. the 22nd and the 25th were holding solidly. Then the 26th and 24th passed through to continue the advance and finish the day's assignment at the reserve positions of Nun's Alley, down the hill about half a mile nearer Lens.

In some ways the 25th and 22nd had the best of the first half-hour. They had been out and away before the counter-barrage came down. All the way along as far as they had to go, they moved before it was shortened enough to catch them. The 24th and 26th were not as lucky. They were just far enough behind to have some of it hit them head-on. Because of this their early casualties were more severe. Again, by the luck of the draw, the right two 25th companies had better going than the left two. On the right, the advance was over open ground without any distinct landmarks. On the left, the way lay astride a German communication trench. The enemy knew this exact position and many of their guns were accurately ranged on it. It seemed almost unbelievable but the right forward 25th company of five officers and about 160 other ranks got through to the first objective with only four men wounded and not a single man killed. The other companies were not so lucky. Near the communication trench a number were killed or wounded.

From the start, counter-attacks were rapid and strong. The Germans were not prepared to give up Hill 70 and were ready to make a sustained effort to take it back. The 25th, holding the original German support line, was soon under fire from enemy guns, not just ordinary whizbangs alone but plenty of 5.9" coal boxes as well. Where old house cellars were available, they offered partly safe shelter from everything except a heavy shell. One cellar suffered a direct hit from a 5.9. Out of eight men inside, seven were killed outright. The one survivor was rescued after an hour of digging, suffering severe shock with leg wounds and a broken arm. A falling beam held up enough of the roof to keep him from being crushed until his friends could get to him. The bodies of the others when recovered were taken to the rear for burial by carrying parties composed of German prisoners on their way back from the forward trenches.

In successfully completing their part of the battle the 26th and 24th also suffered heavily. The Germans were holding strong reserves at Lens. They started sending in counter-attacks soon after 7:00 a.m. The Canadian artillery and heavy machine guns gave them fits, greatly reducing their effective strength before they could get close to the lines we were holding. Even so, some did get through at different points. There were at least four heavy counter-attacks between 7:00 and 9:00 a.m. Hand-to-hand fighting developed with bombs, bayonets, rifles and Lewis guns. At times the 25th sent men forward to help hold the forward line and drive the Germans out. For three full days and nights the battle raged at one point or another. At some spots supplementary attacks with fresh troops improved or consolidated the Canadian positions. From August 15th through 18th twenty-one German counter-attacks developed.

It took another five days of continuous action before both sides held off long enough to dig and consolidate where they stood. On one occasion the Sixth Brigade mounted an attack at the exact minute the enemy started one of its own. The two sides met head-on in no man's land and slugged it out hand-to-hand until exhausted. In the end it was a draw with both back where they had started. A great deal of gas was used. The whole area was saturated with German mustard gas. It was all too easy, particularly when moving at night, to fall into a mustard gas shell-hole without knowing what it was. On the hands it was not immediately felt. An attempt to get a quick wash or possibly a shave often could put some of the gas on the face as well. When the blisters started to form a day or two later they turned into messes of yellow running sores.

Men suffering from severe mustard gas burns were sent to a special hospital at the seaside near Boulogne. Clothing was thoroughly disinfected or where necessary replaced. Two or three times each day they went to the beaches to bathe in the clean salt water and dry out in the air without towels. At first the bite of that cold salt water on open sores was tough to take. Within about ten days even very bad cases were well enough to return to full duty without any permanent bad effects. It usually took several months for the deep scars to fully fill in. To combat chlorine gas, in addition to the box respirators carried by all ranks, the troops were supplied with glass capsules filled with pure ammonia. Whenever even suspicious of chlorine gas, the gauze-covered end of a capsule was cracked on a rifle butt or some other hard surface. Then the pure ammonia fumes were inhaled right down into the lungs: unpleasant at times but sound protection against severe damage. Severe chlorine gas cases were a different matter. Even if not immediately fatal, the lung damage could never be fully overcome. Many men were condemned to months of lingering illness and early death as a result of chlorine gas poisoning.

On the night of 22/23 August, after a full week of fighting, the Second Division was relieved by the Third Division. The 25th, along with the rest, moved back to rest and reorganize. As the action tapered off later in August through September and October, the Canadian Corps securely held Hill 70 and the Germans never did get it back. The fighting at the hill and around other parts of the suburbs of Lens cost the Canadians nearly 10,000 casualties but in the process they cut to ribbons five crack German divisions and threw the whole German battle plan out of gear. It was the first full corps action under the command of General Sir Arthur Currie. Its complete success was a remarkable tribute to his leadership.

Following relief from Hill 70 the 25th moved back to rest billets near Gouy Servins. Reorganization began at once. Reinforcements came up from the base at Etaples. Others started over from Bramshott in England. There was a special dinner on the evening of August 25th, given by the officers' mess in honour of the Fifth Brigade commander, Brigadier General J.M. Ross, DSO.[42]

Operation Order – Secret[43]
The Mess President DSO 25th Cdn Battn

1. *Intention.* The 25th Cdn Battalion assisted by HQ 5th CIB will carry out a raid on the Commissariat situated at q.35.0.7.0.

---

42 John Munro Ross (1877–1937) was a manufacturer in Vancouver with extensive militia experience, including service in South Africa. He volunteered in November 1914 as a major and adjutant of the 29th Battalion, which he commanded January-July 1917. Promoted to brigadier general in July 1917, he commanded the Fifth Brigade until August 1918 and the Tenth Brigade from October 1918 to demobilization.

43 This tongue-in-cheek document is included in Clements's manuscript.

2. Zero hour has been fixed for 6:30 p.m. on the night of August 25/
   26th, at which hour troops will assemble as previously laid down.
3. *Barrage*. In order to assist the attacking troops the chef has been
   ordered to put over a barrage as shown in Appendix 'A,' Barrage
   Table, overleaf.
4. *Dress*. Battle order will be worn, less belts, arms and equipment.
   The QM has arranged for special entrenching tools to be placed in
   the assembly position, so these need not be carried. Steel helmets
   will not be worn.
5. *Water*. The MO has been instructed to see that all drinking water
   is properly treated before the attack and troops are warned that
   owing to the chemicals used, the water may have a light yellow or
   even a dark red colour but that will not make it unfit for drinking.
6. *Bands*. The Bands of the 5th CIB and 25th Battalion will play the
   troops over during the attack and will continue to play until the
   position is consolidated.
7. *Casualties*. All casualties will be removed as quickly as possible.
   This does not apply to 'Dead Soldiers,' for which a special party
   has been detailed. Estimated Casualty Reports will be rendered by
   10:30 p.m. These must be on time as Bde Office will send remind-
   ers if our report to them is delayed.
8. Bangalore torpedoes and smoke bombs already issued will not
   be lit until signal is received from HQ. Our box respirator affords
   complete protection.
9. Second water bottles will not be issued owing to the difficulty in
   accounting for same to Brigade afterward.
10. Identity discs must be worn in a conspicuous place in order to
    facilitate the identifying of bodies after the attack.
11. *Salvage*. No salvaged articles will be removed from the field not-
    withstanding Bde orders to the contrary. A special party has been
    detailed for this purpose.

F.D. Dodsworth, Lieut[44]
Mess Secty, 25th Cdn Battn

---

44 Francis Duncan Dodsworth was born in England in 1888 but immigrated to Canada
   and was a commercial traveller, living in Pictou, Nova Scotia, with his wife, Kath-
   erine, when the war broke out. Because he had served in the British territorial army
   for four years and in the 81st Militia Regiment, he joined the 106th Battalion with the
   rank of lieutenant. He served overseas in the 25th Battalion.

Appendix 'A'
Barrage Table[45]

6:30 – 6:35 p.m.	*Burning Oil* Projected by No X Special Company Corps of Batmen
6:35 – 6:40 p.m.	*Fishtails*
6:40 – 6:50 p.m.	*High Explosives*
6:50 – 7:00 p.m.	*'Roasting Fire'* by massed artillery assisted by pom poms, whizz bangs, shrapnel and trench mortars
7:00 – 7:05 p.m.	Rifle Grenades *and Liquid Fire*
7:05 p.m.	At this hour the barrage will lift but intermittent fire will be kept up with shrapnel, Mills bombs (all numbers) and liquid fire.

Program of Music
by

5th CIB Band		Bandmaster J. Wallace
25th NS Pipe Band		Pipe Major J. Carson
1. March	Viscount Nelson	Ancliffe
2. March	The Earl of Mansfield	
3. Overture	Lutzpiel	Keler Bela
4. March	The Barren Rocks of Aden	
5. Valse	Fine Lady	Finck
6. March	The Forty Second	
7. Revue	Byng Boys	Ayer
8. March	Scotland Is Ma Haeme	
9. Intermezzie	Secrets	Fletcher
10. March	Happy We Hae Been a Taegether	
11. Gavotte	Les Cloches St Mall	Rimes
12. March	The Cock o the North	
Strathspey	Lord Blantyre	
Reel	A Wee Drap o Whiskey	
13. March	Courcelette	
14. Polka	The Queens	

---

45 One can only speculate, but this may be a list of cocktails.

On August 26th the 25th and 24th Battalions paraded together for a combined divine service at Gouy Servins. Again, on August 27th there was a big parade and inspection by Sir Douglas Haig at Maisnil Bouche.

Note re Commissions

About the time of Hill 70 or shortly after, under General Currie's direction a radical change in the regulations governing commissions came into effect. From the start in 1914 most commissions had been granted in Canada. Accepted candidates were given preliminary instruction at officers' training schools, then posted to battalions being mobilized for overseas. They received additional training as they went along. If their battalions later went into action as complete units the officers went through with them. In battalions broken up for reinforcements the officers were given additional training at schools and bases in England and finally sent to France to replace casualties.

This all too frequently resulted in green young officers without real combat experience being placed in charge of seasoned troops. It was bad for morale and always subject to a small number of the newcomers failing to fully measure up. This was partly overcome at the Somme in 1916 when experienced men from the ranks were raised in the field to commissioned rank. Between the Somme and Vimy Ridge there was some further progress made by sending selected men with several months' trench service back to the Canadian Officers' Training School at Bexhill to qualify for promotion.

Soon after General Currie took over as corps commander new regulations came into effect. Any officers still in reserve in England would be absorbed in France as needed. No further commissions would be granted anywhere until men had first served as NCOs for at least six months in a battalion on active duty in France. During the reorganization after Hill 70 a number of NCOs from the 25th with very fine service records came under these regulations and returned to England to qualify as officers.

The rest period from Hill 70 extended into September. From September 6th to 15th there were brigade and divisional sports. Again, the 25th took part in most of the events but failed to make any special showing. About 20 September the battalion moved over toward Mont St Eloi behind Vimy Ridge and then went back into trenches at the Méricourt sector of the Lens front.

The Fish Wagon

At the Souchez Valley the Canadian Railway Construction Corps set up a control centre as a junction for several sections of light railway serving the slopes of Vimy Ridge toward Arras and throughout the back areas. These connected with various standard-gauge railheads. As the months passed the system was extended to form a connecting network behind the whole of the British front. At Souchez, along with the regular yards there was a well-equipped machine shop. Several former members of the 25th who had railway and engineering experience before enlistment transferred to the Railway corps and were stationed at Souchez Junction. Along with others of a similar background they somehow got hold of an old Model T Ford car.[46] In the machine shop it was cut down to fit the light railway gauge and fitted with flanged iron wheels to correspond. Once finished, they could scout around the back country and cover a whole lot of ground in a hurry.

To increase its utility they built a covered trailer with sides which could be opened in fine weather. It was fixed so that it could take seats when not being used for cargo. No one knows where or how a hand-operated foghorn off a Lunenburg salt banker got to Souchez at that time. Somehow one did. It was promptly installed on the Ford and its trailer. In the 25th and elsewhere the whole outfit became known as the fish wagon.

The battalion connections already noted suddenly became very useful to the inner cabinet of the Thinkers' group. By devious arrangements the fish wagon, gassed and lubricated by army supply, could be induced to appear in charge of an ex-25th crew at the nearest point convenient to the battalion camp. With a day's rations and the necessary supply of emergency fluids, a tour of the back country could carry the tourist group almost to within sight of the English Channel at Dunkirk and back before the call to duty had to be answered again.

The right to the post of foghorn operator was a special privilege taken in turn by the entire passenger list. It was a competition to see who could produce the loudest and longest blasts. It was a sad day when the battalion was moved too far away to maintain working contact with the Souchez railway junction.

---

46 The Model T, introduced in 1908, was Henry Ford's first commercially successful car.

Chapter Eighteen

Dirty Jobs

Passchendaele

While the Canadian Corps was exploiting the capture of Vimy Ridge by biting out pieces of the suburbs of Lens and keeping the Germans off balance, British forces started another offensive in Flanders. On June 7th the mines which had been successfully planted under German trenches on the Messines-Wytschete Ridge were blown. Many of these had originally been dug by the tunneling company of Cape Breton coal miners detached from the 25th Battalion late in 1915. Working parties from the 25th had put in more than one dirty night carrying forward boxes of high explosives to load those same mines. The whole face of the ridge on a frontage of some eight miles was shattered. Many of the defenders were eliminated. The British forces overran the ridge, penetrating several miles before being contained by determined resistance from heavy and fresh German reserves.

Since return from the Somme battles the Canadian Corps had been part of the First British Army under General Horne.[47] Early in October 1917 it was transferred to the Second Army under General Plumer,[48]

---

47 Commissioned into the Royal Artillery in 1880, Henry Sinclair Horne (1861–1929) served in the South African war and was inspector of artillery during 1912–14. Upon the outbreak of war, he went to France to command an artillery brigade, then was sent to the Middle East to report on the defences of Egypt and the Suez Canal. He returned to France and commanded the Fifteenth Corps in the battle of the Somme, then commanded the First British Army from 1916 until the end of the war. He was the only British artillery officer to be given command of a field army. He was knighted in 1916 and in 1919 elevated to the peerage as Baron Horne.

48 Herbert Onslow Plumer (1857–1932) joined the army in 1876 and served in India, Aden, the Sudan, and South Africa. In 1914 he commanded the Fifth Army Corps,

then still heavily engaged on the Ypres front in Flanders. To carry out
this movement Canadian divisions in succession were first withdrawn
to GHQ reserve. While the changeover started about October 1st, the
Fifth Brigade, including the 25th Battalion, did not leave the Lens sector
trenches until mid-October. Meanwhile, troops of the Third and Fourth
Divisions were already in Belgium. They had started taking over front
lines to relieve Anzac divisions severely exhausted from a series of
attacks against strong German defences during the previous month of
September.

After a few days in reserve the Second Division started north. Before
leaving, the Fifth Brigade paraded for a farewell inspection and review
by General Horne. The veterans of the 25th had personal memories of
1915 and 1916 in the Flanders mud. They had not any illusions about
future prospects. Those who had joined since heard enough from the
old-timers to feel much the same way. The move was accepted without any enthusiasm: just another dirty job to be done and got rid of
as quickly as possible. The fall and early winter rains were due any
day. All they could foresee was another mud-bath with little reward
and probably severe losses to capture a few thousand yards of shattered mud-soaked Belgian clay. Their worst fears turned out to be all
too sadly true.

The task assigned to the Canadian Corps was to capture and hold the
village of Passchendaele with the high ground on which it stood. There
was little left beyond the cellars of its former houses. General Currie's
advance preparations had been under way since October 1st. The final
plan called for a three-stage operation. The Third Division would make
the first advance. A few days later the Fourth would carry out a second
penetration. Finally, the First and Second Divisions would finish the job
by taking and holding Passchendaele.

The Third Division started the attack on October 26th. The Fourth
Division continued it on October 30th. From the 24th to the 31st the
First and Second Divisions were held in camps outside Cassel and
Hazebrouck. They worked over tapes to perfect the final details of their
coming assignments. On November 3rd the 25th as part of the Fifth
Brigade left Hazebrouck by train for Ypres, thence forward through its
ruins to some broken-down shelters near Potijze.

---

then commanded the British Second Army throughout the war except for a few
months in Italy. He was promoted to field marshal in 1919 and raised to the peerage
as Baron Plumer. He served as governor of Malta from 1919 to 1924 and high commissioner of Palestine during 1925–8.

The location was in open ground between two country roads. Enemy planes were overhead in relays all night, dropping bombs into the whole area. Their efforts were concentrated at or near the roads, as these could be more easily seen at night. Also, bombs landing on them or close by helped to deny or restrict their use for troop movements or transport of supplies. By keeping in the middle as far as possible from either road, the 25th was lucky to avoid any loss of men that night. The transport section on the off side nearer one road was not so fortunate. One bomb hit a line where the mules were tethered and wiped out most of them.

During the night of November 4/5th relief of the Third and Fourth Divisions was completed. This left two fresh divisions at the jumping-off positions ready for the final push. On the Fifth Brigade front the 24th Battalion held the front trench system, such as it was, facing the southerly side of Passchendaele. At zero hour, 6:00 a.m., on November 6th our barrage opened. The 26th Battalion went over and through the 24th to carry out the brigade assault. It quickly captured its part of the village. Three battalions of the Sixth Brigade took the rest of the main village and surrounding high ground further north. Still further north the First Division kept pace, taking all of its objectives right on time.

When the 26th had completed its task in the village, the 24th moved up to fill in and protect the open right flank. The 25th and 22nd came forward from reserve to maintain communications, mop up and con-solidate the captured ground. The next night, November 7th, the 22nd relieved the 26th and the 25th took over from the 24th. The brigade was relieved two nights later and left Flanders on November 11th with the rest of the Second Division to rejoin the First Army at the Lens sector.

The Canadian Corps had carried out its mission to capture Passchen-daele with brilliant success. It cost over 15,000 casualties in little over two weeks of actual combat. Whether the results were worth the price remains a matter over which historians have widely varied opinions. In the 25th there was not any feeling of glorious achievement or particular satisfaction. They had lost some more good men, although not quite as many as some of the other battalions. To them, Passchendaele had nothing to recommend it in any way. It had been two weeks of mud, muck and misery. They were more than glad to bid all of Flanders a 'soldier's farewell' as they moved away.

The Halifax Explosion, December 6th, 1917

Details of the Halifax explosion are too well known to need further review in this story of the 25th Battalion except for one result not men-

tioned in the historical accounts. At that time there were in the 25th a
number of Halifax men who had not seen their homes or families for
over two years. When the first news came through to the trenches facing Lens, the shock to those men can be easily understood. Communications to the stricken city were completely cut. Even normally it
usually took ten days or more to get a reply to a message. Now, beyond
knowing that hundreds in Halifax had been killed or severely injured,
the men in the trenches could not find out what had happened to their
families.

Most of them managed somehow to stay on duty and keep going.
The army authorities made every effort to secure reliable information
about their families and friends. A few men were so badly upset that
they required special attention. Some were relieved to learn their folks
at home were safe and uninjured. Others were not so fortunate. They
had lost family and close relatives killed or seriously injured. As the
real facts became known, a few men were allowed to return to Canada
on compassionate leave. Later, after doing all they could to overcome
family troubles, they were either given full discharge or reassigned as
instructors to the reinforcement camp at Aldershot, Nova Scotia.

Trying to stay alive and healthy under active service conditions in
France with most of the men not directly affected by events in Halifax,
the battalion gradually settled down again to its regular routine. It was
not until they returned in May of 1919 that the 25th men realized the
full extent of the damage and loss of life.

Winter 1917–18

Following return in mid-November from the Flanders area to the Lens
front, the battalion resumed regular trench routine. The dirty wet winter weather made its usual contribution to the joys of the season. Six-
day interchanges with the 24th Battalion continued. About the 20th of
December the whole Second Division was withdrawn to army reserve
for rest and refit. This gave them both Christmas and New Year's in
comfortable dry billets near Bruay.

Reinforcements from England through the base at Etaples brought
the battalions back to full strength. Leaves to England were resumed.
Selected officers and NCOs were sent to corps and army schools for
advanced instruction. This full four-week break was by far the longest
period of relief from front-line service since arrival in France in September 1915.

The division moved back to trench duty in the Méricourt sector on January 16th, 1918. After a couple of tours near Méricourt the Fifth Brigade slipped early in February through Souchez Valley toward the northerly side of Lens, not far from Hill 70. Three weeks later, during the last week in February, the Second Division was again withdrawn to army reserve. That time the 25th was settled very comfortably in good billets at the town of Auchel.

All through the winter rumours circulated that the Germans were planning another all-out offensive. The peace treaty of March 3rd, 1918, between Germany and Russia increased the threat. Large forces were returning from the eastern front into positions in Flanders and France. It seemed only a need to wait for the winter weather to moderate and the ground to dry out enough to permit movement of heavy military equipment and men.

The Germans had another reason for early action. The United States had been in the war since April 6th, 1917. It had naturally taken some months for it to organize and begin to move large numbers of men to Europe. By late 1917 and early 1918 its efforts slowly began to show. If the Germans hoped for any substantial success, it was vital for them to strike with everything they had before the American forces could become fully effective.

Through the tours of trench duty forward of Vimy Ridge ingoing troops were continually warned to keep alert and prepared to stand fast against any attack which might develop. Possibly those at a comfortable distance behind the front lines knew more than they cared to tell the PBI up forward. There was actually far less worry in the extreme forward areas than anywhere else. The further back the greater the wind was up and the wilder and more widespread the rumours. On one trip over the ridge on the way into the Méricourt front line a staff major at the entrance to a brigade headquarters passed out some words of comfort to a 25th company commander. The comment went something like this:

Staff Major: 'Hello X. You better watch out. There is a good chance they may come over this time, right where you are going to be.'

Voice from the rear in the gathering darkness: 'What the hell are you worrying about? You'll have a four-mile start on me.'

Staff Major, coming to attention and saluting smoothly in the general direction of the voice: 'Brother, how right you are and I hope to keep it that way. Good luck my friend until we meet again.'

Note: That fine young staff officer was killed at Amiens on the 8th
of August close up behind the advancing infantry while trying to
maintain contact and keep his headquarters correctly informed of the
progress of the attack.

The first to arrive from the United States were doctors and medical
technicians. They quickly joined established base hospitals, casualty
clearing stations and hospital trains. As combat troops began to reach
France late in 1917 and early 1918, it proved easier to move men than
to supply them quickly with many essential auxiliary services. Transport was a specially difficult problem. To help out, the Canadian forces
had to part with some of their already scarce horses and mules. Up to
that time the regulations covering weight of extra baggage per officer
carried by the transport section had never been strictly enforced. Each
officer was entitled to his bedroll and two blankets, plus parade and
walking-out clothes with necessary amounts of other clothing and personal effects.

For trench duty the officers were not treated any differently than their
men. They dressed in regulation army tunics with nothing but cloth
stars on the shoulder straps to show their rank. This was a regulation
sensibly put into effect after the Somme in 1916 to prevent officers from
becoming easy targets for enemy snipers. The officers had to do their
own carrying while on forward duty exactly the same as the men. They
only had access to bedrolls and spare clothing while in reserve. Otherwise, their effects were kept at the QM Stores and on the move were carried in transport wagons. With the loss of a number of horses and mules
plus wagons to arriving American units, a rigid no-fooling order was
laid down: forty pounds maximum per officer. All excess out, no exceptions. The quartermaster was supplied with a beam scale to enforce the
order. Overweight bedrolls had to be brought down to forty pounds or
they would not be loaded on the wagons.

The circus prior to the next move was quite a show. Long-treasured
souvenirs such as brass shell nose-caps, extra Luger pistols, field
glasses, surplus supplies of soap, towels, underwear and socks all came
to light. What to keep? What to dispose of and how? Any chance to trade
or secure some part of the value? No amount of protest or persuasion
had any effect: forty pounds total or off the wagon. The words of blessing for quartermasters in general and all higher authority, with equally
friendly references to the United States, flowed freely. There were some
real bargains in excellent souvenirs available to those prepared to add
them to their personal backloads. Like everything else in the army, what

could not be avoided had to be endured. The forty-pound limit stuck. It was never entirely forgotten or willingly accepted.

The German Spring Offensive 1918

There cannot be any attempt here to cover all the details of the fighting in the spring and early summer of 1918. This record is concerned mainly with the story of the 25th Nova Scotia Battalion and to some extent the immediate companion units in the Fifth Brigade. As February gave way to March with the battalion as part of the Second Division in army reserve at Auchel, the rumours continued to spread.

Finally, on March 21st the long waiting period ended. The Germans let go with their full strength against part of the British front held by the Fifth and Third Armies. The Second Division at once stood to awaiting orders to move. Officers and NCOs away on instruction courses were quickly recalled. All upcoming leaves were cancelled. For the next two days the division continued training. Then on March 24th the Fifth Brigade moved back toward Arras. The 25th occupied one of its former camps near Mont St Eloi. There was little clear information on what was really going on further south.

Through March 25th and 26th the battalion furnished strong working parties to dig and wire reserve trenches. On the evening of the 26th orders came to break camp and move south at full speed. That night they marched for ten hours. By next morning they were off the road in open fields near Bienvillers au Bois. It looked as if another forced march could put them back into the same ground on the Somme where they had fought so gallantly around Courcelette in 1916. In this movement the Second Division was temporarily detached from the Canadian Corps and transferred to the British Sixth Corps, part of the Third Army under its former commander, General Byng.

With the battle raging on a wide front, all movements had to be on a day-to-day, almost hour-to-hour basis. By the morning of March 27th the situation further south had improved. Meanwhile, another serious threat had developed. The Seventeenth Germany Army was making a strong effort to break through just below Arras, behind Vimy Ridge, to capture it from the rear. After a short rest the Fifth Brigade was turned around to return north. It marched for another ten hours. By midnight of the 27th it had occupied reserve trenches behind the threatened front near Bretencourt and Ficheaux.

A heavy German attack on March 28th drove our forward lines back again. The defenders' already depleted strength was further reduced. On the night of the 29th the Second Division moved to take over part of the front line. Along several miles of frontage where the enemy had been briefly held and contained, fresh full-strength units were taking over. Fortunately, the weather was kinder than usual, a little foggy but at least not raining. The 25th relieved the remnants of a battalion of its old friends, the Gordon Highlanders. After a week of steady fighting a rearguard action there were only two officers and about sixty other ranks of the Gordons still grimly holding on. To replace them the 25th was bringing in full trench strength of some 600 officers and men.

On the 25th's right was the 1st Battalion of the British Grenadier Guards, on the left our own 26th Battalion, both also up to full strength. Further to the left other Second Canadian Division battalions held ground southeast of Arras nearer to the Arras/Cambrai road. The 25th trench area was closer to Mercatel, facing Neuville-Vitasse and the Arras-Bapaume road. Advance parties of battalion scouts and guides had done an excellent job. The relief went smoothly and fast. Within an hour after dark the forward companies had taken over and the exhausted Gordons were on their way to a well-deserved rest.

Contact with the Guards was made across a light country road on the right. The line at that point was solid. The trench was only a shallow ditch with a few bits of barbed wire out in front. The immediate problem was the lack of any contact with the 26th on the left. There was a wide-open hole there. A report confirming relief of the Gordons and the open gap on the left flank was rushed back by runner to battalion headquarters. The company commander led a small scouting party into the opening to investigate further. The first big surprise came through discovery of a very large abandoned British supply dump behind a steep bank in an old gravel pit. There were piles of picks and shovels, coils of barbed wire, sandbags, boxes of iron rations plus assorted other supplies. The most astonishing find was a large number of new Lewis guns still in their original cases just as they had been shipped from the works in England. These were supported by cases and cases of fully loaded new firing drums all ready for use in the guns.

A few minutes later there was noise of movement on a path nearby. It was the scout officer with two scouts from the 26th. He was working ahead of his forward company to locate and join up with the 25th. The guides supplied to it had been badly informed and lost their way in the dark. Without delay 26th men were brought up and the open break was closed. From then until daylight carrying parties from both units and from the Guards, who had also been informed, came and went steadily to secure everything from the dump they could use to advantage. Normally there were six men to a Lewis gun crew. Split, with other riflemen added, this provided extra crews.

Guns from the dump, cleaned of grease, were spread throughout the front and close-support companies. Stacks of loaded drums were piled beside each gun. Within two hours there were sixteen fully serviced guns in the 25th Battalion's front line. The close-support company had an equal number in place. The Guards and the 26th were equipped the same way. Extra picks and shovels were used to deepen the shallow trench system. There was not enough time to build regular barbed-wire fences. Coils were broken open and spread loosely into long grass in front, providing excellent protection until more permanent defences could be built.

Just before dawn on March 30th the front-line company commanders held a short meeting. It was certain that at daylight the Germans would move forward in their established pattern. There had not been time during the night to accurately locate the enemy troops. Question: how close to let them come before taking defensive action? It was agreed to leave the decision to the Guards' front-line commander. The Canadians would hold fire until he fired the first shot. After that everyone would be free to open up with everything they could bring to bear.

To make matters even more ducky, it seemed likely the Germans would not know the relief had taken place. They had halted at darkness to consolidate and regroup a fair distance short of our new trench positions. The 25th men with their companions on both sides had been able to work steadily all night without danger in preparing for the next morning's attack.

German assaults had changed greatly from earlier years. There were no more mass formations in solid lines. They now came forward in small separate groups, probing and searching for weak spots through which to penetrate. Defenders cut off were forced to retreat fast to avoid capture.

Daylight came quickly. The men of the 25th stood quietly to their guns. Along the whole front it was so still that it was almost possible to taste the silence. There was not a sound as in the distance small groups began to show against the skyline, coming forward steadily. Tension mounted as they drew closer. The waiting men found it almost unbearable to withhold fire at such open targets. Before long the attackers sensed that something was wrong. Forward movements slowed down.

Some could be seen halting to exchange messages. A few of the leaders were within 100 feet of the defending trench lines.

Then a single shot rang out from the Guards' trenches. A split second later the frontage exploded in a tremendous crash of machine-gun and rifle fire. Nothing quite like it had ever happened. The enemy had walked head-first into a trap, caught out in the open under murderous fire from heavily manned defensive positions. Those not wounded or killed on the spot broke and fled. Many of the closest were shot down as they ran. Others fell flat trying to avoid being hit.

As the attack turned into a complete rout, some of the defenders went over the top. Bayonets fixed and firing from the hip, they chased the fleeing enemy. In a short time the chase was recalled with the nearest enemy forces almost a mile away. A few prisoners were picked up. Some wounded and others were winkled out of hiding places. From that time on the German High Command lost all stomach for further attacks in that area. The threat to Arras and Vimy Ridge had been crushed, the front solidly reestablished.

Chapter Nineteen

Cleaning Up

The Chinese Labour Corps

There was a large Chinese Labour Corps compound near Mont St Eloi. The Chinese seen in Canada were usually small Cantonese types. Those in France were much larger, tall strong men reported to be Manchurians from northern China. According to the Estaminet Times and similar sources of news current in the 25th, these Manchurians worked under some sort of contract between the British and Chinese governments.

Although carefully checked before loading on shipboard, they smuggled along enough female company to ease the strain of the long voyage to France. On arrival at Marseilles, the whole lot went through a general clean-up. Heads were shaved, all clothing was burned and new clothing was issued. In the process the females were easily detected. The ladies were promptly sent back to China and their male friends went on by rail to the rear of the battle areas in northern France. There is not any record of how these unfortunates managed for female company after that.

They were not fighting troops. They were only brought to France as labourers and worked unloading supply trains, helping to maintain and extend the railroad systems or on other construction jobs at safe distances behind the fighting areas.

Once, while at St Eloi, the 25th sent their pipe band to give a concert at the Chinese compound. There must have been some appreciation of such strange sounds. The band duly returned intact, a bit unsteady from the effects of a mixture of unknown origin to which they had been generously treated. Next day a delegation under escort delivered a message of thanks to the 25th. It was a scroll about three feet wide by six feet long, made from heavy wrapping paper inscribed with Chinese writing. Lacking any Chinese scholar able to read the scroll, it had to be accepted as favourable comment. A few suitable small gifts were hastily gathered and given to the delegates. They finally departed looking highly pleased with the results of their visit. If that scroll still exists and could be located, it would make an interesting exhibit at the military museum in the Citadel at Halifax.

They knew all about the advantages of the tea-break idea. When leaving the compound for a day's work, each man carried everything he owned with him. They seemed to feel that anything left behind would not be there on their return. The cooks and helpers came along with stocks of tea. Iron dixies were carried Chinese-fashion, hung on both ends of carrying poles. Before any work could start, fires were lit, water boiled and tea made. The workers had all they wanted then and throughout the rest of the day. Otherwise, no tea no work.

At the time of the German smash on March 21st, 1918, the Chinese compound was a safe distance in the rear, well out of shelling range. The Chinese were used to the noise of shellfire in the far distance. They knew where it was coming from and what it meant. With the first partial success of the enemy attacks the noise came closer. The nervous tension mounted. When the flash and smoke were close enough to be seen, even if still a safe distance away, the dam broke. The whole lot burst out back through the Mont St Eloi railhead, down the rails toward the English Channel. Lacking the regulation steel helmets, many lashed tin pans or enamel washbasins on their heads, using wool mufflers for ties. Carrying all personal effects, they went through the station at a fast clip downline toward the town of St Pol.

The Railway Transport Officer (RTO) at Mont St Eloi was far from happy or too certain about the immediate future. As a precaution he had a boxcar loaded with his records and personal effects. It was attached to an engine with steam up on a siding and headed downline. As it turned out, the enemy attack was held. He did not need to use his private escape train but he certainly was all set for any emergency.

Some time after the last of the Chinese had disappeared, the head of the column began to arrive at St Pol. They had covered a fair distance. By then they were even more hungry than usual. Without being asked, they took charge of a well-stocked YMCA canteen. Before enough army assistance could be organized to start rounding them up, they had eaten the entire canteen stock. Most of the travelers were gathered in fairly quickly. They were held under guard until it was safe to return them to the Mont St Eloi camp. It took longer to catch every last one. Tales later heard in the 25th indicated some few got as far as the Atlantic seacoast near Bordeaux. After the war ended, the 25th was far away. It was too busy trying to get home itself to pay any attention to how and when the Chinese finally got back to Manchuria.

Security and Censorship

The High Command had definite ideas about what was right and proper to maintain maximum security and prevent military informa- tion from reaching the enemy. Strictly enforced regulations were in effect. All letters from the front were censored before going forward. In battalions such as the 25th, outgoing mail was gathered daily as nearly as conditions would permit.

Among other duties, company commanders assisted by platoon offic- ers read over all open letters before sealing to be mailed. Any parts con- sidered dangerous were first blotted out. For men not wishing to reveal their thoughts too openly there were special forms available in limited numbers. These were collected sealed by the senders, then sent to a rest base to be opened and censored by special officers not acquainted with the writers.

After reading forty or fifty letters in a rush, officers could hardly remember any of the details. Even when they knew the writers and the intended receivers they kept whatever they remembered to them- selves as a matter of honour. No decent officer would think of betraying the confidence of his men by discussing such private information with others.

Most of the letters were very much of a pattern. After reading a dozen or more, the job became routine, something to be cleared up as soon as possible. Once in a while a real gem came along. The censoring party could be pardoned if he briefly shared the thoughts expressed before passing the contents forward. Two samples which follow seem to be worthy of honourable mention:

Dear Mother:
It's a bugger. Here I am soaking wet for a week. Food is cold and poor. My clothes are lousy and there are rats all over the place. Last night a mouse bit my ear while I was trying to get some sleep in a dirty dugout. I need a shave and a

bath but don't know when I will get any. My feet hurt and my shoes are nearly
worn out. I have only one pair of socks left. I have not had a letter from you for
six weeks.

>   *Hoping you are the same,*
>   *Your loving son,*
>   *Dan*
> *PS I am enclosing you ten dollars but not this week.*

Dear Maisy:
If I last another week my leave comes up and I will be on my way to Lon-
don to see you again. If you enjoy the birds, bees and flowers take a good
look at them before I get there.
>   *After that you will not see anything but the ceiling for the next six days.*
Hold everything and hope for the best.
XXXXXX
Arthur
>   *X*
>   *X*
>   *X*
>   *X*

Welcome Little Strangers

At one point on the Neuville-Vitasse-Mercatel front a narrow road
crossed no man's land from the enemy lines through the Canadian
trenches. After dark a listening post manned by a corporal and two or
three men was always set out in front along a roadside ditch.

On a very foggy night a few weeks after the German March offensive had been halted, the 25th men at the post heard sounds of horse
transport coming toward them along the road. They quickly alerted the
main front line behind them. A minute or two later, out through the fog
came a small cart drawn by a pair of light ponies. The men at the post
cut off its retreat while others from the trench made prisoners of the two
young Germans riding on the cart.

In the thick fog the driver had somehow lost his way and had driven
through his own front line without being heard or seen. The cart was
loaded with special food and other goodies for the German front-line
officers. Unless they had quick access to replacements they would be

on short rations for the next twenty-four hours at least. They were no doubt very unhappy about the whole business.

The cart and its drivers, minus the supplies, was sent back to battalion headquarters right away. The prisoners were promptly turned in for the usual processing through intelligence. For a few days the battalion transport section managed to hold and use the cart and the ponies. In the end they were forced to turn them in through a shortage of extra food for the animals, plus strict regulations against the use of non-military equipment.

Summer with the Third Army

Between April 8th and 10th the First Division was released from the Third Army. It rejoined the Third and Fourth Divisions in the Canadian Corps under General Currie. At that time the corps held the line in front of Vimy Ridge and Arras from Hill 70 to the Scarpe River. The Second Division remained with the Third Army for another three months. It was not released to rejoin the Canadian Corps until just before July 1st, 1918.

For a few days after the action on March 30th, which marked the end of the German effort to penetrate behind Arras, regular reliefs were not possible. The 25th was taken out for a couple of days, then put right back in again. A more routine relief by the 24th Battalion on April 9th put things back to some kind of order again.

Work had gone on steadily to improve the trench structure. Heavy barbed-wire barricades were set up and a good system of communications established. On April 9th the Germans launched another heavy attack between La Bassée and Armentières in Flanders. They overran ground held by Portuguese troops. During the following three weeks British and French forces were pushed back to the approaches to Ypres. By the end of April the attacking forces were exhausted. Unable to make further progress, the offensive broke down. No further attacks developed in that area for the remainder of the war.

It was about that time that the following appeared in battalion orders throughout the Canadian Corps: 'The practice of referring to our noble allies the Portuguese as the Portugooses must cease forthwith. In future, anyone guilty of a breach of this order will be severely dealt with.'

From April through May and June the Second Division as part of the Third British Army held lines below Arras in front of Mercatel and Neuville-Vitasse. No man's land was wider than normal in many places. During the first few weeks a number of German patrols were ambushed and destroyed. As time went on the Canadians just about owned the ground. Every Second Division battalion took a hand at raiding enemy front-line outposts. Sentries were killed, shelters destroyed and prisoners taken. It got to a point where the Germans had to change their front-line troops every two or three days. They were kept under continual pressure and never allowed to rest or relax.

Early in June parties from troops returning from Palestine were sent forward to be given short courses in trench warfare. They had been engaged in open warfare over wide spaces in the eastern deserts and were quite unprepared for existing close contacts between the forces in France and Belgium. One young officer was reported to have innocently asked, 'How far ahead from here are the cavalry patrols?' He refused to believe that the trenches were less than 300 yards apart until he was taken out with a night scouting party close to the enemy barbed wire.

Another story current in the 25th related to an officer who had been left behind to complete clearance of a camp. He was chasing the battalion a day later to rejoin his company. Hurrying along the road in the general direction of the movement, he came upon a crossroads. There were a couple of old British dugouts [sic?] on traffic control at that point. The 25th officer asked if they had seen any Canadians pass that way recently. The reply was about as follows: 'No sir, not us, but when I come on duty this morning me mate said some troops went through here before daylight in a hell of a hurry. By the looks of the ditches they must have been Canadians.'

The old boy was completely right. When Canadians were in a hurry under forced marching orders, they let go of everything but food, water, rifles, ammunition and gas masks. Deficiencies could be made up later after more vital matters had been settled. The 25th officer, also traveling light and fast, followed the littered road ditches and rejoined his company later in the day.

Return to the Canadian Corps

The Second Division was released from the Third Army and rejoined the Canadian Corps just in time to enjoy the great July 1st, 1918, corps sports day at Tinques. The 25th men took an active part but failed to win any of the events. On July 6th the giant muster parade of the pipe bands already noted in the record of the battalion mascot, Robert the Bruce, took place in the same location at Tinques.

The division had completed over ninety days of continuous forward duty, serving in the Sixth Corps of the Third British Army under Lieutenant General Sir Aylmer Haldane[49] and General Byng, the army commander. The 25th spent the two weeks from July 1st to the 15th with the rest of the division, training and refitting. It was in billets a few miles west of Arras in the vicinity of Avesnes le Comte.

Just as it was preparing to go back into the Lens-Arras area, the threat of another drive by the Germans in Flanders developed. The whole division was hustled back and placed in GHQ reserve, ready to move north at a moment's notice. Training continued with rumours a dime a dozen and changing several times every day. First it was to leave next day for Ypres (curses and groans). Next a move back to Lens was predicted, then a return to Neuville-Vitasse-Mercatel. If the Second Division did not know where it would be going, the Germans knew even less, which was just as well as events turned out later.

The influenza then ravaging the world reached France at that time.[50]

A number of the 25th men were temporarily out of action. Their wonderful condition did help to limit the casualties. The battalion doctor deserves special mention. He recognized at once the extreme danger. The care and understanding he gave to every case very definitely saved the lives of many men. They were desperately sick and could easily have died under less skilful attention. With his help the 25th losses were much lower than those of some other units.

A few needed reinforcements brought all the battalions back to full strength by the end of July. Over three years had passed since the 25th Battalion had sailed from Halifax on May 20th, 1915. In that time a green untried body of civilian volunteers had been transformed into a magnificent professional fighting machine. No wonder they were known then and thereafter as the Fighting 25th.

With few exceptions the officers were men of long combat experience who had gained their commissions after many months of battle service

---

49 Sir James Aylmer Lowthorpe Haldane (1862–1950) joined the Gordon Highlanders in 1880 and served in India and in the South African war. He was wounded and captured but escaped and subsequently served as military attaché with the Japanese army during the Russo-Japanese war. He commanded the British Expeditionary Force's Third Division from 1914 to 1916, then the Sixth Corps to the end of the war. After the war, he commanded British forces in Mesopotamia during 1920–2.

50 The so-called 'Spanish' influenza pandemic, which swept across the Western world in 1918–19, was the most devastating epidemic in recorded world history. It killed between twenty and forty million people, more than the First World War.

in the ranks. Most of them had been decorated for outstanding bravery and distinguished service in fighting actions. The senior NCOs were equally well qualified. Many were only a step away from advancement to commissioned rank. The whole battalion was in wonderful shape, full strength, well rested, ready for the next call to action, whenever and wherever it might be.

Chapter Twenty

The Last Hundred Days

The Battle of Amiens, August 8th to 20th, 1918

On the afternoon of July 30th the 25th broke camp. There was a short march to a roadside departure point, then a halt for further orders. Years of experience had brought about many changes. There was less moving of heavily loaded men for long distances on foot in order to save their feet. On arrival they would be far better able to fight effectively.

Within an hour a long convoy of old London buses arrived. The men were packed in and the whole lot got under way. They still thought they were on their way back to Flanders. It slowly became clear that they were traveling southwest instead of north. By next morning the bus convoy had unloaded the battalion near the village of Picquigny on the south bank of the Somme River some fifteen miles west of Amiens. Here they remained in comfortable billets for four days. Light training continued but definite orders for further action were still lacking. Short marches in pouring rain during the nights of August 4/5th and August 5/6th moved them close to Cagny, a short distance below the city of Amiens.

On August 7th (Y-Day)[51] orders for the attack on August 8th started to come through. The plan covered an operation of far greater extent than anyone in the 25th had expected. The Canadian Corps would attack on a three-division front with the French Thirty-First Corps on its right and the Australian Corps on its left. The dividing line between the Canadians and Australians was set at the track and embankments of the Amiens-Chaulnes railway. This ran for several miles in an almost

---

51 'Y-Day' was the military term for the day before a planned attack.

straight line from outside Villers Bretonneaux toward Chaulnes. The Second Division was placed on the corps left against the railway track to connect with the Australians.

The Second Division plan of operation for August 8th called for destruction of the whole German trench system, followed by the capture in succession of three villages – Marcelcave, Wiencourt and Guillaucourt – on the way to the final objective. There would be three stages. The Fourth Brigade would take the trench system and drive the enemy out of Marcelcave. Then the Fifth Brigade would pass through to continue the advance through Pierret Wood, Wiencourt and Guillaucourt. Finally, the Sixth Brigade would pass through the Fifth and advance to selected positions facing the village of Rosières. The distance of penetration into the enemy defences was to be a full eight miles.

During 'Y' night, August 7/8th, the 25th Battalion moved away from Cagny to its assembly position in front of Villers Bretonneaux. Zero hour was set at 4:20 a.m. on August 8th. Right on time, as the barrage opened the Fourth Brigade drove forward through the German trenches. By 7:45 a.m. it had overrun the whole system, including many forward enemy gun positions. It securely held its day's objectives in and around the village of Marcelcave.

The closely following Fifth Brigade passed through the Fourth at 8:20 a.m. (zero plus four hours) exactly on time. Leading the brigade advance was the 26th Battalion on the left against the railway. Here it was in touch with the Australians on the other side. The 24th on its right kept contact with First Division men next to them. The 25th moved 500 yards behind in close support with the 22nd 500 yards further back in brigade reserve.

For the first time since arrival in France almost three years before, the 25th men saw a cavalry regiment in full action. It was momentarily a wonderful sight to watch the squadrons coming up from the rear on the trot, then breaking into smaller groups and finally roaring into a charge at full gallop. Sending men on horses forward against machine guns and field artillery is bad business. The Germans holding the woods and ravines still had enough of both to cut the cavalry attack to pieces. In short order the open fields were thick with dead and wounded men and horses. Other horses now riderless were running wild in many places. Any advantage which may have been gained favoured the advancing infantry. It was able to go ahead faster with smaller losses while the enemy defences were concentrated against the cavalry.

An hour later at 9:20 a.m. the 26th and 24th had taken Wiencourt

and their forward companies were nearing Guillaucourt. The 25th
then joined the 24th. Their combined strength took Guillaucourt. The
advance continued to the brigade objectives on high ground some distance further ahead.

Meanwhile, the 22nd had been mopping up all the way along. It
cleaned out several pockets of resistance bypassed by the forward battalions. Hundreds of prisoners were collected, wounded men assisted
and contacts with the following Sixth Brigade maintained. By 2:15
p.m. the Fifth Brigade was fully established on all objectives. At 4:30
p.m. two battalions of the Sixth passed through, carrying the advance
another mile to its final objective for the day.

August 8th, 1918

As night fell on August 8th both sides hastened to prepare for the next
day. The Germans rushed up reserve divisions to reestablish their shattered defences. The Second Canadian Division was ordered to extend
the advance another four miles. The Sixth Brigade would continue on
its established frontage. The Fifth moved over to the right, widening
the attack to a two-brigade frontage. The Fourth was temporarily held
in divisional reserve.

The eight-mile advance on the 8th had been so rapid that communications were not fully reestablished. This resulted in some confusion in
timing. It was originally intended to move forward shortly after daylight. The Sixth Brigade on the left finally got away about 11:00 a.m. In
the Fifth the order of battle was reversed from that of the previous day.
The 25th and the 22nd would lead the attack. The 24th was in close support and the 26th in brigade reserve. The 22nd started forward about
12:00 noon. The 25th was delayed until 12:30 p.m.

The first heavy resistance developed around the village of Vrely and
took some time to overcome. Both battalions worked forward in short
rushes by small groups. By 3:00 p.m. they had outflanked the village
on both sides. The 22nd cleaned out the north part while the 25th went
through the south end. After a quick re-assembly the attack moved forward again. Using the same tactics, they captured their second objective, the village of Meharicourt. By 5:30 p.m. some 600 yards east of the
village, they had to halt and dig in. They had advanced too fast and
temporarily outstripped other units on both flanks. In this action they
had added four miles to the eight of the previous day and captured two
more villages. The following morning (August 10th), battalions of the

Fourth Division passed through to continue the advance through the villages of Haucourt and Chilly.

Until relieved on the night of August 18th the Fifth Brigade reorganized, holding ground around Meharicourt and Vrely. It marched out to bivouacs at Blagny Wood near Villers Bretonneaux. The whole Second Division left the Amiens area on the night of August 20th/21st. Returning north it rejoined the Third Army on the Arras front. The Third Division followed the next night with the rest of the Canadian Corps a few days later.

The great events of the 'last hundred days' began on August 8th, 1918. It is here worthwhile recording something of the feelings and reactions of the men who took part and saw the action firsthand. The 25th, as part of the Canadian Corps, did its full share in crushing the German defence system to a total depth of fourteen miles. Trenches, machine-gun posts, artillery and supply dumps were overrun and captured with thousands of prisoners taken.

This time, for a welcome change, the weather was with them. There had been a lot of rain on the way in from Picquigny. After so many bad breaks in the past, the Canadians could hardly believe their good luck when August 7th turned warm and dry. From then on through the 8th, 9th and 10th continued clear weather was a tremendous help toward the great success of the whole operation.

At zero hour, 4:20 a.m. on the 8th, the battalion started moving forward from its assembly position. The enemy forward defences were still in action. The way led through the outskirts of Villers Bretonneaux along the railroad track as a direction guide, to follow the Fourth Brigade advance. There was still considerable German counter-barrage fire in spite of hundreds of our guns pouring shells into the enemy lines. Many German batteries had been silenced but many were left in action. It was impossible to dodge all these shells. At some points 25th men were hit and put out of action as the battalion went forward.

In the distance the sky was filled with the flash and smoke of exploding shells. The number and variety of allied planes overhead exceeded anything the men had previously seen. There were dogfights going on in plain sight all over the sky. Reports were current in the 25th that strong forces of cavalry were nearby prepared to join in the attacks where developments might make possible their effective use. Along with the rest of the noise and commotion there were numerous heavy tanks, plus lighter and faster whippets, all moving ahead, adding to the racket and organized turmoil.

Nearing the original trench systems, walking wounded were coming back to the forward field dressing stations. Along with these wounded came the first groups from the thousands of prisoners. Frequently, prisoners assured their own safety by helping to carry stretchers with wounded Canadian soldiers on them.

As an item of interest, the following extract from battalion orders relates to the care of wounded men during the advance: 'The Medical Officer will move forward with the battalion and keep in touch with Battalion HQ. He will attend to as many wounded as possible during the advance. Stretcher bearers will, of course, remain with their platoons. No OR [other ranks] will be detailed to carry wounded during the attack. All must carry on to the objective.' This order is not really as tough as it may seem at first reading. In addition to the medical officer and his small staff, the stretcher bearers with each platoon were expected to give first aid right on the spot. It was the duty of the supporting troops to help clear up the battlefield as they followed along.

Field ambulances and forward dressing stations would come along as quickly as roads or trails could be cleared. The order simply meant that the weight and speed of the advance must not be reduced by sending effective men to the rear with wounded. Others following would take care of them while those still unhurt pressed forward. Another section of the battle orders read as follows: 'Each officer and OR will carry two water bottles which must both be filled on "Y" night and on no account used until after zero. Where possible the spare bottle will be removed during the advance from all wounded men and carried forward.'

The advance continued crossing the shambles of the German trench system overrun by the Fourth Brigade working ahead. Machine-gun fire from both sides was still heavy but enemy shellfire had slackened except from some of their long-range guns. The Fourth Brigade had overcome and captured most of the forward field-gun positions. They were nearing their first-day objective, the village of Marcelcave.

Beyond the trench systems the way led through wide-open country. It was mostly farm country with wheat fields almost ripe and ready for harvest. In small ravines and patches of woodland whole batteries of abandoned German guns remained. There were dead from both sides around these gun positions. Out in the open other men had been cut down by machine-gun fire before those field guns could be captured and silenced. The Germans never were cowards. They fought hard but could not resist the weight and speed of the attack as it rolled over them.

Streams of wounded men and prisoners continued moving toward the rear. Even with the advance in open order under good control and with men well spaced, the hazards increased. More losses developed as they closed up behind the forward Fourth Brigade.

At one point a heavy tank just ahead of the 25th suffered a direct hit from a heavy shell and burst into flames. The crew bailed out fast but the clothing of the last out was on fire. By some 100-to-one chance there was a small pond full of water right beside where the tank had been hit. The poor lad took a head-first dive and put out the fire in his clothing. His face and hands were terribly burned. If he survived at all it must have meant months, possibly years, before any chance of return to normal life.

By 7:30 a.m. the 25th had cleared the last of the trench systems and was nearing its re-assembly positions prior to passing through to continue the attack. At 7:45 a.m. word came through that Marcelcave had been taken, with the Fourth Brigade securely holding all of its objectives beyond the village. Promptly on time at 8:30 a.m. (zero plus four hours) the Fifth Brigade, led by the 24th and 26th Battalions, started to pass through into full combat action toward Wiencourt. Canadian field batteries had been brought forward to give artillery support. They began to add to that of longer-range heavy guns directed against the Germans holding Pierret Wood and Snipe Copse.

The opposition here came from scattered machine guns and several German field guns firing over open sights. Casualties came faster but completely failed to slow down or stop the brigade advance. In a series of rushes directly at and around both sides the brigade drove through the woods. The guns were silenced with surviving defenders being taken prisoner. Along with the 24th and 26th, the 25th pressed forward, leaving Pierret Wood and Snipe Copse for the 22nd to mop up.

Wiencourt was not as strongly defended as had been expected. It fell to the attackers quickly. Halfway toward Guillaucourt there was a large German supply dump that included several piles of lumber. This provided some shelter and a good rallying point at which to gather to organize for the assault on the village. More Canadian artillery was now far enough forward to bring fire to bear effectively. Under that cover, assisted by other fire from Canadian motor machine guns, the brigade advanced. It was able to bypass the village and enter from both sides and the rear. The defenders surrendered quickly as soon as they realized that they were surrounded and their escape was cut off.

Coming out into the open again, more machine-gun fire temporarily delayed the advance. With the help of some surviving tanks and whippets, plus Canadian field guns firing over open sights, the machine guns were overrun and silenced. By 2:15 p.m. the brigade was able to report that it was firmly established on line with all objectives taken. A short time later detachments of cavalry went forward to establish a series of advance posts. At 4:30 p.m. the Sixth Brigade followed the cavalry to finish the day's advance facing the outskirts of the small town of Rosières. At the same time First Division troops had taken Caix to line up in front of Vrely on the right of the Sixth Brigade.

August 9th, 1918

During the night of August 8/9th the Canadian Corps was busy regrouping, bringing up men to replace casualties and preparing to resume the attack the following morning. In the Fifth Brigade the 22nd and 25th would lead with the 24th in support and the 26th in reserve. They also had to sideslip during the night to take over part of the First Division holdings on the right of the Sixth Brigade. Good communications had not been fully reestablished. There was some confusion at first. Instead of the attack going in at dawn as originally planned, it was nearly noon before the 22nd and the 25th were able to get under way toward Vrely. Meanwhile, every hour lost had helped the Germans to bring forward reserves and to strengthen their defences.

The attack on Vrely was a tough job. It had to be made over exposed ground against strong positions held by fresh German reserves. Parties with Lewis guns worked slowly forward along ditches and sunken roads. It was nearly 3:00 p.m. before the 22nd on the left and the 25th on the right had outflanked and driven into Vrely from both sides to finally overcome the defenders. Soon afterward several tanks arrived. With these in the lead, the two battalions went forward again. By 5:00 p.m., after taking the village of Meharicourt, they dug in about 500 yards beyond. During the day they had advanced another four miles to positions dangerously ahead of their supports on both flanks.

On August 11th the Fourth Brigade, after one day's rest in reserve, took over the attack and carried the advance forward again. The Fifth Brigade, badly reduced in strength after two full days of continuous fighting, held positions in front of Meharicourt until taken out on August 18th to begin the journey north to the Arras sector.

There is one further item for the record before closing this part of the story. Plans called for a main casualty clearing station to be established

at a large group of buildings in Amiens previously used as a hospital and asylum. It was later reported that the train carrying the entire
medical staff with all its supplies and equipment had been derailed in a
tunnel somewhere down the main line. Whatever the cause, when the
battle opened on August 8th they were not there. The buildings were
empty without any sign of medical personnel.

The advancing troops were not aware of this situation. Under the
existing orders, all forms of ambulance service were directed to bring
the wounded to this clearing station. Hour after hour as the day wore
on, more and more stretcher cases piled up in the empty rooms, over-
flowing into the courtyards and surrounding open fields. By midnight
there were over 2,000 Canadian and British men lying on stretchers in
various stages of severely wounded condition. In addition, there were
another 700 or 800 German wounded soldiers and an equal number of
French casualties.

A few English soldiers from a nearby signal station did what they
could to help. They circulated with tin cups and buckets of water to
give a small drink to as many as they could reach. Those wounded who
had any small amounts of food shared what little they had with less
fortunate comrades.

The medical staff finally arrived at noon on August 9th. The speed
with which they unpacked and set up to deal with the problem was
beyond praise. The delay was not their fault. They did a magnificent
job but unfortunately in many cases it was too late for some men who
might have been saved by earlier medical care. The wounded were rapidly sorted out, additional anti-tetanus shots were given and urgent
surgery performed. Very soon, hospital trains loaded to capacity were
on their way down to the base hospitals on the channel coast. After
further attention, hospital ships transferred the wounded across the
channel to England. Once the break in the chain at Amiens had been
repaired, clearance of all casualties moved smoothly without further
undue delays.

Heading North Again

In spite of another heavy casualty list, the morale of the men in the
25th was flaming high as they moved away from Amiens. Nineteen-
fifteen, 1916 and 1917 in Flanders and on the Somme had been little but
slaughter and frustration in the mud and misery of the trenches. Vimy
had been wonderful but incomplete. At Amiens, for the first time after

nearly three weary years, they had tasted complete victory. They had never doubted that they would win in the end. Now they sensed the kill. The whole Canadian army was eager to get on with it and clean up the whole bloody mess once and for all.

Furthermore, the infantry at last had evidence that when it went into action it would no longer be alone. So often in previous battles it had been sent in all by itself against heavily manned positions protected by uncut barbed wire and machine guns in concrete pillboxes, supported by masses of both light and heavy artillery with unlimited supplies of ammunition and an enemy air force holding air superiority. Now for the first time our men had support from both light and heavy guns with plenty of shells to blast a way for them through enemy trench systems. They could count on numbers of heavy tanks and fast whippets to help them through barbed wire and deal with dug-in machine-gun posts.

Their own field artillery was able to go forward closely behind to provide cover in sticky spots. The Royal Air Force controlled the air above them. Even if not fully effective against entrenched machine guns or field artillery, the support of mounted cavalry was by no means unwelcome. Altogether, the odds had finally turned in their favour. From then on there would not be any turning back.

The Battle of the Scarpe, August 26th–30th, 1918

From August 21st to 26th the battalion was continuously on the move. Leaving Blagny Wood on the 21st it picked up its bus convoy at a point outside Amiens on the Villers Bretonneaux road. The convoy took it about forty miles north past Doullens to a place just south of St Pol. Arriving about 2:00 p.m. on August 22nd, a march of several miles brought it to billets in a small village.

It moved off again on the morning of the 23rd to a nearby railway siding. A train journey (Army Pullmans: eight horses or forty men) of about twenty-five miles followed by a further seven-mile march ended in billets a short distance directly west of Arras. Another seven miles on August 24th placed them south of Arras near Wailly. From there on August 25th the assembly positions for the action next day were only a short four miles away, between Arras and Beaurains. This was familiar ground for the 25th men. They had spent nearly four months on this front, around Neuville-Vitasse and Mercatel, from March to July 1st before going south to the battle of Amiens.

On Monday, August 26th, the Canadian Corps attack opened on a two-divisional front astride the Arras-Cambrai road. The Third Division was placed north of the road and the Second south of it. The Second attacked on a two-brigade front from the road to a point south of Neuville-Vitasse. The Fourth Brigade was on the left nearest the road, the Sixth on its right, and the Fifth was temporarily in reserve.

The barrage opened and the troops advanced in the dark at zero hour of 3:00 a.m. It had rained heavily during the night. The going was slippery and difficult as the attack pressed forward. At the start progress was rapid as the early hour had caught the enemy by surprise. After daylight it took the two brigades the rest of the day to penetrate a total of some three miles to their objectives.

The Fifth Brigade remained in reserve under orders to continue the attack the next morning. There was more heavy rain on the night of August 26/27th. The broken wet ground delayed early movement. The advance through the Sixth Brigade did not get going until 10:00 a.m. The 22nd, 24th and 26th, placed left to right, led off with the 25th in close support. By 12:00 noon they had taken the village of Chérisy and crossed the small river Sensée along their entire front.

Progress up to and across the Sensée river was helped by effective tank support with covering fire from guns of the Canadian Machine Gun Brigade. On the far side of the river, a strongly held German defence system made further immediate advance too costly. To avoid useless loss of strength and until the situation could be reviewed, the brigade was ordered to discontinue the attack and consolidate where it stood, subject to further orders. They had added two miles to the three of the previous day. By the evening of August 27th the penetration totaled a good five miles from outside of Arras toward Cambrai. The whole Second Division had suffered very heavy casualties. These losses were even more serious because it had not fully recovered battle strength from the battle of Amiens earlier in the month.

The original plans had called for the relief of the Second by the First Division on the night of August 27/28th. This was put off another twenty-four hours. There was another heavy rain that night. At noon on the 28th the Fifth Brigade, in the same battle order as on the previous day, was ordered forward against the strong enemy system known as the Fresnes/Rouvroy line. It was not realized that there were thick wide stands of heavy uncut barbed wire protecting that defence system. These wire barricades had been in place for a long time. They were completely concealed by long grass which had grown up around them. The grass was so thick that the wire could not be seen from planes or detected on aerial photographs. It was only discovered when the advancing Fifth Brigade reached the area and tried to get through. The leading sections of the forward three battalions hung up by this wire were cut down by a storm of fire from concealed machine guns. Reinforcements rushed up from the 25th met the same fate. Progress was impossible. The entire brigade was reduced to less than the fighting strength of a single battalion. It could only back away from the wire to dig in and hold on. The total day's advance was measured in yards rather than in miles.

They had learned once again the same old lesson: human flesh could not penetrate uncut barbed wire backed by strongly manned deep trenches and concentrated machine-gun fire. During the night of the 28/29th the battered remnants of the Fifth Brigade, completely done in after three nights and days of continuous battle, were finally relieved by the First Division, which had just arrived from the Amiens area.

By the time the 25th men reached the rallying points near Neuville-Vitasse they were so completely fagged out they did not give a damn what happened next. All they craved was some place to get a little warm food and lie down to sleep, someplace where they would be warm and dry and left alone. Out on their feet, carried along more by instinct and the skirl of their pipes and drums, they marched as best they could via Beaurains and Achecourt to a shelter at Dainville, just west of Arras. What was left of the whole Fifth Brigade was there. For the moment they were done as an effective fighting force. After what had happened to the Fifth Brigade's attempt to break through the Fresnes/Rouvroy trench system, other methods had to be devised to dispose of that problem.

The First Division found the answer a day later. On August 30th, working first through a gap further south in a British sector, it got in behind the German trench system and cleaned it out lengthwise. At the same time, the Third Division north of the road overran enemy defences on its frontage. By the night of August 30th/31st the Canadian front was firmly established another mile forward facing its next objective, the strong Drocourt-Quéant system. By then the Third Division was in much the same exhausted condition as the Second. It was replaced by the Fourth Division and a British division.

Between August 30th through September 2nd these fresh troops, in a series of brilliant attacks, broke through the whole of the Drocourt-Quéant defences. They were well out into more open country along the Canal du Nord. On the night of September 2nd/3rd the Germans gave up and withdrew behind the canal. The Canadian and British divisions advancing across country established new front lines close up to the canal banks.

The Canal du Nord, September 27th– October 11th

At Dainville from August 30th, the 25th in company with the rest of the Fifth Brigade spent the next five days resting and reorganizing. By September 4th it had received some reinforcements. While by no means back to full strength it had recovered enough to move forward again. From then until September 27th it was constantly moving over reserve and support positions in the recently captured Drocourt-Quéant area. It continued to receive reinforcements as far as they could be supplied from base camps on the channel and in England.

Work went on steadily clearing obstructions, repairing roads and building new ones. On September 27th the corps again went over to the attack. In the centre, brigades of the First and Fourth Divisions supported by British divisions on both sides successfully crossed the only dry section of the Canal du Nord and rapidly overran supporting trenches. While the First Division swung north across the Arras-Cambrai road to widen the frontage, a brigade of the Fourth Division mounted another attack. By nightfall it had taken Bourlon village and Bourlon Wood to put down a firm front further east. In that action the 85th Nova Scotia Highlanders played a decisive part by their entry and capture of Bourlon village.

Successive attacks through the night of September 30th/October 1st advanced to positions facing the Canal de L'Escaut outside Cambrai. During this period the Second Division was not engaged. It was held in reserve for use in the final smash against the city of Cambrai to follow. During the night of October 1st/2nd the First and Fourth Divisions, completely exhausted by nearly five days of continuous battle, were withdrawn. They were replaced by the well-rested Second Division.

The 25th took over from a Ninth Brigade battalion facing the village of Morenchies and a canal bridge known as the Pont d'Aire. Across the canal lay the large northeastern suburb of Cambrai called Escadoeu-vres. The Eighth Brigade of the Third Division, still at good fighting strength, remained holding the Cambrai section of Neuville St Rémy west of the canal. The rest of the Third Division was withdrawn for rest and reorganization, which by then it badly needed.

During the following six days communications were improved and preparations for crossing the canal were completed. The Fifth Brigade was set to make the first crossings. The 25th and 26th would lead with the 22nd following in close support and the 24th held in reserve. In the 25th, as darkness fell on the night of October 7th, last-minute preparations were quietly completed. The start would jump off at 1:30 a.m. on October 8th to surprise the enemy and get strong forces across the canal before heavy opposition could develop. The 25th was detailed to rush the bridges at Pont d'Aire and Morenchies. When taken, they would be left to Canadian engineers to repair and make ready for the passage of guns, tanks and other heavy equipment.

The 26th, with the 22nd following, would cross the water in the canal on hastily placed footbridges on cork floats. To help keep direction in the dark and avoid confusion of identity, the men all wore armbands of white cloth. The night turned very dark and rainy. Everything went smoothly according to plan. The surprise was complete and even more effective because it caught the Germans badly disorganized, preparing for another withdrawal. The 25th headed straight for Escadoeuvres. By nightfall it had cleared out all pockets of German rearguards to establish a firm hold well to the east of the town and north of the Cambrai-Valenciennes road.

At the same time, the 26th and 22nd were slicing through the northeastern part of the main city of Cambrai. The 4th and 6th CMRs [Canadian Mounted Regiments] of the Eighth Brigade, Third Division, broke out from Neuville St Rémy over some partly smashed bridges to keep pace through the centre of the city with the Fifth Brigade men on their right. Other troops from a British division hit the city from the south. As the day progressed, the capture of Cambrai was completed.

By the morning of October 9th it was evident that the enemy was withdrawing further toward another heavily built defence system in the general direction of Valenciennes. It did not give up easily. Whenever in a favourable position he fought strong rearguard actions. During the day the 25th and 26th pushed their advance another mile beyond Escadoeuvres toward the village of Naves. Here they were forced to halt and dig in. Reduced in strength by heavy casualties, they could not penetrate wide bands of uncut wire protecting strongly placed machine-gun posts.

On the following morning (October 10th) battalions of the Fourth Brigade were brought up from reserve to pass through the Fifth. The Germans had again withdrawn. The Fourth Brigade had little trouble clearing Naves, where the 25th and 26th had been held up the previ-

ous day. During the 10th and 11th attacks were pressed further by the
Fourth and Sixth Brigades. The Fifth was kept busy regrouping at a
chateau near Ivry.

On the 12th the Fifth Brigade went in again. With the 24th leading,
it captured the village of Hordain and advanced some further distance
toward Bouchain. The 25th moved in close support with the 26th and
22nd in reserve. Attempts to advance again on October 13th were not
successful, largely due to lack of enough effective manpower. On the
night of October 14th they moved back to billets near Marquion, where
they remained until October 17th. While there they were inspected and
thanked by the Prince of Wales and General Currie.

Valenciennes and the Pursuit to Mons

On October 17th the battalion moved forward again to billets near Cambrai. Another march on the 22nd took them northward toward Fressies
and thence from October 23rd to November 4th to Aniche. The whole
Second Division had been in corps reserve since October 19th/20th and
the First Division since October 22nd.

Meanwhile, the Third and Fourth Divisions in company with British
divisions had been in continuous action. By November 2nd they had
liberated Valenciennes and were pressing rapidly forward against the
rearguards of the retreating German forces. On November 4th the 25th
was moved by bus convoy to Anzin. On the 6th it marched through
Valenciennes to St Saulve. For that night the whole Fifth Brigade was
packed into a local seminary for shelter.

The Second Division was replacing the completely exhausted Fourth
Division. At dawn on November 7th the 25th, leading the van of the
Fifth Brigade, resumed pursuit of the retreating Germans. The 24th
followed closely in support. It was over the Belgian border, across the
Honnelle River. On that day (November 7th, 1918) the 25th carried out
its last combat action of the war. It drove the enemy out of Elouges,
almost within sight of the city of Mons.

The next day the 24th took over the lead and liberated the town of
Dour. The whole brigade then began the slow job of clearing out pockets of enemy rearguards from a series of coal mine buildings and villages facing their frontage. The Germans fought throughout the rest of
November 8th but withdrew again during the night. When the Fourth
Brigade took over the lead on November 9th the way was clear for
several miles. By nightfall it was within three or four miles of Mons.

Closely following the Fourth Brigade, the Fifth again advanced to occupy the small town of Walmes, within sight of Mons. Here it was halted to await further orders. Just ahead of it the Fourth Brigade south of the Valenciennes-Mons road and the Seventh Brigade north of it were working their way slowly into the city suburbs.

The entry into the main city was left to the Seventh Brigade while the Fourth pushed past the southern side to maintain pressure on the retreating German rearguards. During the night of November 10th/11th the historic city of Mons fell to the Canadian army. The first break-in was made about 11:00 p.m. on November 10th with entries at other points following around 2:00 a.m. on November 11th. By daylight the entire city had been cleared of all enemy resistance. When the ceasefire came into effect at 11:00 a.m. that day, the advance lines were almost five miles beyond the city limits.

Chapter Twenty-One

The Long Road Home

November 11th, 1918: The Armistice

During the afternoon and night of November 10th, while the Seventh and Fourth Brigades were working their way into Mons, the Fifth was holding about three miles away at Walmes, awaiting orders for the next move. For several days rumours of peace developments had been current. Early on the morning of November 11th the confirmation came through: all hostilities would cease at 11:00 a.m.

Troops would hold their positions at that time, maintaining fully organized control subject to further orders. As the news spread throughout the world, excitement mounted. In every city, town and village people went wild with joy. The demonstrations in places like London, Paris and New York were almost beyond description. At home in Canada people turned out everywhere to celebrate the victory which had taken over four long years and immense sacrifice in lives as well as wealth to bring to a successful end.

In contrast, the reaction in the active service battalions such as our own 25th was strangely different. After years close to the noise and turmoil of battle, the sudden silence as the fighting ceased seemed to communicate itself to the men. Ordinary military routine had to be fully maintained. Guards and sentries held to their posts. All other duties carried on as usual, with the battalion held ready for instant response to possible orders to resume the advance.

The realities were slow in reaching them. A few men got drunk but there was not very much strong drink of any kind quickly available. Here and there recently liberated civilians dug up hidden supplies of wine and shared them with the first Canadian soldiers they met. The general mood was one of relief and quiet thanks for delivery from further battle hazards.

Somehow a great deal of the meaning of their recent activities had suddenly vanished. It was much too soon for them to think clearly or deeply about the future. If there was one thought shared by every officer and man it was 'how soon will I get home and free from all the restrictions of military life?' Of all people then alive, the front-line soldiers were more quiet and showed less excitement than any others. Slowly they began to develop a feeling of relief from the tensions under which they had worked for so long. Among themselves, in small groups of close friends, their thoughts turned more toward the future.

Another strange result was that some men even experienced a feeling of dread toward return to civilian life. Their thinking went something like this. After all, the army feeds and clothes me. If I get sick or hurt there is a fine medical service ready to take care of me. None of this costs me anything. It is all free. When my turn comes, I get a leave and free transportation, with a wide choice of places to visit. I cannot be fired or lose my job. With a little care I can avoid unpleasant punishment for my military sins. Everything is decided for me and I do not have to think about it. All I need is to do what I am told without argument or question. On top of all that, $1.10 a day is good spending money with plenty of cigarettes at tax-free prices, plus generous free rum issues (not so good but still dry enough to burn and not completely choke me). Just what do I get in civilian life by way of replacement for all these blessings, particularly now that the fighting is over and the danger of being killed in action no longer exists?

The truth was that these men were dreadfully tired, almost beyond human endurance. Between August 8th and November 11th they had been fighting one battle after another for nearly 100 days. Take a look at the following list:

Battle of Amiens	August 8th to 19th
A Week Later	
Battle of Arras and the Scarpe	August 26th to September
Three Weeks Later	
Battle of the Canal du Nord and capture of Cambrai	September 27th to October 11th

Capture of Valenciennes and pursuit to Mons   October 12th to
                                                 November 11th

Is it any wonder that they were unable to immediately respond to the
news of the armistice with the same outbursts of emotion which swept
through the outside world behind them?

The March to the Rhine

The period of uncertainty following the armistice did not last very long.
On Sunday, November 17th, representatives from the 25th took part in
the great Canadian service of thanksgiving in Mons cathedral. Meanwhile, the two senior divisions (the First and Second) were preparing to
march again as part of the army of occupation in Germany. The distance
by road from Arras through Cambrai and Valenciennes to Mons was
roughly sixty-five miles. It had taken seventy-seven days of continuous battle between August 26th and November 11th. The march which
started from the Mons area on November 18th to cross the Rhine River
to the outpost lines beyond Bonn meant another 250 miles on foot.

The first fifty miles past Charleroi to Namur was not too tough.
The road was fairly good and the weather was cool but dry. The 25th,
marching as part of the Fifth Brigade, covered the distance comfortably
in a week, reaching Namur on November 25th. After that the going got
really bad. The weather changed, with day after day of cold early winter rain. The roads got worse: either narrow hard stone cobble or sticky
mud. Boots wore out with replacements next to impossible to obtain. It
was all the army service corps could do to get enough food ahead. At
times they could not even manage that, so the men went hungry and
had to make the best of it.

The way lay through the hilly forest country of the Ardennes southeast toward Germany. On December 5th, eleven days after leaving
Namur, the 25th crossed the German border at the village of Boho. Led
by Robert the Bruce ahead of the pipe band playing 'Blue Bonnets over
the Border' and with an honour guard proudly carrying the Union Jack,
the battalion marching at attention with bayonets fixed swung grandly
past a small reviewing stand. For a brief few minutes heads went up,
shoulders were squared and sore feet were forgotten.

They were the 25th from Nova Scotia. They meant every German
in sight to know it and to recognize what it meant to them that day to
be Canadians. Eight more days of weary marching, at times as far as
twenty miles a day, brought the battalion to the west bank of the Rhine.

Shortly after 10:00 a.m. on December 13th, 1918, the 25th in parade order, bayonets fixed and flag flying, crossed the Bonn-Beuel bridge. It was pouring rain as General Currie took the salute from the reviewing stand. From the bridge they went forward to take up positions in the Cologne area outpost line at Siegburg-Waldorf.

Occupation in Germany and Garrison Duty in Belgium

The duties of occupation were fairly easy. It was largely a matter of showing the flag and control of traffic between the occupied zones and the rest of Germany. The main benefit was freedom from long route marches in pouring rain, with a chance to rest and catch up on much-needed sleep. Replacements for worn-out boots and clothing were brought along as rapidly as possible. There were strict orders against any show of fraternizing with local people. The novelties of the situation wore off quickly. The Canadians were very ready in mid-January to welcome relief by other British divisions.

The 25th, along with the other Fifth Brigade units, left the Bonn area on January 19th, 1919. It moved by train back to the town of Arvelais, about ten miles west of Namur. In spite of very rough train accommodation, it was a welcome change from the long route marches going into Germany a few weeks before. On return to Belgium it was assigned to garrison duty as part of the British army reserve. Replacement of worn-out equipment continued. In a short time all the men were once more fitted with sound boots and respectable clothing.

The main problem was in finding enough to do, to prevent any serious lapse of discipline or excessive unrest. As the weeks passed, lack of definite indications of an early return to Canada made men edgy and harder to control. The Canadians were volunteers and not regular professional soldiers. As long as there was fighting to do they had accepted the necessity of military organization. In principle they agreed with the man who said, 'My father taught me how to work but he never taught me how to like it.'

In spite of some unrest, the time was not entirely wasted. The immense task of documentation in preparation for return to Canada was pushed forward as fast as the available staff could cope with it. All this work done in Belgium helped later to shorten the transit period in England. Entertainment by various concert parties, particularly the famous Dumbells[52] of the Third Division, helped to relieve the boredom

---

52 The Dumbells were a concert party formed in 1917 by members of the Third Divi-

of garrison duty during these dreary winter months of waiting. On
March 3rd, about six weeks after moving back from Bonn to Arvelais,
a divisional sports day was held at Namur. The 25th had entries in a
number of the events but without any outstanding success. The good
news finally broke in April. Orders came through to prepare for early
departure for England.

Homeward Bound

After nearly three months of semi-frustration, the battalion entrained
on April 5th en route to Le Havre. From Arvelais to England via Le
Havre took five days, including the channel crossing on April 9/10th
and train from Southampton to Witley Camp in Surrey. Preparations
were hatched for an early return to Canada. As quickly as possible all
ranks were given leave of from eight days up to two weeks. Men from
the 25th were detailed to form part of the Fifth Brigade detachment in
the great peace parade through the streets of London on May 3rd. The
salute at the march-past was taken by HM King George V.

During the following week, documentation was completed, medical
and dental clearances finished and the last pay was issued. Because of
family connections some men did not return to Canada with the battalion. They were permitted to take their discharges in England. On
May 10th the battalion went by rail to Southampton to board the giant
liner *Olympic* on the last long leg of its homeward journey. It seemed
particularly fitting that the whole four battalions of the Fifth Brigade
which had worked and fought together side by side through four long
years should return to their homeland on the same ship, still united in
their regular brigade formation.

Journey's End

At daylight on the morning of May 15th, 1919, the *Olympic* picked up its
position off the entrance to Halifax harbour. The first sight of land at the

---

sion to build the morale of Canadian troops – often on the front lines – with a program of popular songs and skits about life in the trenches. The group took its name
from the Third Division's emblem, a red dumbbell that signified strength. Many
of their patriotic songs were published, and the sheet music to their theme song,
'The Dumbell Rag,' sold more than ten thousand copies. They played a four-week
engagement in 1918 at the Coliseum in London and subsequently enjoyed a successful career in Canadian vaudeville.

end of a homeward ocean voyage always does something to any traveler with even the slightest trace of feeling and sentiment toward his own country. For all the Fifth Brigade men and particularly the Nova Scotians of the 25th Battalion, this was a moment of fulfilment of all of their dreams and longings of the past long four years.

Excitement mounted as they crowded the rails to watch the land come closer as the great ship slowly entered the harbour to make its way up to the same dock at Pier Two from which the original battalion had sailed away on the *Saxonia* on May 20th, 1915. There were hundreds of people at the ends of every wharf and pier, waving and shouting a tremendous welcome. Every ship and tugboat in the harbour had its whistle tied down at full blast. There were salutes being fired from the Citadel and the whole city was out to show its pride and affection for this special battalion of its own kith and kin.

There is not any way of conveying in words the feelings of these men as they waited for the final tie-up and the interval before the gangplanks were put down and freed. The other battalions would be going inland by train. For the 25th this was the end of its journey, so it was brought off first. As quickly as possible, it was drawn up in parade formation and moved out through the dock gates into the city streets. Led by Robert the Bruce ahead of the pipe band, it marched through wildly cheering crowds to its old home at the armory, facing the North Common at Cunard Street.

The rest of the day was spent greeting relatives and old friends. At 8:30 p.m. there was an official reception and concert. The record of service speaks for itself. It should always be preserved in memory of all those brave young men who so truly upheld the honour of their country throughout those dreadful four years. That night a few surviving members of the Thinkers' group held a last secret meeting not part of any official record. Those still alive will remember it well. No one else knows anything about it. It was a king-sized event while it lasted.

The next morning, May 16th, 1919, the battalion paraded as an organized unit for the last time. It was drawn up on the Common and after a quick inspection marched back to form up on the great floor in the armory building for the final brief ceremony. The officers were called to fall out and take positions facing their men. For a few brief seconds a strange silence prevailed. Then came the last command. The words rang out: '25th Battalion, Nova Scotia Regiment, Dismiss.' There followed the sharp turn to the right, the stamp of the heels to complete the turn, and for one split second they stood without movement. As they broke away, the great battalion which had been their home and for so long the mainspring of their being vanished into history, leaving them to face the uncertainties of the future in a cold civilian world.

Before departing for their homes in the city and throughout the province, the men were given their last pay, transportation vouchers and discharge papers. By nightfall the building was empty except for a few men staying overnight, unable to make travel connections until the next day.

The passing years have taken their toll. The roll grows shorter every year. Soon they will all be gone but each year during the week of September 15th – Courcelette Day – in some Nova Scotia town the members of the 25th Battalion Memory Club gather at a legion hall for a reunion. For a few hours the old battalion lives again. There is a parade led by a local band to the town war memorial for a short service of tribute and the laying of a legion wreath. Returning to the legion hall, old friends gather and the old stories are told and retold. The ladies of the legion branch put on a fine dinner. Then as the evening passes, they gradually break away to their homes with the silent hope that they may be spared and be well enough to make the meeting again next year.

Appendix:
Nominal Roll of Officers,
Non-Commissioned Officers
and Men of the 25th Battalion[53]

Officers

Rank	Name	Address[54]
Lieut Col	Le Cain, George Augustus	Round Hill
Lieut Col	Sponagle, John Addy	Middleton
Major	Bauld, Duncan Stanley	Halifax
Major	Conrod, William Humphrey	Halifax
Major	Jones, Alfred Nagle	Halifax
Major	MacKenzie, James Grant	Westville
Major	MacRae, Donald Alexander	Baddeck
Major	MacKenzie, Lawrence Howard	Stellarton

53 This list includes the original officers, non-commissioned officers, and enlisted men of the 25th Battalion and is based on a document published by the Department of Militia in 1915. However, cross-checking with the *Soldiers of the First World War* and *Virtual War Memorial* website databases revealed several errors, which have been corrected. The symbol + next to a name indicates that the man was killed in action or subsequently died from his injuries. It should be remembered that approximately 4,500 additional men served in the battalion during the course of the war.

54 The addresses listed here were those given by the men when they enlisted and usually are those of their next of kin, not necessarily their own place of residence. Unless otherwise indicated, all addresses are in Nova Scotia. It should be noted that those whose home addresses were outside Nova Scotia enlisted in the province. Many such men were former Nova Scotians who returned home in order to enlist. Those who gave British addresses had immigrated at some point prior to 1914 and were living in Nova Scotia in 1914.

Major	Weston, Arthur William P.	Halifax
Captain	Graham, Edwin Ernest	Arcadia
Captain	Holt, Charles Wesley	Amherst
Captain	Logan, Jotham Wilbert	Truro
Hon Captain	MacPherson, Donald[55]	Sydney Mines
Captain	Margeson, Joseph Willis	Bridgewater
Captain	Medcalfe, William Bolton	Halifax
Captain	Purney, Willard Parker	Liverpool
Captain	Tupper, James Howard+	Bridgetown
Captain	Whitford, Walter Lyon+	Chester
Lieutenant	Brooks, Ernest John+	England
Lieutenant	Bullock, Lawrence Newsom	Saskatoon
Lieutenant	Cameron, William Archibald	Saint John
Lieutenant	De Lancey, James Arnold+	Middleton
Lieutenant	Eville, Claude Kirkby	Birchdale
Lieutenant	Grant, James Alan	Halifax
Lieutenant	Grant, James Warren	Amherst
Lieutenant	Johnstone, Lewis Howard+	Sydney
Lieutenant	Longley, Harold Graham	Paradise
Lieutenant	MacAloney, Charles William	Halifax
Lieutenant	Morgan, Elmer	Bear River
Lieutenant	Mosher, Clarence Moyle	Mahone Bay
Lieutenant	Murphy, Vincent Patrick+	New Ross
Lieutenant	McKay, Kenneth L.	Inverness
Lieutenant	McKinnon, Dougald	Woodbine
Lieutenant	McLeod, Harvey A.	Salt Springs
Lieutenant	MacNeil, Gordon Michael	Iona
Lieutenant	McNeil, John Donald	Sydney
Lieutenant	Newnham, Thomas F.	Halifax
Lieutenant	Roberts, George Edgar	England
Lieutenant	Smith, Bronwin Howard	Halifax
Lieutenant	Stairs, John Cuthbert+	Halifax
Lieutenant	Tanner, Frederick Inglis	Pictou
Lieutenant	Young, George Renny	Kentville

---

55 Born in Boisdale, Cape Breton, Rev. Donald MacPherson (1872–1959) was a Catholic priest who joined the 25th Battalion in April 1915 as a chaplain. He had previously served for three years as chaplain to Cape Breton's 94th Militia Regiment. Chaplains were given the honorary rank of captain. MacPherson subsequently rose to the honorary rank of major.

Other Ranks

67315		Adams, Horace W.	Brookfield
67004	L Sgt	Adamson, John Alexander	Westville
67629		Addicott, Thomas	New Aberdeen
68286		Adey, Enoch B.+	Adytown, NL
68271		Adshade, David William	Collingwood Corner
67968	L Cpl	Akins, William Alexander	Falmouth
68041		Allan, Adam+	Sydney Mines
67522		Anderson, De Blois	Bridgetown
68088		Anderson, George+	Birkenhead, England
67775		Anderson, Greatorex Frederick	Annapolis Royal
67094		Anderson, Robert N.	Dipper Harbour, NB
67093	Cpl	Anderson, Thomas+	Montrose, Scotland
67242		Anderson, William	Westville
67521		Anderson, William Clyde+	Sydney
67131		Andrews, Alfred	Upper Gullies, NL
68177		Andrews, Sydney	Stellarton
68082		Anthony, James	Paisley, Scotland
68060		Appleton, John George+	Westville
67210		Arbuckles, William	New Glasgow
67741	Cpl	Armitage, Arthur Edwin+	Halifax
67700		Armstrong, William Banford	Burlington
67586		Arsenault, Angus	Abrams Village, PE
68287		Arthrell, William Gerald+	Broughton
67835		Ashworth, John+	Reading, MA, USA
68039		Atkins, Murley	Darling's Lake
67842		Atwood, George Lamont	Dartmouth
68070		Auld, George	New Delaval, England
67312		Aulenback, Harold B.	Maitland Forks
68132		Austin, Otis Frederick	Collingwood Corner
67215		Baigent, Harry	Portsmouth, England
68405		Bailey, Aaron+	Old Bonaventure, NL
67538		Bailey, Ernest	Trinity, NL
67794		Bailey, Newton	Newhampton, England
68220		Bain, Edmund	Digby
68275		Bain, William+	New Aberdeen
68470		Baird, Charles	Dalwellington, Scotland
68360		Baker, Harry Singleton	Arcadia
67851		Barkhouse, John Henry	Kentville

67121		Barlow, Arthur	Denaby Main, England
68282		Barlow, Herbert James	Glace Bay
68453		Barnes, Frank	Edmonton, AB
67655		Barteaux, Ervine Lester+	Morristown
67108		Bartlett, Leo	Sydney
67411		Bates, Mark Wilfred+	Louisbourg
67451		Beaton, John S.+	New Waterford
68008		Beattie, John Rorison	Sydney Mines
68240		Beck, John	Ardwich, England
68402		Beck, John Cecil	Halifax
67591		Bedford, Andrew	North Sydney
67774	Sgt	Beeler, Gordon Lester	Lequille
67452	Cpl	Bell, Jacob	Sydney Mines
67572		Belliveau, Anthony	Lower West Pubnico
68388		Bennett, Charles Clarence	Halifax
67782	CQM-Sgt	Bennett, Charles W.	Halifax
67819		Bennett, Edgar Cecil+	Halifax
68128	L Cpl	Bennett, Harold Wilfred+	Halifax
67852		Bennett, Hugh	Sydney Mines
68398		Bennett, William	Port Caledonia
67752	Cpl	Bensted, Harry George	England
67625		Bezanson, Howard	Sydney
67622		Billard, William Gordon	North Sydney
68235		Bills, Edward+	Walsall, England
		Bing, Edward Charles Cameron+	New Southgate, England
67193	Sgt	Bird, Steve Carman+	Amherst
67821		Birkenhead, William James	Halifax
67160		Bishara, Gabriel+	Saint John
67817		Black, Charles Aubrey	Amherst
67338		Black, Elmer	Linden
67796		Blackburn, Edward	Halifax
67224		Blair, Gordon	Stellarton
67788	Sgt	Blakeney, Harold Kingsbury	Halifax
67346	L Cpl	Blakney, Ora W.	Hilden
67618		Blehr, Otto+	Sydney
67813		Blenkhorn, Lorne Glen	Canning
67124		Bliss, Dennison Dorr	Amherst
67288		Bolivar, Joseph	Lunenburg
67701		Bonang, Harry	Halifax
67035		Borden, Wilkie	Westville

67853	Boudreau, William	Maria, NB
68214	Boulter, Edward	Sydney Mines
68192	Boulter, John	Sydney Mines
67214	Bourges, John+	Asnières, France
68036	Boutilier, James	Springhill
68272	Boutilier, John Jacob	Dartmouth
68288	Boutilier, William	Caledonia
67734 Sgt	Bowen, John William	Paterson, NJ, USA
68081	Bowen, Walter	Landore, Wales
67384	Bowser, Victor Andrew	Ship Harbour Lake
68444	Boyd, Alexander	Sydney Mines
67898	Bradbury, John W.	Birmingham, England
67751	Bragg, Charles	Halifax
67388	Brain, Charles A.	Swindon, England
68429	Brand, David	Halifax
68432	Brand, William	Halifax
67511	Brennan, Guy	Halifax
67910	Brewer, Thomas William	New Waterford
67743 Sgt	Brice, John R.	Halifax
67424	Brogan, Frank	Sydney Mines
68161	Brogan, Patrick	Sydney Mines
68094 L Cpl	Bromly, Arthur	Palmer's Green, England
67762	Brooks, Albert Edward	Halifax
67892	Brown, Frederick	Parrsboro
68010	Brown, George	Florence
67176	Brown, George	Sydney Mines
67913	Brown, George H.	Sydney Mines
68454	Brown, Harry	Windsor
67391	Brown, Hugh D.	Hoodstown, Scotland
67072	Brown, James+	New York, NY, USA
68027	Brunt, Vincent+	Halifax
68290	Brushett, Colin	New Aberdeen
67700	Bryant, Frederick	Pictou
67303	Brydle, Frederick James	Mount Uniacke
68289	Buckley, Frank Henry	Glace Bay
67147	Buckley, Murdock	East Margaree
67195	Budd, Victor Percy	Eastney, England
68411	Budger, Harry	Halifax
67136	Burchell, Robert	Halifax
68247	Burke, Ambrose	North Sydney

67759		Burke, Bernard Frederick+	Portuguese Cove
68157		Burkholder, Nathan H.	Osterville, MA, USA
68392		Burns, James	Halifax
67975		Burns, Jonathan+	New Waterford
67606		Burrage, Abraham	Neil's Harbour
68292		Burridge, William	New Haven
68291		Burton, Norman	Twillingate, NL
67714		Butler, James Kenneth+	Berwick
68058		Byrne, John	Halifax
67069		Byrne, William+	St Peter's Bay, PE
67014		Cain, Robert	Liverpool, England
67605		Caldwell, Charles	New Waterford
67758		Callow, Edward	Halifax
68259		Cameron, Edward Daniel+	Sydney
67532		Campbell, Angus	Campbell's Mountain
68343		Campbell, Charles Smith+	Glace Bay
67382		Campbell, Cyril	Amherst
67434		Campbell, George McKay	Truro
67703		Campbell, John	Sydney
68188		Campbell, John	Bowhill, Scotland
67146	Cpl	Campbell, Murdoch G.	Whycocomagh
68465		Cann, James	Sydney Mines
68346		Cann, James+	Glace Bay
67192	Sgt	Canning, Ernest	Maccan
68239		Cant, James	Dundee, Scotland
67138		Carmichael, Andrew	Coalburn, Scotland
68278		Carmichael, David Kenneth+	Northeast Margaree
67831		Carr, Edward Francis	Halifax
67970		Carr, William	Sydney Mines
67267		Carrigan, Daniel	Westville
68446		Carruthers, George+	Sydney Mines
68445		Carruthers, Joseph E.	Sydney Mines
68139		Carson, John	Greenock, Scotland
67977		Casey, John	Kilkenny, Ireland
68102		Chalmers, George+	Turriff, Scotland
67188		Chapman, George+	Amherst
68265		Chew, Frank Arthur	Shoeburyness, England
68012		Chiasson, Arthur	New Waterford
67617		Chiasson, Harrison	New Waterford
67165	Cpl	Chipman, Donald	Yarmouth

67186		Chisholm, Alexander William	Amherst
68387		Chisholm, Joseph Martin	Long Point
68001		Christie, John	Cromarty, Scotland
67489		Clamp, Harry Edward	Carsholton, England
67588		Clark, Bestwick+	Halifax
67769		Clark, Frank Avery[56]	Windsor
68074		Clark, James	Liverpool, England
68067		Clark, John M.	Victoria Vale
68379		Clarke, Ernest	Manchester, England
67236		Clay, George+	Westville
68433		Clements, Robert J.	Kingston, ON
67156	CQM-Sgt	Clements, Robert Nehemiah	Yarmouth
67032		Clemson, Charles	London, England
67955		Cockburn, George	New Waterford
67632		Cockburn, William	New Waterford
67841	Sgt	Collings, John Francis Patrick+	Dartmouth
67272		Collins, Edgar	Florence
67539		Colpitts, Fenwick	Moncton
67049		Comstock, Carl De Wolfe	Hantsport
67041		Connolly, Edward Lewis	Milford Haven Bridge
68098		Cook, Arthur Hilton	Ohio
67207		Cook, Clarence	Ohio
68252		Cook, George	North Sydney
68422		Cook, James	Halifax
68145		Coolen, Ross Curvin	Halifax
68000		Corbin, Raymond John	Weymouth
67400		Corkery, Richard+	Sydney Mines
68293		Corkum, John William	New Aberdeen
68013		Corkum, Wyeth Herbert	Bridgewater
67329		Cormier, Archibald	Grand Etang
67180		Corr, James Francis	Emerald Junction, PE
68384		Covey, Milton	Indian Harbour
68133		Cowan, Thomas	Dublin, Ireland
67650		Crane, Frank	Sydney Mines
67799		Creelman, Harry Eugene	Old Barns
67222		Culton, Reginald	Stellarton
67290	Cpl	Cunningham, Michael	Ballinasloe, Ireland

---

56 The 25th Battalion war diary reports that he died in December 1915, but he survived
the war and died in Windsor in 1945.

68464		Curnew, Benjamin	North Sydney
67933		Currie, Bernard	Glace Bay
67448		Currie, John Dan	Stellarton
68295		Currie, Ronald	Glace Bay
68410		Curtis, Charles+	New Basford, England
68294		Curtis, William+	Glace Bay
67854		Cuzner, Joseph	Sydney Mines
68276		Dakin, Francis	Wincobank, England
68126		Daley, John Byron	Fredericton, NB
67021		Dalley, George Austin	Sault Ste Marie, ON
67054		Daniels, Robert	London, England
68365		Dart, Edward	Halifax
67776		Davidson, Peter	Aberdeen, Scotland
67240	L Cpl	Davies, Edward	Westville
67080		Davies, Joseph	Newton, England
68195		Dawe, Benjamin	Sydney Mines
68447		Dawe, James L	Florence
68350		Dawe, Walter	Conception Bay, NL
68249		Dawe, William B.+	Sydney
68253		Dawson, Charles	Sydney
67601		Daye, Samuel	North Sydney
67613		Dean, John+	Pilley's Island, NL
68243		Dean, Kerr	Accrington, England
67464		Dease, Everett	Yarmouth
68406		DeBay, Howard	Ship Harbour
67309		Delaney, Hiram Frederick+	Yarmouth
68213		Delaney, William+	New Waterford
67900		Deveau, John	Yarmouth
67683		De Wolfe, Alfred B.	Stellarton
67260		Dickens, Henry+	Birmingham, England
67855		Dickie, Ebenezer C.	Kingsport
67856		Dickie, Harry Burgess+	Lower Canard
67416		Diggins, Michael+	Sydney Mines
68077		Dillon, John Newland	Leith, Scotland
67857		Dixon, James	Glace Bay
67988	Sgt	Dobson, Arthur Wesley	Amherst
67008		Dolan, John D.+	Washington, DC, USA
67042		Dolan, Michael	New York, NY, USA
68297		Donaldson, John	West Bay
67331		Donaldson, Robert Burns+	Nappan Station

67712	Donovan, Arthur	Sydney
68342	Donovan, Colin Francis	New Aberdeen
67914	Dorey, Lewis William	St Margaret's Bay
68436	Dorion, Pius+	North Sydney
67858 Sgt	Dorman, Lloyd Arthur+	Newtonville
68395	Doubleday, Percy John+	Halifax
68335	Doucette, William Charles	New Aberdeen
67068	Douglas, Alexander H.	London, England
67698	Doward, Joseph Henry	Glace Bay
68004	Dowdy, Edward James	Westville
67732	Dowell, George	Leicester, England
67334	Dowling, Venanties	Amherst
68061 L Cpl	Down, James Frederick	Margaretsville
68101	Doyle, Michael	Sydney
67925	Duffett, Albert George+	St John's, NL
67299	Dunphy, Lawrence	Trepassey, NL
67241	Duncan, Alexander+	Manchester, England
67536	Dunne, James+	Dominion
67341	Dupuis, Benjamin	Amherst
67573	Dwyer, Thomas	Conception Bay, NL
68176	Dymond, John Henry	Halifax
67321	Eaton, Scott	Canning
67343	Eaton, Stewart B.+	Granville Ferry
68361	Edmonds, George Francis	Bridgewater
68030	Edmunds, Frank	Sydney Mines
68069	Edwards, Frank	Glace Bay
68035	Elsworth, Daniel	Springhill
67563	Embree, George W.+	Port Hawkesbury
67755	Emery, Calvin	Port Hawkesbury
67157	Emin, Leslie	Yarmouth
68298	England, James	Glace Bay
67336	England, Otto	Amherst
67410	Erickson, John	Florence
67969	Ernst, James	Halifax
67922	Erving, Joseph	Newferry, England
68355	Etchells, Ezra	New Waterford
67593	Etchells, Frederick	New Waterford
68356	Etchells, Joseph+	New Waterford
67556	Etchells, Peter	New Waterford
68389	Evans, Jack	North Vancouver, BC

68381	Fagan, Peter	Montreal, QC
67783	Fage, James	Hastings
67155	Falt, Millard	Yarmouth
67797	Farley, Albert John	Halifax
67120	Farmer, Isaiah	Conisborough, England
68014	Farquharson, John Archibald	Sydney
68427	Farrell, John+	Miles Platting, England
67859	Farrell, Philip+	Glace Bay
67181	Faulds, James+	Springhill
67952 L Cpl	Faulkenham, Byron	Dalhousie West
68367	Faulkner, Charles Gordon	Dartmouth
67166	Fells, Roy	Yarmouth
68057	Fenwick, Robert	Westville
67587	Ferguson, Frank+	Broughton
68423	Ferguson, Harold McCully+	Halifax
67860	Ferguson, James G.	New Waterford
67443	Ferguson, John+	Louisbourg
67765	Fillmore, Carroll	Collingwood Corner
68419	Finn, Patrick+	Halifax
67311	Fisher, Aubrey Clair+	Newton Mills
67172 L Cpl	Fisher, Thomas	Montreal, QC
68437	Flanagan, Abraham George+	Bass River, NB
67505	Flanagan, Thomas	Halifax
67949	Fleming, James	Bathgate, England
68233	Fleming, John Robert	Letterkenny, Ireland
67269	Fleming, Lawrence	New Aberdeen
67099	Fletcher, John	Halifax
67111	Fogarty, Albert	Sydney
68223	Fogarty, James A.	Hazel Hill
67428	Follett, William Henry+	Conception Bay, NL
67158	Forbes, Andrew	Yarmouth
67592	Forbes, Cedric E.	Sydney
68228	Forbes, James R.	New Glasgow
68461	Fortune, Frank	Sydney Mines
67114	Foster, David	Springhill
67542	Foster, Thomas	London, England
67218 Sgt	Frampton, Robert+	Stellarton
67265	Frampton, Victor	New Glasgow
67884	Francis, John T.	Halifax
68052	Fraser, Cyril Jeremiah	Halifax

67344	Fraser, John W.	Springhill
67911	Fraser, William J.	Mulgrave
68234	Frizzell, Percy Lyman	Glace Bay
67502	Frizzell, Vernon M.	Winnipeg, MB
68015	Fullerton, James	Saltcoats, Scotland
68160	Gaddes, Alexander	Florence
68268	Galloway, Graham	Halifax
67433	Ganner, Michael	Dartmouth
68450	Gardiner, Andrew+	Sydney Mines
67066	Gardiner, Horace E.	Upper Gagetown, NB
68299	Gardiner, John+	New Aberdeen
68340	Gardiner, Joseph+	Glace Bay
67563	Gardner, George	Halifax
68251	Gardner, Michael+	Sydney Mines
67097	Gass, Cyril	Shubenacadie
67275	Gear, James	Salmon Cove, NL
67031 Cpl	Gibbons, Henry	Roseville, Australia
67238	Gibbons, Robert	Westville
68093	Gibson, Ernest	London, England
67725	Gibson, Lawrie B.	Parrsboro
67306	Giles, Matthew+	Yarmouth
67399	Gill, Isaac E.	Earsdon, England
68417	Gillis, Alexander	New Waterford
68417	Giroux, Gedeon	Black Lake, QC
68233	Gledhill, Thomas	Broughton
67702	Glover, James+	Sydney Mines
67177	Godartt, James	Weymouth
67720	Godbold, Herbert William	Coventry, England
67753	Goddard, Louis+	Halifax
68175	Golding, Lewis	New Aberdeen
67888	Goodwin, Courtney	Baie Verte, NB
67159	Gordon, Albert+	Yarmouth
67113	Gordon, Ernest	Sydney Mines
67554	Gordon, William George	Sydney
67724	Gould, John William	Amherst
68341	Gouthro, John	Glace Bay
67202	Graham, Jerome	Murray Hbr North, PE
67729	Grant, Ernest Robert	Gabarus
67102	Grant, Frederick Edwin	Sydney
68125	Grant, James William	Amherst

67162		Graves, Richard	Yarmouth
68401		Gray, Albert Sydney	Prince's Lodge
67512	L Cpl	Gray, Mitchell	Methil, Scotland
67912		Gray, Robert+	Sydney Mines
67937		Grayley, George William	Lockeport
68121		Grimmer, Walter Parker	St Stephen, NB
67442		Groves, John Dan+	New Aberdeen
67417		Guthro, Levi	Sydney Mines
67348	Sgt	Guy, Basil John Taylor	Joggins Mines
68370		Guy, George William	Birmingham, England
68369		Guy, John+	Birmingham, England
67861	L Cpl	Haddow, Samuel+	Cambuslang, Scotland
67353		Haigh, Albert	Joggins Mines
68111		Hall, Gordon William+	Bridgewater
68078	L Cpl	Hall, Harry	Southall, England
68117		Hall, John Raymond	Sheet Harbour
68368		Hall, William Eaton	Arbroath, Scotland
68129		Hallamore, Sidney Raymond	Middle Cornwall
68201		Hamilton, James	Sydney Mines
68147		Handley, Frederick	Halifax
68393		Hannan, Peter Edward+	Halifax
67350		Harding, Albert James+	Bournemouth, England
68207		Harding, George Albert	Paradise
67294		Harlow, Glen Allan	Sable River
68441		Harnett, Thomas Mussen	West Orange, NJ, USA
67772		Harnish, Guy Prescott	Lequille
67640		Harper, Charles	Wales, UK
67173	Sgt	Harper, John	Old Hill, England
67124	Sgt	Harper, Samson	New Waterford
68038		Harris, Ernest+	Bonavista, NL
68267		Harris, James Henry+	Halifax
67811		Hartling, Aubrey William	Port Dufferin
67503		Harvey, John+	Truro
68300		Harvey, Michael	St Mary's, NL
68200		Hastie, William	Sydney Mines
67286		Hatch, Elmore	River John
67552		Hatcher, Daniel	North Sydney
67978		Hatfield, Alfred Parker	Smith's Cove
67302	Cpl	Hatfield, Arthur Wellsley+	Sand Beach
67716		Hawdon, William Charles	Amherst

67248	Sgt	Hawes, George Edmund	Westville
67906		Hay, Alexander L.+	Kilmaurs, Scotland
67194		Hayes, Chester+	Trail, BC
68237		Hayes, William	New Aberdeen
67803		Hayes, William Henry	Halifax
67262		Hayler, Albert+	New Glasgow
68301		Healey, Martin	Holyrood, NL
67477		Heaver, John	Brighton, England
67012		Henderson, Duncan+	Kintyre, Scotland
68467		Henneberry, Edward	Mullinavatt, Ireland
68466		Henneberry, William	Mullinavatt, Ireland
67475		Hennessy, Alonzo	Springhill
68079		Henry, James	Victoria, BC
67092	Sgt	Henry, John Francis	Halifax
68426		Hernon, Edward	Halifax
68054		Herron, David	Blantyre, Scotland
67296		Hersey, Adelbert+	Yarmouth
67163		Hersey, William	Yarmouth
67196		Hervey, George Edward	Round Hill
67829	L Cpl	Hetherington, William Lancelot	Dartmouth
68236		Higgins, Herbert	Stellarton
67931		Higgins, Hugh L.	Sydney Mines
67672		Higgins, John+	Hough, Ireland
67932		Higgins, Michael	Glasgow, Scotland
67488		Hignett, Irwin	Pawtucket, RI, USA
68400		Hill, Albert+	Halifax
68273		Hill, John Henry	Chesterfield, England
67845		Hill, John Richard	Sydney
67480	Sgt	Hills, Gerald George	Leytonstone, England
67998		Hilton, William Henry+	Halifax
67830		Hiltz, Clifton A.+	Kingsport
67862		Hiltz, Harry Wentworth	Kingsport
67863	C Sgt-M	Hinchcliffe, Frank W.+	New Glasgow
67326	C Sgt-M	Hire, Walter	Amherst
67584		Hockley, Charles William	Halifax
67664		Hodges, Herbert Norman	Berwick
67950		Hodgkinson, John	Shenley, England
68186		Hodgkinson, Joseph+	Shenley, England
67465		Hogg, Donald	RFD 2, Yarmouth Co
68337		Holland, John	McKay's Corner

68428		Holland, John Stanley	Aylesford
67789		Hollands, James George	Halifax
67749		Holmes, Charles Beckett	Halifax
68471		Holmes, George Ranfield+	Pitsmoor, England
67393		Hood, Arthur W.	Yarmouth
67349		Hood, Ernest+	Joggins Mines
68281		Hooper, Charles A.	Small Heath, England
67243		Hooper, William	Stellarton
68042		Hopley, Thomas	New Glasgow
68441		Horne, Wilbert	Charlottetown, PE
67549	Cpl	Houghton, Archibald	Sydney
67381	Cpl	Houghton, John Caswell+	Church Street
67052		Howell, John Henry	London, England
67467		Hubbard, Edward+	Yarmouth
68187		Hughes, Reginald	Coleford, England
67380	Cpl	Hughes, William	Somerset
67864		Hulme, George	Little Bras d'Or
67116		Hulme, James	Little Bras d'Or
67926	CQM-Sgt	Hunt, Charles Wilfrid	Chertsey, England
67889	Cpl	Hunter, Bruce	Athol
67184		Hunter, Roy	Amherst
67723		Hunting, John Alfred	Greenwich, England
67387		Hurley, Thomas Dennis	Halifax
67760		Hurrell, William	Thornvale
68438		Hutchinson, Hugh Eldred	East New Annan
68091		Imber, Sidney	Brixton, England
68154		Ingram, Thomas Frederick	Wavertree, England
67419		Ives, George	Sydney Mines
67550		Jack, Douglas	North Sydney
68244		Jack, Edward+	Sydney
68185		Jackson, Alfred+	Mexborough, England
68164		Jackson, Daniel	Sydney Mines
67045		Jackson, Leonard	Bromley, England
67254		Jackson, Thomas Nicholson	Westville
67738		Jeffrey, Heber	Pleasant Lake
67134	L Cpl	Jenkins, Alfred H.	Llangattock, Wales
68123	L Cpl	Jenner, Hugh Berton	Truro
67363	L Cpl	Johns, William G.	St Paul, MN, USA
68469		Johnson, Albert+	Brighton, England
68458		Johnson, Thomas	Florence

68459		Johnstone, Robert	Sydney Mines
67114		Jones, Arthur	Florence
67084		Jones, John Henry	Halifax
68130		Joudrey, Charles+	Liverpool
67801		Just, William+	Halifax
67802		Kane, Thomas Bernard	Amherst
67954		Karney, William	New Waterford
67352		Kay, Joseph	River Hebert
67153		Keeley, William+	Sydney
68062		Kelly, Douglas	Central Clarence
68303		Kelly, James+	Fox Harbour, NL
68404		Kennedy, James+	Halifax
68304		Kennedy, Joseph Patrick	Reserve Mines
67119		Kennedy, Nicholas+	Dominion
68377		Kernaghan, Francis	Murroe, Ireland
68026		Kernick, John Joseph	Sydney Mines
67089		Kidston, William Foster	Spryfield
67175		King, Ernest	Sydney Mines
67791		King, Leslie John	Harcourt, NB
68302		King, Percy+	Twillingate, NL
67836		King, Raymond	Walthamstow, England
67290	Sgt	King, Roy Hiddlestone+	Lunenburg
68455		Kinsman, Maxwell Everett	Centreville
67079		Kirkwood, Thomas C.	Beith, Scotland
67233	Sgt	Kitchen, Richard	Stellarton
67915		Kizer, Frank D.+	Round Hill
67853		Knight, Douglas Bruce	Halifax
67899		Knowlton, Charles	Oxford
67778		Laird, John+	West Hartlepool, England
67764		Lake, Harry	Greenmount, Ireland
67190		Lamy, James Ora	Amherst
67763		Larder, Clinton Bannerman	Halifax
67893		La Schiuma, John	Parrsboro
67606		Lavery, Arthur	Sydney Mines
67807		Lawson, Patrick John	Halifax
67866		Leahy, Thomas+	Halifax
67896		Leben, Leo	Truro
68306		Le Blanc, Armour	Saint John, NB
67360		Ledingham, Alexander Rogers	St John's, NL
68305		Legett, William Henry	Springhill

67212	Le Lacheur, John Horace	New Glasgow
67082	Lesbirel, Edward	Halifax
68457	Levy, Thomas F.	Windsor
67795 Cpl	Lewin, Richard C.+	Northampton, England
67396	Lewis, Leonard Fash+	Sydney
67565	Lewis, Ralph	St John's, NL
68216	Lingley, James E.	Paradise
67189	Linsdell, Charles Frederick+	Amherst
67551	Little, Ernest+	Stellarton
67559 Sgt	Livingstone, James	Big Glace Bay
67351	Lloyd, John	Rhydymwyn, Wales
67229	Lockhart, Percy	Newville
68143	Lockie, Hugh+	Edinburgh, Scotland
67833 Sgt	Logan, Howard Everett+	Halifax
67440	Lord, George	Grantham, England
67337	Lorette, Abner	Amherst
67024	Lowe, Arthur Ernest	Halifax
68152	Lowe, Joseph	Halifax
68225	Lumsden, Clarence B.	Canso
67497	Lynch, Andrew John	Trinity Bay, NL
67389	Lynch, Daniel	Halifax
67037	Lynch, George+	Halifax
67235	McAllister, Charles+	Westville
67386 L Sgt	MacArthur, William John	Port Williams
67567	McAskill, Daniel Allen	Glace Bay
67498	McAulay, Angus D.	Little Narrows
67496	McAulay, Kenneth Archibald	Glace Bay
67646	McAulay, Lewis Daniel	Sydney Mines
68018	McAulay, Thomas	Troon, Scotland
67806	McClure, W.[57]	
67784	McCullum, Charles Roy	Hastings
67934	McDaniel, Peter	Margaree Forks
67005	McDermott, John	Halifax
67187	McDermott, Percy	Amherst
68049	McDonald, Alexander	Sydney Mines
67413	McDonald, Alexander Rorie	Sydney Mines

57 There is no information on him in either the Nominal Roll or the *Soldiers of the First World War* database, but this may be William C. McClure, who was born at Moose River, Nova Scotia, in 1874 and was living in Amerset when he married in 1906.

67127	Cpl	MacDonald, Allan	Mira Gut
67666		McDonald, Archibald	Glace Bay
67333	Sgt	McDonald, Benjamin F.	Amherst
68391		MacDonald, Burton	Sherbrooke
67648		McDonald, Charles H.	Glace Bay
67523		MacDonald, Cyril	Sydney
67627	Cpl	McDonald, Daniel D.+	Beinn Bhreagh
50442		McDonald, Daniel	Sydney Mines
68352		McDonald, Daniel Joseph	Grand Narrows
68277		McDonald, Daniel Murray	Glace Bay
68037		McDonald, Daniel R.+	New Waterford
68311		McDonald, David	Dominion
68109		McDonald, Duncan	Sydney
67412		McDonald, Edward+	New Aberdeen
67395		MacDonald, Finlay	Sydney
67518		MacDonald, Frederick Burt	Sydney
67070		McDonald, John	Halifax
68006		McDonald, John Hector	Truro
68151	L Cpl	McDonald, John Henry	Springhill
67404		McDonald, John Nelson	Dominion
68316		McDonald, Neil	Glace Bay
67624		McDonald, Ronald Campbell	Caledonia Mines
67585		McDonald, William Douglas	Glace Bay
67602		McDougall, Albert	New Waterford
68270		McDougall, Michael	Grand Mira
67679	Sgt	McDowell, Andrew	Bally Kelly, Ireland
67621	Cpl	McEachen, Allan F.	North Sydney
68349		McEachern, Alexander	North Sydney
67115		McEachern, Daniel	Riverton, PE
67060		MacEachern, Warren+	Sydney
68418		McEachran, Archibald+	Victoria, BC
68442		McEwan, William	Florence
67509		McGrath, Lloyd	Port Wade
67223		McGrath, Rufus+	Stellarton
67110		McGregor, Alfred Vincent	Sydney Mines
67106		Macgregor, Andrew	Leith, Scotland
67564	C Sgt-M	McGregor, Frank	Cain's Bay
67104		McGuigan, Frederick	Sydney
67139		MacInnis, Gordon L.	Mira Gut
68317		McInnis, John	Glace Bay

67140		McInnis, John C.+	Quebec City, QC
67457		McInnis, Joseph+	Glace Bay
68142		MacIntosh, Henry Duncan	Lunenburg
68029		McIntosh, Norman	Sydney Mines
67128		MacIntyre, Alexander James	Sydney
68205		McIntyre, Allan+	Ben Eoin
67525		McIntyre, John+	Florence
68338		MacIntyre, John William	Reserve Mines
67547		McIntyre, Roderick	Sydney Mines
67948		McIntyre, Ronald	Sydney Mines
67947		McIsaac, Archibald	New Waterford
67277		McIsaac, Archibald+	Inverness
67234		McKay, Henry G.	Westville
67529	L Cpl	MacKay, Hugh	Big Intervale
68195		McKeigan, Angus James	Sydney Mines
68280		McKeigan, John A.+	Glace Bay
68354		McKenzie, Francis	Glace Bay
67688		McKenzie, James William	New Glasgow
67402		McKenzie, John	Sydney
67548		Mackenzie, John+	Glasgow, Scotland
68320		McKenzie, John James	Caledonia Mines
67531		McKenzie, Leo+	New Glasgow
67347		McKim, William Ellis+	Brookdale
67582		McKinlay, John	Revere, MA, USA
67694		McKinlay, Wilfrid	Sydney
68322		McKinnon, Allen+	Sydney
67566		McKinnon, Hugh+	Beaver Cove
68440		McKinnon, James Burton	Truro
67909		McKinnon, John C.+	North Sydney
68345		McKinnon, Malcolm John+	Glace Bay
67561		McKinnon, Neil A.	Beaver Cove
67323		McKinnon, Roderick	Sydney Forks
67920		McKinnon, Victor Clarence	Mill Village
67270		McKinnon, William	Sydney
67122		MacKinnon, William V.	Sydney Mines
68359		McLean, Daniel Jacob+	Glace Bay
67179		Maclean, Frank John	West River
67563		McLean, John Archibald+	South Bar
68339		McLean, Lauchlin A.	Glace Bay
68127		MacLean, Neil Archibald+	Big Island
67407		McLean, Peter	Glace Bay

68449	McLean, Peter J.	Sydney Mines
68183	McLean, Robert	Reserve Mines
67946	McLellan, Alexander	New Waterford
67213	McLellan, Daniel	Trenton
67560	McLeod, Jack	Grand River
67685 Cpl	McLeod, Kenneth	Sydney Mines
67394	McLeod, Samuel	Coxheath
67717 Sgt	McLeod, William Roy+	Bridgetown
67818	McMullen, Bert R.	Shubenacadie
67415	MacMullin, Daniel	Sydney Mines
68386	MacNamara, Herbert	Halifax
68072	McNeil, Angus	Dominion
68248	McNeil, Angus	Janesville
67895	McNeil, Daniel James	River Hebert
67890	McNeil, Hugh+	River Hebert
67678	McNeil, James	Hamilton, Scotland
68336	McNeil, James+	Glace Bay
68310	McNeil, John	Caledonia Mines
68312	McNeil, John	New Aberdeen
67870	McNeil, John A.+	New Waterford
68319	McNeil, John Joseph	New Aberdeen
67630	MacNeil, John Murdoch+	Montreal, QC
67623 L Sgt	McNeil, Murdock A.	Gillies Point East
67612	MacNeil, Stanley	Sydney
67990	McNeil, Thomas	Westville
67409	McNeill, John O.	Sydney
67030	McNeill, Malcolm	Halifax
67607	McNeill, Robert	New Waterford
67938	McPhee, Hugh	Sydney
68197	McPhee, Hugh Archibald	Sydney Mines
67904	McPhee, Joseph S.	Sydney
67634	McPherson, Angus+	Bridgeport
68009	McPherson, James	New Waterford
67244 Cpl	McPherson, James Bedford	Westville
68112	MacPherson, Lloyd	Oxford
67459	McPherson, William	Sydney Mines
67657	McQuarrie, John Daniel	Strathlorne
68274	MacQuarrie, Malcolm William+	Middle River
67989	McQuillan, Charles Edward+	Halifax
67307	MacRae, James	Loch Flemington, Scotland

68318		McRae, Malcolm	North River Bridge
68202		McRae, Thomas	Sydney Mines
68314		McVarish, Stephen	Reserve Mines
68425		McVicar, Angus John+	Halifax
68206		Maling, Reginald Avoy	Bear River East
67885	L Cpl	Mallinson, Ernest Robert M.	Halifax
67063		Malone, Patrick	Belfast, Ireland
67028	L Cpl	Manley, Albert	Halifax
67085		Mann, James Curtis Stanlyn+	Halifax
67827		Mansley, Theodore	Halifax
68149		Marlowe, Franklin James	Richer, QC
68396		Marryatt, Everett+	Halifax
67669		Marshall, Ernest	Westville
67369		Martin, Cyril Allan	Halifax
67125		Martin, Herbert	Sydney
68104		Martin, William	Yarmouth
67368	C Sgt-M	Mason, George	Kensal Rise, England
68173		Masson, James Hamilton+	Broughton
67868		Matheson, Albert	Wood's Harbour
67438		Matheson, Carl Preston	Springhill
67639	Sgt	Matheson, Guy MacLean	Baddeck
68308		Matheson, Herman	New Aberdeen
67365		Matheson, Wilson	Sydney Mines
67230		Matthews, Elijah	Chesterton, England
67261	L Cpl	Mayfield, William	Mulgrave
67985		Meagher, Thomas Rockland+	Cobalt, ON
67403		Mercer, Arthur Lawrence	New Aberdeen
67981		Meredith, Henry	Wales
67366		Merritt, Charles	Halifax
67945		Michaels, Philip+	Glace Bay
67871		Michell, John	St Lawrence, NL
67034		Mickle, James	Greystones, Ireland
67178		Middleton, Henry	Scone, Australia
67001	Sgt M	Miles, Harry Frederick	Halifax
67118		Miles, James	Dominion
67006	Cpl	Millar, Edward+	London, England
67182		Millard, Herman	Springhill
67773		Miller, Arthur Stanley	Annapolis Royal
68394		Miller, William Thomas	Halifax
68119	Cpl	Milligan, James	King's Head

68408	Millington, Samuel	Grand Bank, NL
67056	Minnick, Starratt	Port Medway
67619	Mitchell, Aubrey	Camborne, England
67513	Mitchell, Charles Edward	Sydney
68383	Mitchell, John Joseph	Halifax
68397	Mitchell, Joseph Albert	Montreal, QC
67887	Moffatt, Guy+	River Hebert
67595	Moffatt, Millin	Dominion
68307	Molloy, James+	Caledonia
68007	Monaghan, William	Cambuslang, Scotland
67378	Moore, George Leroy+	Florence
67756	Moore, Harry B.+	Burin, NL
67903	Moore, Henry+	London, England
67285 Cpl	Moore, Noble+	Winnipeg, MB
68003	Moore, Norman B.	Kentville
67423	Moore, Richard	Sydney
67544	Moore, Willard Anderson+	North Sydney
67226	Morrell, Ralph	Stellarton
68097	Morgan, George	Bristol, England
68378	Morley, Charles	Stamford, England
67739	Morris, Harry	Bath, England
68047	Morris, Thomas+	New Waterford
67545 Sgt	Morrison, Daniel	Blue's Mills
67439	Morrison, David	New Waterford
67614	Morrison, Donald	Florence
67984	Morrison, John+	New Waterford
67171	Morrison, Kenneth Dan	Loch Lomond West
68421	Mosher, Carl+	Garden Lots
67239 L Cpl	Moss, Harry	Westville
68390	Moss, John+	Halifax
67846	Moulton, James	North Sydney
67648	Moulton, Stanley	Burin Bay Island, NL
68140	Mountain, Samuel	Springhill
68084	Mowatt, Jack	Thurso, Scotland
67237	Muir, Hugh	Glace Bay
67314	Muise, Arthur	Yarmouth
67167	Muise, Manning	Yarmouth
67939	Munro, Ernest	Yarmouth
68115 L Cpl	Munro, George Crawford+	Halifax
67250	Murdock, William H.+	Pictou

67027 Cpl	Murphy, James Frederick	Halifax
68309	Murphy, Michael Robert+	New Aberdeen
67942	Murphy, Victor Carl	Wolfville
67943	Murray, Maurice+	Sandy Cove, NL
67164	Murree, Gordon S.	Yarmouth
67615	Myers, Charles	New Waterford
67620	Myers, George E.+	Sydney
67681	Myers, Joseph+	Trenton
67301	Nadeau, William	Digby
67947	Napier, Alexander	East Wemyss, Scotland
68153	Naubert, René+	Ottawa, ON
67330	Neal, Frederick J.	Amherst
67462	Neitz, Charles	Yarmouth
67466	Neitz, William Henry+	Yarmouth
67015	Neville, Leroy	Liverpool
68372	Neville, Patrick Charles	Halifax
68224	Newell, Harry	Canso
68250	Newstead, Walter	Broughton
67287	Nicholl, George	Bridgewater
67686	Nicoll, William Irvin+	Mira Gut
67872	Nicholson, Daniel Philip	New Waterford
67220	Nicholson, Peter James+	Stellarton
68095	Nicholson, Vince Leroy	Vancouver, BC
67484	Nickerson, Warren	Wood's Harbour
67671	Nickerson, Warren	Clark's Harbour
67569	Nielson, David	Glace Bay
68323	Nolan, Michael H.	Glace Bay
67960	Norse, Thomas E.+	Middle Cornwall
67924	Noseworthy, Allan George	St John's, NL
67377	Noyes, Chester	Joggins Mines
68992	Oakes, Frederick L.	Liverpool, England
67780	Oakley, Frank	Halifax
67317	O'Connell, Harold	Yarmouth
67530	O'Connell, William	North Sydney
67873	Ogilvy, Sydney S.	Kingsport
68347	O'Handley, Daniel Archibald	Glace Bay
67705	O'Hanley, Daniel Alexander+	Marble Mountain
67216	Ohrling, Cecil Carl	Stellarton
67217	Ohrling, Harry	Stellarton
67633	Oram, Charles	Baddeck

67645		O'Reilly, Frederick	New Waterford
67661		Orton, Joseph	Dominion
68324		Osmond, Stephen	New Aberdeen
67815	L Cpl	Page, George	Earlsdon, England
67086		Paine, John Ernest	Halifax
67786		Pallott, Percy Arthur C.	Halifax
68191		Parfitt, George	New Aberdeen
68452		Parker, Cecil+	Upper Newport
67305		Parker, Lamont Anthony	Whitinsville, MA, USA
67824		Parkes, Edward Joseph	Halifax
68048		Parsons, Charles	Sydney Mines
68327		Parsons, Frederick	New Aberdeen
67677		Partington, Thomas	Westville
67055		Paterson, David	Edinburgh, Scotland
68116		Paton, Arthur Herbert	Westville
68158		Patterson, Hugh K.	Sydney Mines
68092	Sgt	Patterson, John	Brampton, England
67468		Patterson, Sheridan Larry	Wood Mountain, SK
67810		Paul, Frank A.	Halifax
68096	L Cpl	Payne, Robert+	London, England
67959		Pender, John+	Halifax
67961		Pentz, Richard Arthur+	Hantsport
68242		Petrie, Hilary	New Waterford
68326		Petrie, John George+	New Aberdeen
67680		Petrie, Joseph	Sydney Mines
67169		Petten, Eleazer	Kelligrews, NL
67293		Phalen, Oswell	Charlestown
67373		Pickavance, Albert+	St Helen's, England
68351		Pickard, William Joseph	Glace Bay
67996		Pickering, Alexander S.	Halifax
68325		Pickup, Francis	Caledonia Mines
67508		Pierce, Alvan Linscott	Lockeport
68184		Pilley, Archibald+	Caledonia
67074	L Cpl	Pineo, Ralph	Waterville
67608		Pledge, Thomas	Sydney
67719		Pogson, Joseph	Halifax
67754		Polsen, Helvardt	Copenhagen, Denmark
67785		Power, Hugh	St John's, NL
67071		Prime, Reginald Francis+	Heaton Moor, England
67995		Purcell, Frank P.	Halifax

68380	Purcell, Reginald	Halifax
68463	Pyke, Robert Reeves+	St Lawrence, NL
67405	Pynn, Frederick	Sydney
67874	Quinlan, Milton	Port La Tour
68106	Raeside, Alexander	Airdrie, Scotland
67747	Rafter, Frederick	Halifax
68231	Ralphs, Henry	Reserve Mines
67901	Randle, Ebenezer	Horsley Heath, England
68020	Randle, William F.	Sydney Mines
67043 Cpl	Ranford, Thomas	Worcester, England
68279	Ransom, John	North Sydney
68144	Read, George Albert	Halifax
67253	Reay, Edward+	Stanley, England
68424	Reid, Mack+	Halifax
67707	Reid, Sim+	Sutherland's River
68181	Rennie, Henry	Reserve Mines
67875 Cpl	Rhind, Jack A.	Stewiacke
68232	Rhodes, William	Reserve Mines
67117 Cpl	Richards, William+	Sydney
67609	Richmond, James+	Tracadie
67456 L Cpl	Roberts, Richard	Ushaw Moor, England
67604	Roberts, Roderick	Caledonia Mines
68099 L Cpl	Robertson, Alexander G.	Stillman
68246	Robertson, James	Barry Dock, Wales
67137	Robertson, Robert	Sydney Mines
68415	Robinson, Michael Joseph	Glace Bay
67279	Robinson, Samuel	New Glasgow
67492	Robinson, Thomas	Glace Bay
68122	Robinson, William Frederick+	Round Hill
67697 L Cpl	Roby, James	Lancashire, England
67454 Cpl	Roche, George E.+	Bedford
67967	Roger, Walter+	Clydebank, Scotland
68090	Rogers, Arthur	Tottenham, England
67231	Rogers, Harry	New Glasgow
67992	Rogers, Harry Irving	North Weymouth, MA, USA
68284	Rogers, John	Glace Bay
68462	Rogers, John Joseph	Port-aux-Basques, NL
50443	Rolfe, Albert Dennis	Halifax
67757 L Cpl	Rolfe, William D.	Halifax

67174	Ronayne, Charles Burchell+	Sydney Mines
67528	Roper, Prescott	Sydney Mines
67020	Rose, Reginald	Halifax
68261	Ross, Albert+	Bayfield, NB
67081	Ross, David	Not Stated
67535	Ross, Donald Fraser+	North Sydney
67201	Ross, Edward	Stellarton
67596	Ross, Frank	Northeast Margaree
67320	Ross, John	St Croix
68141	Ross, Murdock Alexander	Springhill
67638	Ross, William	North Sydney
68385	Rowley, Worthington Randolph	Halifax
67039	Roy, Arthur	Elm Tree, NB
67211	Ruault, Francois	St Pierre & Miquelon
68215	Ruggles, Guilford	Paradise West
68190	Rushton, Robert	New Waterford
67064	Russell, Herbert	Halifax
67455 L Cpl	Rutter, Thomas	Fredericton, NB
68065	Ryan, John Gregory	Play Cove, NL
67300	Ryan, John W.	Mulgrave
67295	Salvage, John	Yarmouth
67731 CQM-Sgt	Sands, John Frederick	Dartmouth
67342	Saunders, Clarence Bernard	Sydney
67661	Schofield, Charles William+	Wolfville
67631	Scott, George Brown	Sydney Mines
67133	Scott, John	Sydney Mines
67713	Searle, Edwin	Lostwithiel, England
68162	Shadforth, Frank	Sydney
67897	Sharpe, George+	Maccan
68103	Shaw, John Edward	Halifax
67087	Sheppard, Albert	Halifax
67673	Shoul, Camille+	Inverness
68182	Silver, Harlis	Glace Bay
68005	Simcox, Benjamin	Liverpool, England
67781 L Cpl	Simmonds, Sydney	Halifax
67849 L Cpl	Simmons, Norman Guy	Glace Bay
68443	Simpson, Robert	Chicago, IL, USA
67516 L Cpl	Sinclair, George W.	New Waterford
67359 Cpl	Singer, James Leith	Windsor
67590	Skillen, John	Whifflet, Scotland

67877	Slaney, Alonzo+	St Lawrence, NL
68407	Slater, Jack	London, England
67958	Slater, John	Barry Docks, Wales
67356 L Cpl	Slater, Thomas H.	Halifax
68031	Small, William+	Tillcove Mines, NL
67191	Smart, James	Amherst
67142 Cpl	Smith, Charles Albert	Norwich, England
67517	Smith, Christopher	Sydney
67170	Smith, Daniel	Port Morien
68022 Cpl	Smith, Frederick	Wood's Harbour
67421	Smith, Graham	Sydney
67425	Smith, Harold G.	Halifax
67183	Smith, Harry Webster+	Halifax
67878	Smith, Hersey Southcote+	Smithville
67392	Smith, Horace+	Advocate Harbour
67374	Smith, John L.+	Port Morien
68199	Smith, Murdoch J.+	North River Bridge
68435	Smith, Stanley	Halifax
67135	Smith, William+	Sydney
67495	Snow, Samuel+	Harbour Grace, NL
67741	Sollows, Frank	Yarmouth
67103	Somers, John E.	Sydney
68353	Soulsby, Thomas	Glace Bay
68043	Speakman, James	New Waterford
67879	Spicer, Robert W.+	Wolfville
68375	Spicer, Thomas Rupert+	Halifax
68448	Squires, Gregory+	Pool's Cove, NL
68328	Squires, Robert	Glace Bay
67740	Stafford, Charles B.	Halifax
67048	Stafford, John+	Ipswich, England
67273	Stallard, Sidney	New Glasgow
67426	Stark, James	Cardonald, Scotland
67628	Steele, Thomas	Northern Bay, NL
67430	Stewart, John+	Reserve Mines
67880	Stoddart, David	Wood's Harbour
68221 L Cpl	Stokes, William	Chelmsford, England
67635 Cpl	Stone, George Henry	Norwich, England
68439	Strang, John	Sydney Mines
67345	Strickland, Garfield	Port-aux-Basques, NL
67964	Stubbard, Walter+	South Bar

67568	Stubbert, Amos	Florence
67256	Sullivan, James Walter	Canso
67100	Surette, Louis	Yarmouth
68165	Sutherland, Alexander+	Sydney Mines
68204	Sutherland, John	Sydney Mines
67727 L Cpl	Sutherland, Mack W.	Oxford
67668	Swinimer, Guy Ernest+	Peggy's Cove
68085	Tann, Walter+	Great Yarmouth, England
67268	Taylor, Alexander+	Sydney
67078	Taylor, Alfred+	Liverpool, England
67771	Taylor, John Edward+	Windsor
68414	Taylor, Joseph+	Halifax
68238	Telfer, Walter James	Boston, MA, USA
67390	Thomas, Charles Edwin	Tyldesley, England
67283	Thompson, Arthur	Truro
67297	Thompson, Dana	Weymouth Falls
67966	Thompson, John	Dartmouth
67825	Thompson, John Thomas	Granby, QC
68203	Thomson, John	Florence
67971	Thomson, John Stevenson	Blackridge, Scotland
50445	Thurber, Edmund Gibbs	Wolfville
67636	Thurgood, Abraham	Gabarus
67143 Cpl	Tickle, John Peter	Bow Island, AB
67693	Timmins, Thomas Joseph	Brewood, England
67318	Titus, Thomas E.	Yarmouth North
68110 L Cpl	Tolson, George Lundy+	Boston, MA, USA
67570	Toon, Thomas	Leicester, England
68087	Topp, Egbert Bethridge	Auckland, NZ
67917	Torrie, Gavis A.	Digby
67644	Tottle, Leonard Ernest	Bristol, England
67662	Turner, John E.	Haverhill, MA, USA
68460	Turner, Matthew	Whitles Bay, NL
68329	Turner, William Charles	Caledonia Mines
67414	Tutty, Robert	Sydney Mines
67838	Tynan, John James+	Halifax
67406	Valentine, Joseph	Dominion
68374	Vaughan, John Michael	Halifax
67647	Vickers, Sidney Ballentine+	Sydney Mines
68023	Waylein, Robert	Cape Canso
67354	Walker, Harry	Fleetwood, England

68053	L Cpl	Walker, John Stewart	Sydney Mines
67453		Walker, Peter	Glasgow, England
67355	Sgt	Walker, William Alfred	River Hebert
68108	L Cpl	Wallace, Albert	Camberwell, England
67327		Wallace, Howard Vincent	Halifax
67839		Walsh, John	Derrynane, Ireland
67805		Walsh, Thomas William	Halifax
67735		Walters, Isaac	Northampton, England
68373		Walton, Peter Walter	Liverpool, England
68059		Walton, Thomas	Stellarton
67808		Ward, Frank	Halifax
68412		Ward, George	Halifax
68034		Ward, William	Paradise, NL
68086		Ward, William	Preston, England
68330		Wareham, Willis	New Aberdeen
67982		Warnell, William	Halifax
67736		Waterfield, Joseph H.	Dartmouth
67479		Watkins, Hugh Walter	Church Street
68174		Watson, Andrew George	Strathbane, Scotland
68083		Weare, Cecil+	Hitchin, England
68398		Webber, Nelson Albert	Lakeville
67308		Weddleton, Frederick Walter+	Lockeport
68146		Weller, Albert	Thakeham, England
67765		Welsh, George	London, England
67787		Wensley, Frederick	Exford, England
67533		West, Albert	Penge, England
68113		West, St Clair	Liverpool
67792	L Cpl	Westwood, John	Halifax
68468		Wheadon, Clifford	Ellershouse
67150		Wheeliker, William H.+	New Aberdeen
67418		Whelan, James	St Jacques, NL
67332		White, Edward	Amherst
67837		White, Milton	Purcell's Cove
68172		White, Ralph	Kirkintilloch, Scotland
67375		White, Robert	Aylesford
67474		White, William James	Arlington, England
68180		Whitehouse, John Henry	New Waterford
68451		Whitman, James	Mahone Bay
67013		Whitworth, Harold James	Lincoln, England
68148		Wicks, James Henry	London, England

67335		Wiggins, Joseph	Amherst
67022		Wigginton, Charles Thomas	Halifax
68262		Wight, Norman Daniel Franklin+	New Waterford
67247		Wilcock, George	Sydney Mines
67761		Wilkinson, George T.	Plymouth, England
67534		Wilkinson, Leonard	New Aberdeen
68100	L Cpl	Williams, Edward James	London, England
67905		Williamson, Henry	New Waterford
67130		Willmot, Percy Charles+	Sydney
68382		Wilson, Benjamin	New Waterford
67524		Wilson, John Thomas	Dominion
67514		Wilson, Murray	New Waterford
68332		Wilson, Richard Thomas+	Glace Bay
68376		Wilson, Walter McLaren	Halifax
68331		Wilson, William	Dominion
67571		Winnard, James	Daubhill, England
68138	L Cpl	Wintrup, Harry	Galashiels, Scotland
67709	Cpl	Wise, John	Trenton
67983		Withers, Obadiah Clark	Saint John, NB
67737		Woods, Ernest	Pontypridd, Wales
67057	Sgt Bugler	Woods, Patrick	Liverpool, England
68241		Wooley, Thomas	Louisbourg
67067	L Sgt	Wort, Henry James	Halifax
68333		Worthington, Robert	Glace Bay
67062		Wright, Arthur	Alston, England
68420		Wright, Sidney Melvin+	Dartmouth
67692	L Cpl	Wynn, John R.	New Glasgow
67274		Yates, Frederick+	Sydney Mines
67112	Sgt	Yates, Henry	Sydney Mines
67059		Yeomans, Charles+	Derby, England
67881		Young, Calvin	Glace Bay
68263		Young, Daniel	Glace Bay
67882		Young, Elsworth+	Glace Bay
68076		Young, Samuel	Five Mile Town, Ireland
68403		Zong, James	Halifax
67460		Zwicker, Francis	Mahone Bay

Recommended Reading

Anonymous. *Canada in the Great World War*. 6 vols. Toronto: United Publishers, 1919–21.

Beatty, David Pierce, ed. *Memories of the Forgotten War: The World War I Diary of Pte V.E. Goodwin*. Port Elgin: Baie Verte Editions, 1988.

Bird, Will R. *Ghosts Have Warm Hands*. Toronto: Clarke Irwin, 1968.

– *Thirteen Years After: A Great War Veteran Revisits the Old Battlefields*. Toronto: Maclean, 1932. Reprinted. Ottawa: CEF Books, 2001.

Cook, Tim. *At the Sharp End: Canadians Fighting the Great War, 1914–1916*. Toronto: Viking, 2007.

– *Shock Troops: Canadians Fighting the Great War, 1917–1918*. Toronto: Viking, 2008.

Cowley, Deborah, ed. *Georges Vanier, Soldier: The Wartime Letters and Diaries, 1915–1919*. Toronto: Dundurn, 2000.

Dancocks, Daniel G. *Legacy of Valour: The Canadians at Passchendaele*. Edmonton: Hurtig, 1986.

Duguid, D. Fortescue. *The Official History of the Canadian Forces in the Great War, 1914–1919*. Vol. 1. Ottawa: King's Printer, 1938.

Hayes, Joseph. *The Eighty-Fifth in France and Flanders*. Halifax: Royal Print and Litho, 1920.

Lewis, Ralph. *Over the Top with the 25th*. Halifax: H.H. Marshall, 1918.

MacDonald, F.B., and John J. Gardiner. *The Twenty-Fifth Battalion, Canadian Expeditionary Force: Nova Scotia's Famous Regiment in World War One*. Sydney: Privately published, 1983.

MacGregor, Francis. *Days That I Remember*. Windsor: Lancelot, 1976.

Mathieson, William D. *My Grandfather's War: Canadians Remember the First World War*. Toronto: Macmillan, 1981.

McClare, Dale, ed. *The Letters of a Young Canadian Soldier during World War I: P. Winthrop McClare of Mount Uniacke*. Dartmouth: Brook House Press, 2000.

McElhenny, G.C. 'The 25th Battalion.' In *Nova Scotia's Part in the Great War*. Ed. M.S. Hunt. Halifax: Nova Scotia Veteran Publishing Co., 1920. 70–91.

Morton, Desmond. *When Your Number's Up: The Canadian Soldier in the First World War*. Toronto: Random House, 1993.

Morton, Desmond, and J.L. Granatstein. *Marching to Armageddon: Canadians and the Great War, 1914–1919*. Toronto: Lester & Orpen Dennys, 1989.

Nasmith, George G. *Canada's Sons in the World War*. 2 vols. Toronto: John C. Winston, 1919.

Nicholson, G.W.L. *Canadian Expeditionary Force, 1914–1919*. Ottawa: Queen's Printer, 1962.

Pedley, James H. *Only This: A War Retrospect, 1917–1918*. Ottawa: Graphic, 1927. Reprinted. Ottawa: CEF Books, 1999.

Rogers, Peter G., ed. *Gunner Ferguson's Diary*. Hantsport: Lancelot, 1985.

Rutledge, Stanley A. *Pen Pictures from the Trenches*. Toronto: William Briggs, 1918.

Tennyson, Brian Douglas. *Percy Willmot: A Cape Bretoner at War*. Sydney: Cape Breton University Press, 2007.

Walker, Frank. *From a Stretcher Handle: The World War I Journal and Poems of Pte Frank Walker*. Charlottetown: Institute of Island Studies, 2000.

Index